Published in 2009 by Myrdle Court Press, London, UK
in association with This Is Not A Gateway

ISBN 978-0-9563539-0-0

Myrdle Court Press is an independent publishing company that advances
ideas generated by emerging urbanists.
Unit 24 Myrdle Court, Myrdle Street, London E1 1HP
www.myrdlecourtpress.net

Designed by Karolin Schnoor
www.karolinschnoor.com

Printed and bound by Imprint Digital, Exeter, UK
Bookwove cream paper

supported by:

CRITICAL CITIES

IDEAS, KNOWLEDGE AND AGITATION
—————— *from* ——————
EMERGING URBANISTS

VOLUME 1

edited by
DEEPA NAIK *&* TRENTON OLDFIELD
THIS IS NOT A GATEWAY

Contents

Preface

JEMMA BASHAM

I am delighted to write this preface to the Critical Cities publication on behalf of the HCA Academy. The HCA Academy supports the inter-disciplinary approach that This Is Not A Gateway uses in this book. We feel it is important to support the work of young and emerging urbanists developing inter-disciplinary platforms to take risks and think about space and place differently. The book itself demonstrates the rich insights that can be gained from bringing people from a range of backgrounds and occupations together and the valuable learning that can be shared.

The subject of this book is of relevance to all practitioners seeking to build sustainable communities, as cohesion is the strength of the 'social glue' that binds us all together. The global recession has highlighted the importance of cohesion as a driving impetus for sustainable economic growth, bringing people and communities together to withstand the added socio-economic pressure.

In our contemporary world it is important to understand cohesion as an embedded part of building sustainable communities. This book will help practitioners quickly get to grips with how cohesion can be addressed in their specific locality. The HCA Academy acknowledges This Is Not A Gateway's work, first through the *Creating the Future Award*, and now in supporting this publication. We see the potential of this book to be used as a tool for sharing critical knowledge, to reach new audiences and ultimately to affect space and place.

BIOGRAPHY : Jemma Basham is Knowledge Manager at the HCA Academy.

The HCA Academy (formerly the Academy of Sustainable Communities) is the external skills and expertise arm of the Homes and Communities Agency (HCA). It supports the HCA's partners to deliver better places by providing access to practical training and resources. Its current priority is to give people tools and know-how to deal with the recession and prepare for the upturn.

Acknowledgements

We would like to thank the HCA, in particular Paul Spooner, Jemma Basham, Diane Sadaoui, Trudy Birtwell and Zabir Moghal, for their belief that this publication could make a contribution to expanding the field, prising open learning avenues and highlighting emerging practitioners and thinkers. Thank you to the HCA Academy for funding the production of this book.

It has been wonderful to work alongside the contributors to this book, who are all in their own way forging new means for critical engagement with our cities. We are grateful for the opportunity to continue learning from each of them.

The book itself would not have been possible without the early guidance we received from Charlotte Troy of CT Bureau. We are especially grateful to Barbara Murray for her expert advice on all aspects of producing this book along with her splendid editing skills. It remains a pleasure and inspiration to work with illustrator and designer Karolin Schnoor. We thank her for proposing ways to translate a series of salons and a three-day festival into a book that would be enjoyable to read and a useful resource.

Many of the questions expanded on in this book surfaced during the festival, which would not have been realised without the financial support from openvizor.com and the international knowledge of the organisation's founding director, Abbas Nokhasteh. Through conversations with him in the years preceding the first festival we agreed there was the potential for different ways to think through the quite unnecessary barriers erected around official conferences and discourse. We thank him for helping build the festival as a platform so the ideas being worked on by an ever-wider collection of emerging urbanists could converge and be circulated.

We are indebted to Keiko Yamamoto and Hamish Dunbar for hosting much of the festival in their wonderful Café Oto, and we would like to thank Britt Hatzius for introducing us to them. Sam Aldenton, the manager of Bootstrap Company, immediately understood what we were trying to do with the festival project. We would like to thank him for opening many doors, including those of a disused underground bunker for its first art exhibition! In total, 11 venues housed festival projects. We are especially grateful to Emma Jones from Hackney Co-operative Developments, Maria Benjamin and Ruth Höflich from Guestroom, all the folks in Space 1 Studio, The Angel public house in Rotherhithe and Metropolitan Workshop. As the festival was a platform for broadening current discourses in urban theory and practice, we had the very good fortune to work alongside remarkable individuals and organisations from across Europe that are curious, engaged and also invested in this pursuit. We would like to thank them for collaborating with us and organising their events with the best DIY ethos and outcomes. We would also like to thank the many audience participants who contributed to the festival and salon discussions, some of whom are now organising their own events in the forthcoming festival.

The festival wouldn't have happened without the contributions of Becky Lipsey and Sidonie Roberts, our two interns, for which we are immensely grateful. We would also like to thank the Romanian Cultural Institute and SDNA who provided equipment. The team from Leaders In Community were critical in ensuring events ran smoothly and the spaces were safe for which we are most grateful.

The first 'fertilising' our organisation received was from Ekow Eshun and Iram Quraishi at the Institute of Contemporary Arts, London, and Maria Georka of the Cultural Leadership Programme. We are would like to thank them for seeing the potential of the project and setting us on our way. We are enormously grateful to the kind and super-productive folks at public works who hosted our first salons. We would like to thank Arts Council England, in particular Hassan Mahamdallie and James Holden, for working with us to establish the salon platform as a way of bringing diverse practitioners and theorists together.

Our steering committee provided vital support, a number of great ideas and an ever-expanding network for our organisation. We would like to thank each of them: Abbas Nokhasteh, Alessio Antoniolli, Andreas Lang, Chris Sharpe, Dominic Church, Ellen Haukas, Hilary Powell, Joost Beunderman, Kathrin Böhm, Korinna Thielen, Lina Gudmundsson, Lisa Cholmondeley, Nanna Nielsen, Polly Brannan, Rehan Jamil, Sepake Angiama and Talia Braun. Recent steering committee members include: Ben Campkin, Ellen O'Hara, Ruhul Abdin and Fiona Whitty.

Karolin Schnoor would like to thank Seif Al'Hasani, Tom Flynn, Tilmann Hielscher and Jacqueline Wagner for their generous help and patience.

04

Thank you to all the festival and salon participants:

Murali Shanmugavelan, Sarah Butler, Ana Laura Lopez, Lewis Eldridge, Sam Appleby, Anne Woods, Nat Roberton, Moustapha Traore, Braves Garcons d'Afrique, Pink et Brown, Le Movement des Indigènes de la République, Penny Skerrett, Bram Thomas Arnold, Eleanor Wynne Davis, Winston Whitter, Maria Benjamin, Ruth Höflich, Alex Haw, Indy Johar, Dan Edelstyn, Kristina Miechinski, Laura Braun, Irit Rogoff, Pamela Laracca, Diana Ali, Natalia Skobeeva, Craig Edwards, Nick Smith, Victoria Bean, Anna Colin, Kelly Foster, Peter Fry, Nic Groombridge, Ricky Burdett, Isola Art Center, Manu Luksch, Paul Mackie, Jaimes Meyhew, Richard Reynolds, Mark Simpson, Liza Fior, Ben Todd, Faisel Rahman, Nadia Katz-Wise, Craig Taylor, Chris Bailey, Paul Shepheard, Nelly Alfandari, Auro Foxcroft, Susan Parham, Effie Williams, Ellen O'Hara, Jaffer Kolb, Alan Pipe, Tea Mäkipää, David Ubaka, Karin Woodley, Andrea Phillips, Mary Whittaker, Sonia Metha, Andy Pratt, John Pandit, Helen Burrows, Gavin Alexander, Tony Nwachukwu, Charlotte Troy, Abbas Nokhasteh, Keiko Yamamoto, Hamish Dunbar, Valentina Floris, Ben Foot, Eileen Simpson, Ben White, Emma Engkvist, Joost Beunderman, Polly Brannan, Rehan Jamil, Lisa Cholmondeley, Chris Sharpe, Phil Gusack, Elizabeth Fonseca, John Oduroe, Paul Goodwin, Ben Campkin, Lina Gudmundsson, Bill Parry-Davies, Mara Ferreri, Heather Ring, Hilary Powell, Gesche Würfel, Tristan Fennell, David Kendall, Caroline Knowles, Joanna Zawieja, Léa Ayoub, Alan Thompson, Omair Barkatulla, Ania Dabrowska, Liz Obi, Cathy Ward, Sarah Evans, Matthew Gandy, Sukhdev Sandhu, Karolin Schnoor, Louis Moreno, Peter Hall, Dariusz Wojicik, Maria Kaika, Max Nathan, Andew Harris, Lawrence Webb, Inua Ellams, Subhadassi, Melanie Abrahams, Rakhee Kewada, Sophie Hope, David Ogunmuyiwa, Matteo Belfiore, Roberto Tranchese, Francesco Rossini, Salvatore Contaldo, Berger&Berger, Thomas Raynaud, Mariella Annese, Cristiano Torre, Nadia Jamil, Pierangelo Izzo, Vera Autilio, Raffaele Guaragna, Gianfranco La Torraca, Andrea Abita, Mario Casciu, Torange Khonsari, Francesca Rango, Tessa Garland, Stephen Cornford, Milica Robson, Christien Garcia, Becky Lipsey, Sidonie Roberts, Alice Fung, Silvija Stipanov.

INTRODUCTION

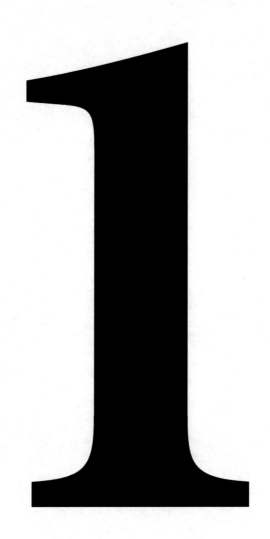

City-thinking
For City-building

RICKY BURDETT

*The city in its complete sense, then, is a geographical
plexus, an economic organisation,
an institutional process, a theatre of social action,
and an aesthetic symbol of collective unity.*

Lewis Mumford, 'What is a city?' *Architectural Record*, 1937

A few decades have passed since we first became aware that the world is a single system, integrated and synergetic but also small and fragile. We now know, for the first time in human history, that the majority of people on the planet are living urban lives. Despite the current global recession, projections tell us that this trend will continue. Seventy-five per cent (75%) of the global population is expected to concentrate in cities by 2050 – mostly in mega-cities of several million people each and massively urbanised regions stretching across countries and continents. It is precisely because of the scale, pace and immediacy of this new urban reality that we need to turn our attention to thinking about cities, and not just building them. And as this intellectual investigation evolves, it becomes clear that the work of urban activists, academics, commentators and actors – involved in organisations like This Is Not A Gateway (TINAG) – will become more and more important, feeding ideas and provocations from city-thinkers to city-builders.

The scale of the new urban context is difficult to grasp. While only 186 million people lived in cities of over a million or more in 1950, this figure reached one billion in 2000 and will grow to 1.8 billion by 2025. For mega-cities of ten million or more, the increase is twice as fast: from 23 million in 1950, to 229 million in 2000, and to 447 million in 2025. Europe, North America and Oceania became mostly urban before the 1950s and Latin America during the 1960s, Asia will hit that mark around 2024 and Africa by 2030. Much of this urban growth is occurring in areas where poverty and deprivation are rife; where cities have the potential to either integrate or separate. In addition, the relentless pace of urban change is likely to be fuelled by the environmental impacts of climate change, with more people – climate change refugees – abandoning exposed agricultural areas in favour of the relative protection and promise of the city.

But, what does this speed and vastness mean for both those who inhabit and those who build the city? How can the model of urbanity that has supported human existence for centuries serve us to comprehend the emerging form of 'cityness' that the new century of massive global urbanisation is delivering? What is the complex relationship between urban form and city life; how to intervene and bring about positive change? These are some of the questions that my colleagues and I have been addressing at the Urban Age Programme at the London School of Economics for the last years, focusing on the interactions between the physical and the social in some of the world's major 'global' cities such as Istanbul, Mumbai, Sao Paulo and London. But the more I have worked on these issues, the more I realise that deeper questions about the relationship between the individual experience of the urban dweller and the macro-scale of the city are out-of-step with each other. Urban policy, it seems, is largely framed in a functional paradigm that attempts to quantify our everyday experience rather than establish a set of human or even existential values.

For me, the quintessential urban paradox of confrontation and promise, tension and release, social cohesion and exclusion, wealth and poverty, is a profoundly spatial equation with enormous democratic potential. Ultimately, the shape we give society affects the daily lives of those who live and work in cities across the world. The creation of a small gymnasium, a cultural centre or a landscaped open space at the heart of a slum dignifies the existence of disenfranchised communities, and can fundamentally transform people's lives. As architects, planners and city-makers we engage every day in creating the very infrastructure that can either enable social interaction or become a source of exclusion and domination. But, we need to ask deeper and harder questions about the social impacts of built form to create more equitable policies that will shape our cities.

The world's most extensive city-regions are rapidly being formed in southern Asia and coastal China, areas expected to concentrate close to half of the world's urban population within a couple of decades. According to the United Nations, Mumbai – India's dynamic powerhouse – is set to overtake Tokyo as the world's largest city by 2050, but nowhere is the dizzying velocity of this transformation as tangible as in the largest Chinese conurbations. As Shanghai grapples with the social challenges of integrating a 'floating population' of rural in-migrants numbering perhaps five million people, it continues to grow at a breathtaking rate in both height and breadth, with nearly 3,000 buildings over ten storeys high in a city that had less than 300 such buildings only ten years ago. Fuelling this growth is not only in-migration but also the desire of existing residents to increase the amount of personal space they inhabit. The average amount of space per person has tripled in just over a decade, from less than 4 metres per person to over 12 square metres, still a modest figure compared to the averages of most western countries. Beyond Shanghai and Beijing, Shenzhen is the most well-known of the many instant million-plus cities of China, each with their own airport or opera house, that have emerged out of the largest rural to urban migration movement in the history of humanity – again only in the short span of a few decades.

But rapid urbanisation is not always paralleled by the exponential economic growth and comprehensive infrastructure investments of the Asia Pacific region. Demographic pressures are bound to continue – by 2015, with each passing hour, Lagos will add 67 new residents, Kinshasa 34 – leading to a disproportionate concentration of young people in the southern hemisphere that coincides with a global imbalance of social indicators such as literacy and income levels. In Egypt, one child is born every 20 seconds and many people move to Cairo within the space of one generation. In this city, over 60% of the population lives in informal settlements with buildings up to 14 storeys high in a city with only 1 square metre of open space per person (each Londoner, by contrast, has access to 50 times that amount).

Even Johannesburg, the economic and cultural engine of southern Africa, is challenged to maintain its current levels of infrastructure provision in the face of a growth scenario whereby its population may double in a matter of decades. In this post-apartheid city that is struggling with crime, fear, segregation and AIDS, there are attempts to bring people back to the abandoned downtown – from which in the last decade many businesses fled to anonymous corporate areas on the urban fringes – with small-scale projects around transport hubs (or 'taxi ranks') that are designed to re-humanise the public realm of the city otherwise hidden behind security fences and inside gated communities. Given the social risks associated with exponential growth, the global urgency of an urban agenda for Africa cannot be over-stressed, in a continent that is expected to have a slightly larger share of the world's urban population than Europe by the year 2030.

There is a growing awareness that the urban agenda is a global agenda. The environmental impacts of cities are enormous, due both to their increasing demographic weight and to the amount of natural resources that they consume. Every aspect of urban living has significant implications for the planet – from the billions of people driving cars along metropolitan highways, to the energy required to either heat or cool buildings and to bring in food, often from the opposite corner of the world. In the developed economies, it is estimated that over 50% of energy is consumed by buildings and 25% by transport. Thus, a slight change to this energy equation in cities will have a massive impact on the global stage. It has been argued that the degree of dispersion of urban forms can be related to consumption of non-renewable resources and emissions. On this front, the cities of more developed countries bear a particular responsibility towards the global commons – the per capita levels of energy consumption and global warming emissions in these countries are the highest in the world.

A new generation of urban leaders is rising to meet these challenges. In Europe, for example, many big-city mayors are implementing important urban reforms that will enable their cities to be more competitive in the global economy and smarter producers of knowledge and culture. These cities are responding to contemporary social challenges, in some cases accommodating the large-scale influx of new residents and in others managing demographic decline without imploding irreversibly.

Urban leadership is acquiring a growing momentum around the world, from metropolitan coalitions for smart growth and growth with equity in the United States, to the big-city governments in China whose social reforms may allow for less segregated urban settlements and more integrated labour markets. But much more fresh thinking needs to be done. Some of the most innovative urban interventions of the past 20 years have in fact come from grassroots organisations in Latin America, a region otherwise mired in macro-economic problems and widening social inequalities. Following the exemplary case of Curitiba in Brazil, Bogotá today stands out as a perhaps unexpected best-practice case of egalitarian urban transformation. The effect of a series of co-ordinated actions by successive mayors has turned a once violent, car-dominated city facing dramatic levels of in-migration from its rural hinterlands, into a calm and well-managed city that still exudes the passions and experiences of its syncretic Latin American culture.

In our book *The Endless City* we conclude that what is needed most now is a wake-up call for urban policymakers and city-builders. If cities are the organising units of the new global order, then a broad range of policies and practices at the city, national and supra-national levels need to be overhauled, reordered and integrated around new spatial realities and paradigms. We note that the barriers between specialised and self-referential disciplines, professionals and bureaucracies need to be broken down. We promote the notion that innovation needs to be shared across networks of urban researchers, practitioners and policymakers, across the developing and developed worlds, in order to build cities that are prosperous, sustainable and inclusive.

I have not yet been to a TINAG event, but I know that it is a forum where these questions are certainly being asked. As a 50+ academic who belongs to some sort of institutionalised urban 'tribe', I sit on the other side of a self-constructed professional fence. In many ways, that is the point. TINAG refuses to abide by conventions. It defines itself by saying what it isn't. It pokes at the establishment but wants to engage with it. Producing ideas through dialogue is TINAG's *raison d'être*. And it is urgent now, to engage, to bring different urban 'tribes' together, to do away with 'professional fences', to facilitate city-thinking *for* city-building.

BIOGRAPHY

Ricky Burdett is Director of LSE Cities, an international centre supported by Deutsche Bank at the London School of Economics. He is co-editor with Deyan Sudjic of *The Endless City* (Phaidon, 2008).

Emergent Agitation

Knowledge as Urban Politics

DEEPA NAIK & TRENTON OLDFIELD

The Urban Age is upon us. In less than two generations, over 75% of the world's rapidly growing population will live in cities. Most of these people will endeavour to establish work and create a sense of home in massive urban conglomerations: mega–cities, such as Mumbai, Shanghai, Lagos and Dhaka, and hundreds of huge, often interconnecting, urban developments. At the same time, some existing cities will shrink as people and finances move elsewhere.[1] These unprecedented statistics have critical implications for our planet, as well as undeniable potential.

Out-of-step

Statistics provided by Ricky Burdett (see 'City-thinking *For* City-building') highlight the scale, pace and immediacy of this rapid urbanisation. Crucially, Burdett argues that there is 'an opening', an 'out-of-step', between the knowledge at hand and the knowledge needed by 'city builders'. Why is there this condition of being out-of-step, especially at a time of increased emphasis on understanding urban realities? A study of the forums (exhibitions, conferences, festivals and publications) where official knowledge on cities is produced and exchanged reveals a stark reality: 'invitation only' policies and high fees, among other factors, limit participation to a narrow group of professionals and academics.[2] In parallel, educational institutions teach a selection of predictable texts. This has resulted in increasingly self-referential circuits of knowledge. It is, ironically, as if the events and aftershocks of 1968 had never ruptured the disciplines concerned with the built environment. While cities are expanding, official 'gateways' into urban discourse are reducing.

And yet, a vast body of knowledge exists and is being expanded by vigorous, unexpected and heterogeneous agents, and cells of new knowledge are continuously surfacing. Unsurprisingly, this knowledge is generated and shared most often 'from the ground up' by those that inhabit the city, those that work alongside them and those thinkers within governments, think tanks or private companies that have not been seduced into only promoting and enabling the notion of 'erase, stretch, relinquish'.[3] The sites propagating new knowledge are most often outside of 'the urban industry', and the agents of these new possibilities and practices seem to come together around shared notions of complexity, texture, rigour and potentiality. Is it not time for a re-understanding and re-formulation of the disciplines and, above all, of the participants involved in making space? Is it not time for urbanism to undergo a transformation similar to that of sociology opened up through cultural studies, or art history re-examined in the light of visual cultures? This is not a moment to bemoan or to react against the current structures that are thought to be limiting and limited, but an opportunity to produce new conditions.

Following Alinsky, the need to act arises from recognising 'the world as it is'. Research data from UN-Habitat and Urban Age make explicit the significant implications of urbanisation on people's everyday lives. Statistics detailing the number of tall buildings constructed in Dubai and the accelerating concentration of financial and political power in a handful of cities are set against 'stomach dropping' and clearly unacceptable levels of poverty, injustice, monopolisation, collusion and exploitation. Our discussions with those working both within and outside spatial practices made it clear that the out-of-step between official knowledge and on-the-ground realities was causing burning frustration for many. Personal and professional experience in a diversity of arenas[4] brought us in contact with sites of relevant, critical knowledge and practice. These sites are often independent but also include clusters of research groups and leaders within innovative companies pushing out beyond their institutions. We were constantly working alongside people with remarkable ideas and projects that we thought colleagues in other fields should know about. These were not binaries, but missed opportunities resulting from a perceived isolation from each other. Like Jemma Basham, Ricky Burdett and countless others, we recognised the urgency, desire and mutual need for barriers to be broken down, for ideas to be made accessible and for an expanded dialogue to begin. It was clear to us that a platform was needed – one that would circulate these multiple fields and sites of knowledge. Encouraged by colleagues and associates, we set out to create a platform that would demonstrate the potential of coming together.

On-site

While traditional notions of power are no doubt being re-thought, 'the city' is certainly no art gallery and no playground (much as some would like to imagine it that way). Anybody who suggests otherwise is likely to have never had their home or livelihood threatened, nor worked alongside built-environment professionals. They might be revealing their sense of resignation, their incapacity to act, or perhaps protecting their benefactor's income stream. Clear and un-romanticised understandings of the dynamics of power are more pertinent than ever as people increasingly assert their right to agency in their lives. While cities attempt to consolidate their capital and influence, diverse bodies including transnational corporations, NGOs, citizen groups and popular movements compete for power.

Every movement and action in a city is a negotiation, each square foot belongs to a profit-making spreadsheet, every design is reviewed, every notion of 'citizenship' is contested. The work of Michel Foucault[5] and Gayatri Spivak[6] provides a useful lens to question power-knowledge mechanisms, along with the exclusion and marginalisation of certain groups resulting from the maintenance of power within the urban industry. The question of how we might approach these realities, as significantly more people demand agency in their cities, has been guided by the practices of both Saul Alinsky[7] and Paulo Freire[8].

The openness of visual cultures and the work of theorists such as Stuart Hall, Irit Rogoff and Nicholas Mirzoeff[9] have also been enormously influential in our thinking. Arguing for an engagement with a range of approaches and disciplines, these thinkers persistently allow us avenues in considering how to propose the city as a site of knowledge and potentiality. Writing about the A.C.A.D.E.M.Y exhibition[10], Irit Rogoff asked: "Where are the unseen possibilities that already exist within these spaces – the people who are already working there and who bring together unexpected life experiences and connections ... the paths outward which extend beyond the museum, the spaces and navigational vectors which are unexpectedly plotted within it."[11] It is this curiosity and continual questioning how spaces and knowledge can be unbound from established limits and expectations that have informed our thinking. We know that language frames thought and the usefulness of visual culture can also be demonstrated by a consideration of shifting terms such as criticism, critique and criticality, potentiality and actualisation; terms that alter in convergence with the changing conditions they seek to address. The significance of this is not to deepen an understanding of a fixed object of study, in this case 'the city', but rather to create the possibility of prising open the field, making its complexities explicit, and allowing for unexpected actors to propel ideas forward.

Ricky Burdett's pursuit to build 'a knowledge and practice bridge' between social- and political-science thinkers and built-environment professionals, firstly through his students, and more recently through the research-led Urban Age Project, has also been motivating. His approach emphasises that cities are not only a theoretical notion but also remarkable sets of statistics with social and political implications. Cities are here 'now', and there are endless practical realities that elected and employed decision-makers must address throughout a working day. Ricky Burdett also wants to ensure that when political decisions are made the decision-makers are informed of the issues at stake. His articulation of the extent of practical failures, alongside the limited array of professionals involved in developing policy and productions of space, has been another motivating factor.

Surfacing

Who are the people and what are the activities already contributing to this shifting consciousness? Our project started with questions raised via an open call for participation. Individuals and groups from across Europe and beyond, whose central reference in their work or thinking is 'the city', got in touch. With the help of our steering committee, we considered various propositions of where and how we could make the most worthwhile and provocative contribution. The resulting four prime areas of production for This Is Not A Gateway are salons[12], festivals, publications, and a library and archive[13].

This Is Not A Gateway's festival was inaugurated[14] with the aim of making visible the shifting approaches to urbanism and the wider participation in creating cities. Though we welcome further understanding of what is evidently wrong, who and what are out-of-step, the festival was not set up to produce a collision by revealing corruption in official regeneration practices, questioning academic reading lists, detailing the absurdity of highly sponsored architectural institutions and their simplified events; nor was it intended to reveal the widespread frustration felt towards artists who turn up on public housing estates insisting that participating in publicly funded projects is 'good' for local residents. The focus was on opening up the field, providing public opportunities for offering rigorous and constructive alternatives, and stimulating multi-party participation in forging new sets of questions.

Constructed on a micro-budget and volunteer hours, the festival was bound together by an ethos of peer-to-peer learning, inter-disciplinary exchange, initiating networks and DIY urbanism. It sought to make apparent the most current questions being explored by emerging urbanists. An architectural magazine correctly described it as 'not your usual conference'[15]: it was entirely free, it was held outside of institutions, the programme was primarily participant-led, and the majority of activities were organised by women and ethnic minorities.

While research and instinct suggested there was need and desire for such an event, it was unclear whether anybody would come to the festival. Both the attendance and contributions across the three days were much more than we had anticipated. The public that came along included community workers, activists, artists, regeneration managers, theatre directors, students, writers, journalists, local councillors, government policymakers, think-tank researchers, gardeners, chairs of resident associations, as well as established built-environment professionals and theorists. Unfortunately (and embarrassingly), we neglected to collect any statistics. While observations and anecdotal evidence are inadequate, we feel comfortable to suggest that over 500 people attended across the three days and, though most were based in London, we know that people travelled from Croatia, Germany, Poland, Denmark, Italy, Switzerland, Romania, Netherlands, France and Australia to attend.

The festival was held in the offices of designers, architectural firms and charities, with a wonderfully busy café as the central hub, and there was a vibrant atmosphere apparent from the very start that signalled a stimulating and fruitful interaction. There was also a pervasive sense of productive agitation as the surrounding neighbourhood of Dalston Junction was, and still is, in the throes of 'express speed gentrification', accelerated not least by the development of a new railway line and the 2012 Olympic Games.

The impetus for founding This Is Not A Gateway was a need to articulate the shift currently apace within our rapidly transforming cities; one that is changing the way cities are being thought through, studied, researched and produced, resetting both the questions that inform urban space and those who are framing them. As the urban industries are prised open, this approach will encourage the engagement of the multiple agents shaping space. It is our hope that there will be no more than five editions. This Is Not A Gateway will then, we hope, be redundant, 'surplus to requirement', as it will have contributed towards advancing an approach that will be taken on board, become 'second nature'.

Critical ideas, articulated cities

Critical Cities is the first of This Is Not A Gateway's publications. It builds on projects, films, exhibitions, discussions and workshops from the festival and preceding salons. Without a doubt, the most difficult part of producing the book was editing the content and unfortunately we were unable to include each activity. As a result, the book does not act as a comprehensive record, detailing each project or idea that arose during the year and a half of activity. Instead, by bringing together a collection of critical papers, visual essays, conversations and actions, we hope to begin articulating where the new sites of knowledge are surfacing, who the agents are and what the potential might be.

It was important for us to produce a book, as books remain a cornerstone of cultural production. The development of new technologies such as print-on-demand means the production and circulation of books has even greater potential. The majority of the contributors to *Critical Cities* have not been published before. The authors inhabit a number of fields: practicing architecture, open-source software writing, academic teaching, filmmaking, community organising, law, journalism. Publishing this book allows their ideas to circulate to new audiences. The book is divided into four sections: Legalities of Space, Home & Migration, Public Memory and Creative Destruction. These section 'titles' arrived only after we reflected on the programme and once we read all the contributions. They indicate the pressing areas of concern being considered and expanded upon by emerging urbanists at present. The sections offer a lens to enter the material. The themes do not create rigid boundaries and many of the essays can be read through the filter of another title.

In the course of our work, including publishing this book, it has become apparent that the sense of an 'out-of-step' is experienced not only by the gatekeepers within the urban industry but also by myriad others: architects questioning why their field has been limited and tempered; managers of regeneration schemes questioning why existing culturally significant buildings are demolished and replaced with shopping centres; activists questioning how increasing poverty margins are condoned in the development of cities; NGOs questioning why official urban conferences continually exclude their propositions; academics questioning how the study of 'cities' moved out of geography and became a genre in itself; artists questioning the everyday and individual experience of urban life; local politicians questioning the implications of global migration flows on their jurisdictions; real-estate financers questioning the sustainability of their financial transactions.

Clearly, as we enter the 'Urban Age' there is something of a state of expectancy, of suspense and awkwardness resulting from the proliferation of questions in a diversity of sites. This sense of being 'unsettled' acts as a catalyst – it is that which propels people to agitate, to reframe questions, to produce new possibilities.

BIOGRAPHIES

Deepa Naik and Trenton Oldfield co-ordinate This Is Not A Gateway.

Deepa Naik is a writer, educator and organiser based in London, UK. She has worked with public works, Art for Change and the Serpentine Gallery, and has co-ordinated special projects with Irit Rogoff (Goldsmiths) including: De-Regulation (MuHKA 2006, Herzliya Museum of Contemporary Art 2006, Berlin 2010); A.C.A.D.E.M.Y: Learning from the Museum (Van Abbemuseum 2006); SUMMIT: non-aligned initiatives in education culture (Multitude e.V. 2007); and Eye Witness Conference (Birkbeck School of Law 2008).

Trenton Oldfield is an urban practitioner, writer and organiser based in London, UK. He was Co-ordinator of the Thames Strategy – Kew to Chelsea, Project Manager at Cityside Regeneration, a Community Development Worker in North Kensington. He has been active on the boards of the Westway Development Trust, London Citizens, British Urban Regeneration Association and Subtext. He is currently writing a book on the socio-political history of fenced green spaces in London.

1. For more information see, Ricky Burdett and Deyan Sudjic (eds), *The Endless City* (London: Phaidon, 2008).
2. Since 2007 we have been collecting data on urban forums, including price, professional fields and communities represented, gender and ethnicity of speakers.
3. 'Erase, stretch, relinquish' is introduced here as a term to summarise both the thinking and the actions leading built-environment decision-making processes. Rather than re-using existing building and making use of the ideas put forward by local residents, buildings are demolished. 'Erasing' is understood as both easier and more efficient. Demolition produces an empty canvas suitable for an alien 'typology' to land. The new typology 'stretches' all aspects of the site including size, height and programming – the main aim being to 'stretch' the profit margin for the developer and the tax revenues for the local authority. 'Relinquish' is the stage when almost everyone that has benefited from 'stretching' moves on: the developer either sells the site or passes on management responsibilities; the local authority no longer owns anything and struggles to answer who does own what or why none of the facilities promised have been built; and the neighbours 'relinquish' or resign themselves to the fact that their neighbourhood will never be what it could have been.
4. Our professional and voluntary experience has spanned academic work, regeneration project management, activity on committees and boards, education projects on housing estates and in local schools, regeneration initiatives and public art commissions.

21

5.   See for example, Michel Foucault, *Discipline and Punishment* (Paris: Gallimard, 1977).
6.   See for example, Gayatri Chakravorty Spivak, *Death of a Discipline* (New York: Columbia University Press: 2005).
7.   See for example, Saul Alinsky, *Rules for Radicals: A pragmatic primer for realistic radicals* (New York: Vintage, 1989).
8.   Paulo Freire, *Pedagogy of the Oppressed* (New York: Continuum, 2007).
9.   See for example, Kuan-Hsing and David Morely (eds), *Stuart Hall: Critical Dialogues in Cultural Studies* (London: Routledge, 1996); Irit Rogoff, *Terra Infirma: geography's visual culture*, (London: Routledge, 2000); Nicholas Mirzoeff (ed.), *Visual Culture Reader* (London: Routledge, 1999).
10. A project that posited the museum as a site of learning. A.C.A.D.E.M.Y: Learning from the Museum, Van Abbemuseum, Eindhoven (16 September – 26 November 2006).
11. Irit Rogoff, 'Turning', e-flux Journal #0, www.e-flux.com/journal/view/18 (accessed 18/08/09).
12. The informal salon discussions culminated in post-salon essays, some of which are produced in this publication. The salons were kindly hosted by art and architecture collective, public works. The generosity and support in sharing their studio enabled us to hold the salons outside institutions and bring in new audiences.
13. We aim to launch the online Library and Archive in the next two years. It will make available the polarity, scale and heterogeneity of work being produced across the globe 'on cities'. The search engine will produce material from different disciplines and different voices.
14. The inaugural festival was held in Dalston, East London, from 24-26 October 2008. Over 40 events including discussions, workshops, exhibitions, film screenings and a walk were held across 12 venues.
15. Jaffer Kolb, 'Open Gate Policy', *Architectural Journal*, 28 June 2008.

LEGALITIES OF SPACE

Introduction

DEEPA NAIK & TRENTON OLDFIELD

Competing uses, increasing populations and changing values raise urgent questions of resistance and agency in urban settings. It is clear that a diversity and volume of co-existing actors are challenging how their cities and communities are being shaped. The contributions in this first section – essays, conversations and art projects – reveal ways in which space and place are being re-proposed, not by real-estate financers or architects, but by filmmakers, lawyers, academics, artists and scientists. The material spans multiple geographical locations and contexts – from the redevelopment of East London and the Isola neighbourhood in Milan, to informal social spaces created by guest construction workers in Dubai.

Bringing the material together is not to allow for a universalised theory of spatial resistance, but rather to demonstrate how numerous critical practices, operating on micro scales, are thinking beyond seemingly opaque structures in significant ways. These multi-faceted, heterogeneous and increasingly linked actors are determined to wrestle (with ferocity, speed and scale) the tactics of misplaced, un-requested or 'lost-in-translation' development in their neighbourhoods and cities.

What does it mean to challenge or resist these structures? For the authors, to challenge is not to tear down but instead to achieve greater agency, not only over how their city is built, but also over how it is conceived. The texts show that movements, communities and individuals are not simply reacting to perceived threats but are, instead, framing new questions, proposing their own plans and formulating their desires for urban renewal, regeneration and city–building. The key sites of knowledge and momentum are shifting.

The section highlights a number of emergent sites of knowledge, starting with the locality of the festival. Dalston Junction is an area of East London undergoing over-scaled redevelopment due to pressure to meet not local but international requirements for the forthcoming 2012 Olympic Games. The opening paper by Dalston-based lawyer Bill Parry-Davies addresses the question: What power do local people have to protect their environment and communities in the face of apparently unstoppable development proposals? 'The Legalities of Development and its Resistance in the UK' exposes the legal, social and political factors that communities need to understand and offers the practical experience of OPEN[1] in counteracting undesired development proposals. It expands on questions raised during the festival workshop DIY Urbanism: Legalities of Organising[2], which featured a screening of Winston Whitter's film *Legacy in the Dust: The Four Aces Story* documenting the multiple community movements that converged in an attempt to prevent the demolition of a cultural landmark. Originally built in 1886, the building in question had been home to the renowned Four Aces Club, which was pivotal to black music in Britain during the previous 33 years and had hosted Bob Marley, Stevie Wonder, Ben E. King and Bob Dylan. Importantly, Whitter's film also reveals the numerous attempts by local residents to re-present ideas and aspirations for its ongoing use. During the workshop discussion, it was clear that participants had an urgency to learn lessons about the deployment of legal precedents that might have prevented the demolition of this and other sites. The paper highlights how an existing legal framework is a response to conceptualisations and theoretical understandings of the society it is located in. The law is as important as any other site for intervention by urbanists.

In the second paper, Mara Ferreri continues this exploration of the production of counter proposals and the notion of 'desire' in contested urban spaces, by drawing on the experience of the Isola Art Center and OUT in Milan. Such practices produce critical insight into the mechanisms of power and knowledge that drive urban redevelopment. Furthermore, they enable the potential to consider alternative modes of producing and inhabiting space. The paper elaborates on concerns that emerged during a film screening and discussion hosted at the festival, Isola Art Center.[3] The film *Isola Nostra* follows the collective's efforts to communicate the cultural, historic and social value of the existing buildings through a series of events, art interventions, media campaigns and architectural proposals. Eventually, despite several years of active campaigning and organising, the buildings were demolished via a process that did not have a legal code of reference. Mara Ferreri argues that this act replaced a site of potentiality with unimaginative and proscriptive luxury flats and predictable shopping districts. The responsible local authority for the Isola neighbourhood, not unlike Dalston, attempted to address persistent and pressing statistics of poverty, under-funded housing, limited employment opportunities, low education and tax rates with an 'urban renewal scheme'. In shorthand this meant 'erase, stretch, relinquish.'[4] No doubt lawyers, accountants, journalists and time will reveal how this methodology was the easiest theoretical position and reflex for urban decision-makers. It is here that Mara Ferreri sees the potential borne by collectives like Isola Arts Center and OUT, amongst others, and made available in the compendium *Urban/Act: A handbook for alternative practice*.[5] She proposes we should move away from traditional forms of opposition and conflictive urban planning and pay more attention to the work done by these groups, made tangible by French sociologist Anna Querrien's notion of 'desire archives'. The paper argues that the use of imagery to represent spatial desires should be undertaken not when a threat arises (as is most often the case) but as a constant process between individuals and communities, re-shaping the values and ideas underpinning who and what cities have the potential to be.

The importance of small acts as a way of creating potential is evident in the illicit practices of the Guerrilla Gardeners movement. The next paper by Heather Ring, architect and founding member of the Orphaned Land Trust, chronicles her festival event, the Guerrilla Garden Walk.[6] Starting in East London, participants traversed the city – north to south – drawing attention to unofficial gardens planted by individuals who are committed to rescuing land from neglect or misuse. The essay presents an alternative map of the city and a proposition to create a greenbelt of reclaimed spaces. Today guerrilla gardening includes a global network of people who are in constant contact via the internet where their images, resources and knowledge are shared. Richard Reynolds and Heather Ring, two of the movement's modern day evangelisers, have propelled a potent DIY Urbanism example into popular culture. The network membership includes an unexpected diversity of individuals actively forging new understandings of space in their city. The culmination of these acts challenges concepts of land management and land ownership. Each garden proposes and extends the idea of what spaces could be and who might be involved in making them.

The paper 'Olympic Sports, Spirits and Stories: Small Stories and Miniscule Myths' and the conversation 'A Line Is There To Be Broken' turn to questions of representation in conflictive urban spaces. In particular, they explore how artists are involved in both documenting and questioning small-scale sites that result from large-scale policies and legally constructed urban frameworks, such as the 2012 Olympic site.

The festival exhibition A Line Is There To Be Broken[7], brought together the work of Gesche Würfel, Tristan Fennell and David Kendall, and the artists' conversation with theorist Caroline Knowles explores the transformation of urban space in cities across the globe and the role of photographers in documenting these sites.

Gesche Würfel's photographs of seemingly redundant billboards abutting the London 2012 Olympic site open up questions of how regeneration processes resulting from pressures to become 'global cities' could conflict with local needs. Both Tristan Fennell and David Kendall's photographs investigate unofficial and temporary uses of public spaces. Tristan Fennell's work in this exhibition documents architectural structures in Tokyo's parks that have been designed and built by the users: Japan's homeless. The occupants, not shown in the images, are predominantly men over 50, who, as a result of changes in Japanese society due to the globalised economy, are now unemployed. Subsequent financial pressure and ideas constructed around shame have meant significant numbers have left their families to live in these urban parks. David Kendall's work explores how migrant workers in Dubai are re-orienting the new architectural landscape by producing new social spaces to meet. As a collection, the photographs raise important questions about the inter-connected nature of these sites produced as a result of global shifts in capital and about the role of photography and photographers in investigating such spaces. Moreover, they signify sites of knowledge that are often misunderstood or overlooked by researchers.

In her paper 'Olympic Sports, Spirits and Stories: Small Stories and Miniscule Myths' Hillary Powell identifies the ways in which significant legal issues persist in unexpected sites. Most notably, for the author and a growing number of artists, this includes intellectual property rights and copyright law. London's winning bid to stage the 2012 Olympics has resulted not only in laws to purchase and manage a significant slice of the host city, but also in the erection of physical and copyright boundaries. Attempts to limit critical analysis and observation have been surmounted and penetrated by what one might describe as an army of artists. Building on her discussion Salon de Refuses Olympique held during the festival[8], the paper details a selection of the diverse forms of cultural agency operating on the ground and the many participants and residents involved in investigating the 'Olympic-led regeneration', rupturing binaries of 'official' and 'unofficial'. The scale of the Olympic project, along with its proximity to an enormous conurbation of artists, has made this urban site one of the most critically examined; the site and, most notably, the spatial manifestations resulting from the legal frameworks upholding it, have propelled an unprecedented number and range of questions to the fore.

The thoughts and propositions of an emerging political scientist, an engineer and an architectural theorist – the outcome of salons hosted by public works studio, the art and architecture collective – are presented in the final three contributions in this section.

Léa Ayoub's paper, written as a response to the salon Public Air Space[9], provides comprehensive insight into the ideas driving the rapid construction of skyscrapers in the city, and details the implications of these buildings on the experience of urban space and the ongoing exclusion of the public from them. Tall buildings have been likened to what were once inaccessible Royal Parks, or rights of way in the countryside, and the salon asked whether public spaces in skyscrapers could be the new Hampstead Heath, Tiergarten or Lincoln Park? Should everyone have a right to a horizon and what are the next steps to removing the barriers that restrict these views? Léa Ayoub, who has worked for a tall building consultancy, argues that, although current policy encourages and even requires public access to the upper floors, the complex network of partners and interests related to skyscrapers makes it unlikely that public access will be provided unless it is agitated for.

Looking below the ground, Elizabeth Fonseca, an environmental engineer who works for an inner-city local authority, draws our attention to sites where the lack of legal consideration may have significant implications for land quality and projects that propose, for example, 'edible estates'. Her paper, 'Land Quality In Urban Design: How Does a Lack of Standards Affect Sustainable Brownfield Development in England ?', is an outcome of the Medical City salon[10], which investigated the complex relationship between public health and cities. It highlights remarkable statistics – for example, 25% of land in urban settings is contaminated – and disturbing facts – for example, current legislation and guidance in the UK regarding contaminated land and groundwater does not operate on a precautionary principle (in contrast to EU ethos). Although UK legislation requires proactive identification of potentially contaminated land, once identified, a minimal level of remediation is required to deem a development suitable for use (instead of eliminating all known threats). Elizabeth Fonseca argues there are strategies available to prevent risks to public health in industrialised cities and offers examples for a way forward.

The Medical City salon also initiated the final paper addressing the theme 'Legalities of Space'. Alan Thompson, architectural theorist and chair of Art & Architecture, threads a diversity of disciplines through his essay as he outlines the entangled relationship between western medicine and urbanism. Interestingly, he confirms early in the piece that he can evidence little or no influence of the ideas driving the founding principles of architecture on the practice of medicine. Conversely, he highlights how medical ideas have contributed not only to the actual design of urban spaces but also to urban theory and planning itself. 'The Medical City... a story of Venus and Mercury' allows us to chart, through the pertinent example of 'medicine', how ideas shape policies and subsequently laws. From antiquity to the present, the paper maps ways in which spaces have been created as a direct result of concepts related to hygiene and health. Is the rise of 'interdisciplinary urbanism' and the breakdown of specialised and compartmentalised thinking the result of holistic treatment approaches recently adopted in western medicine? Is the recent requirement for mixed-use developments a consequence of contemporary medical theory? Alan Thompson explores whether the founding medical principles of necessity have prevailed over the founding architectural ideas of utopia. Does this triumph of 'medical real-politick' result in an age of rapidly reducing dreams for our cities? What emerges from the essay is how disciplines, such as medicine, that are often overlooked by urbanists continue to flood the ideas and precipitate the laws that shape their everyday practice, and consequently the creation of spaces in our cities. It raises the question: Where are the sites of knowledge that can be drawn on when designing cities?

The theme 'Legalities of Space' arose out of the driving questions that surfaced from the wide range of people and organisations involved in the TINAG festival and salons. This book is unable to provide a comprehensive look at all the workshops and discussions that addressed this theme. Not included are the important workshops organised by Mustafa Traore[11] – lead by organisations such as Les Braves Garcons D'Afrique, based in the Parisian suburbs – which unearthed the implications of French race and ethnicity laws and the resulting spatial manifestations and consequences – injustices that provoke violence, as was the case in the Paris suburbs in 2005 and 2006.

The unnecessary demolition of important buildings and their replacement with alien typologies is now propelling a multiplicity of disciplines across the globe to ask questions about space and cities. Complaint, confusion and resignation are being replaced with a diverse and rapidly growing body of knowledge deriving from a previously unimaginable spectrum of people and locations. The culmination of these critical and multiple new sites of knowledge seems to signal a shift. Existing structures – planning, finance, governance systems – are being rigorously researched and examined in detail while new ideas and approaches are developed and proposed.

This section propels further reflection. Is law not an arena that urbanists ought to know significantly more about and participate within? Should conferences and workshops on regeneration, cities and culture regularly include lawyers? The demand for legal knowledge evident at the festival and salons suggests it is certainly an opportunity. Can change on the ground only occur when a cultural movement runs in parallel and then intersects with the field of law? A superficial survey of recent cultural changes, in fields such as gender, sexuality and human rights, shows that ideas proposed, demonstrated and agitated for by heterogeneous actors shifted to influencing the everyday when the notions driving the movement were understood and subsequently translated into law. Is this a site of rich possibility and what can we do to bring the field of law into the discussion?

1. OPEN (Organisation for Promotion of Environmental Needs) is a community action not-for-profit company founded by Bill Parry-Davies in 2005.
2. Held at Space 1 studio on 25 October 2008.
3. Held at Space 1 studio on 26 October 2008.
4. 'Erase, stretch, relinquish' is introduced here as a phrase to summarise both the actions and the thinking leading built-environment decision-making processes. The demolition of the building housing the Four Aces Club in Dalston is a useful case study. Rather than re-using the existing building and making use of the ideas put forward by local residents it was demolished. 'Erasing' the site was seen as both easier and more efficient. Demolition provided a gap for an alien typology to land. The new typology 'stretches' all aspects of the site including size, height and programming. The aim is to 'stretch' the profit margin for the developer and the tax revenues for the local authority. 'Relinquish' is the stage when almost everyone that has benefited from 'stretching' moves on. The developer either sells the site or passes on management responsibilities; the local authority no longer owns anything and struggles to answer who does own what or why none of the facilities promised have been built. The neighbours 'relinquish' or resign themselves to the fact that their neighbourhood will never be what it could have been.
5. Published in 2007 by the European Platform for Alternative Practice and Research on the City (PEPRAV).
6. Held on 24 October 2008.
7. Installed in Café Oto throughout the festival (23-25 October 2008).
8. Held at Café Oto on 25 October 2008.
9. Held at the public works studio in London on 24 September 2007.
10. Held at the public works studio in London on 14 July 2008.
11. Held at Café Oto on 24 October 2008 and 25 October 2008.

The Legalities of Development

and its Resistance in the UK

BILL PARRY-DAVIES

The UK's town and country planning control system is notorious for its complexity. It is comprised of layers of both law and policy, which may not all be relevant to an individual planning application. We have:

· the 1998 Aarhus Convention at the international level, which has been incorporated into the national law of European Community member states, including in the UK
· central government Planning Policy Statements
· Regional Spatial Strategies (known in London as the London Plan), and
· at local authority level, Local Development Frameworks (these replace Local Plans and Unitary Development Plans).

Each Local Planning Authority (LPA), e.g. a London borough council, has a responsibility to weigh and balance these policies to ensure overall compliance before planning consent is given.

Despite this complex system of checks and balances, we see increasing loss of character and identity in local communities. Historic environments and buildings that form and define the identity of areas over generations are destroyed. Open and green spaces are built over, with the loss of bio-diversity. The emergence of 'Tesco

Town' cloned high streets, dominated by multiple house builders and retailers, eliminates diversity in the local economy. In short, places become indistinguishable from each other and could be anywhere – with the consequent dislocation and alienation of communities.

What power do local people have to protect their environment and communities in the face of apparently unstoppable development proposals? How can local people organise to express their views effectively, in the face of powerful government agencies and retail, industrial and other commercial property interests? How can people effectively influence planning authorities and moderate or even defeat development proposals that may cause irreversible damage to their local economies and environments?

Development schemes often start with 'pre-application' discussions and negotiations between the developer and the local authority's planning officers and elected councillors. Developers seek to persuade planning officers to recommend approval of their proposed scheme to the LPA's planning committees. Major developments may involve significant 'planning gain' payments, made by the developer to enable the local authority to mitigate the effect of the develoment. For example, increased investment in educational, medical, transport or other facilities may be required. In larger residential schemes, a percentage of 'affordable housing' may be required either on or 'off-site', to enable the local authority to discharge its legal duty to house vulnerable homeless people. The attraction of such payments, and a fear of appeals and court challenges if a developer's planning application is refused, means LPAs have to try to balance conflicts of interest.

Local people often don't know of 'pre-application' discussions until they reach an advanced stage. By which time, in principle agreements may already have been reached on the land use, the massing and density of a proposed development, and payments to be made by the developer. Local people alert to sites that attract development interest should use their Aarhus Convention rights and the Freedom of Information Act to request copies of minutes and other records of pre-application discussions from the LPA. Information obtained should then be shared with others with common interests, e.g. business and residents' associations, heritage groups and local citizens. Interested stakeholders can then discuss the scheme and whether alternative ideas could produce more sustainable and beneficial outcomes.

Once registered by an LPA, a planning application must be advertised in a local newspaper and notices circulated to local premises and occupiers affected by the proposed scheme. The public usually has only 21 days to lodge written objections, although consideration must still be given to objections lodged after that date. Arrangements should also be made to meet the LPA's officers to inspect the planning file and to require them, as they are obliged to do, to provide all relevant information and comprehensively explain the application and how it relates to relevant planning policies.

Special rules apply where a scheme affects listed historic sites and buildings or affects designated conservation areas. A substantial scheme may also have to undergo an Environmental Impact Assessment and, because of its strategic significance, the scheme may require prior approval by a higher authority. For example, the Greater London Authority may have to approve before a London LPA can give planning consent.

Written representations should then be lodged with the LPA. Comments and objections to aspects of the scheme should refer to the relevant planning policies. Representations can also be made to impose certain development conditions, if planning consent is to be granted. Where an application is contentious, the LPA will generally refer it to a full planning committee meeting for decision. Planning officers may otherwise approve minor schemes under delegated powers.

A planning officer's report to their planning committee must reflect the appropriateness of the development and set out the arguments both for and against in a fair and balanced way. Objectors should register to speak at the planning committee meeting at which the LPA's decision is to be made. The public Register of Members' Interests should be searched prior to the meeting to ensure that elected planning committee members have no conflict of interest that might give the appearance of pre-determination, i.e. they decided before hearing the evidence. If the report or its presentation to the committee is biased, a decision to reject the application may be the subject of an appeal by the applicant; while a decision to approve the application may be the subject of a court application for judicial review by any objectors.

To challenge the grant of planning permission requires an application to the High Court for judicial review. This must be made as soon as possible, but not later than three months from the date of the planning decision. In view of these timescales, it's advisable to seek specialist advice for a possible challenge in advance of the planning committee meeting and decision.

While legal proceedings may appear to take the campaign out of local people's hands, they still carry the risk that campaigners will become liable for the LPA's, and sometimes even a developer's, legal costs if the court challenge to the planning decision fails. Because an unknown amount of the defendant's costs could be awarded against objectors in addition to their own legal costs, there is a risk of personal bankruptcy. This is one of the biggest obstacles to individuals pursuing legal challenges to environmental injustice.

Adoption of a company structure, to protect directors and shareholders from personal liability, is at the heart of the capitalist system designed to encourage entrepreneurial risk. Developers normally incorporate as companies to enjoy this protection, and local politicians and officers enjoy similar protection by virtue of their status within government. Why should individual community members not enjoy similar protection? How can legal processes be used imaginatively to ensure greater access to environmental justice and community control of environmental campaigns?

One such model to resist inappropriate development is the community action company, OPEN. OPEN is the trading name of Organisation for Promotion of Environmental Needs Limited, a not-for-profit company comprising individuals and organisations from the local communities in which it operates. OPEN's formal objectives are to promote excellence in the quality of the built environment and in the provision of transportation and amenities, to ensure that changes to these have proper regard to the needs of residents and businesses, and the maintenance of sustainable residential and business communities.

The liability of OPEN members is limited by their guarantee to pay £1 if the company is wound up. In other words, if legal proceedings brought in OPEN's name were unsuccessful and a costs order made against OPEN, its members would have a maximum liability of £1 if the company were unable to pay the costs. By incorporating as a company, OPEN can act both as a sword to challenge environmental injustice, and as a shield to protect its members from personal liability.

In practice, OPEN acts as a catalyst to bring people and their organisations together in local fora to campaign under the OPEN umbrella – but at the same time ensuring local ownership and control of the campaign, and reliance on local knowledge and resources. OPEN assists individuals to identify and build on their community's self-interest. It seeks to provide a platform and a vehicle to express people's concerns to protect local character and identity, to advance the needs of local business and residential communities, and to promote diversity and a sustainable social and natural environment.

OPEN is about people being able to participate in change, take pride in their communities, and take responsibility for their environment. People work with OPEN, and join as members and directors, to seek a new approach to regeneration and redevelopment, and to act effectively together as citizens. OPEN has so far operated in North and East London which, in the recent years of property 'boom' and the government's strategic initiatives associated with the UK's successful 2012 Olympic bid, has been the subject of major development interest and commercial pressure.

OPEN began its work in Dalston in 2005, in response to the dereliction of the local built environment and public realm, and with the knowledge that numerous potential development sites had changed hands. Local traders in an increasingly derelict Georgian terrace, which had been transferred from public to private ownership, faced eviction on the grounds of demolition and redevelopment. OPEN members approached English Heritage, which identified the historic terrace as worthy of preservation. Following OPEN's campaign, the LPA's eventual recognition of a historic asset lead to inclusion of the terrace in a new conservation area. The developer's appeal to the Planning Inspectorate against refusal was defeated.

OPEN next became aware of an unlawful attempt by a few local public officials to demolish locally listed Georgian houses and the 1886 Dalston Theatre without planning permission. OPEN sought and obtained an injunction in judicial review proceedings. As a result, the local authority was forced to consult the public as part of a planning permission application and to pay OPEN's legal costs. What emerged was a plan by the local council, and agencies of the Greater London Authority, to demolish historic buildings and redevelop Dalston town centre. By selling the cleared site with planing permission to develop tower blocks of private flats for sale, the local authority hoped to finance construction of a £40-million concrete slab over a reinstated railway station, on which to site a bus turnaround.

With widespread community support, OPEN challenged the demoliton and redevelopment decisions by three sets of judicial review proceedings and obtained court injunctions staying the demolitions for a total period of 18 months. Despite alternative development proposals put forward by the community, it became clear that the authorities had not, and were not willing to, consider alternative plans. Ultimately, a fourth planning decision was made by the LPA, which was procedurally sound and therefore legally 'bullet proof' from further court action. The historic buildings were eventually lost after the government refused to intervene and 'call in' the planning decision, on the basis that the development would provide essential transport infrastructure required for the 2012 Olympics.

Nevertheless, the campaign achieved a 30% reduction in the overall development density. The local OPEN Dalston group is now in discussion with the LPA regarding a conservation-led scheme for the Georgian terrace and ways in which the remainder of the town centre could be improved with community involvement.

In Aldgate, OPEN assisted the local Bengali community to make written and personal representations to the City of London's planning committee. The committee imposed planning conditions on a proposed major office redevelopment including structural works to mitigate the effects of overshadowing residents' homes and gardens.

In Shoreditch, OPEN assisted local associations to make representations to the LPA and higher authorities. This won protection for a historic building by its inclusion in a redefined conservation area. Its redevelopment as a 50-storey tower block may not now go ahead. OPEN Shoreditch also challenged the consent for another tower block, as the local authority's own conservation and design officers' views were not reported to the planning committee. OPEN Shoreditch is now campaigning for a community-based masterplan to ensure a sustainable outcome for the Bishopsgate Goodsyard and the area generally.

Even though individual OPEN members have no personal liability for costs awarded against the company, its directors have a duty to act reasonably, i.e. to protect OPEN from the risk of unquantified costs awards that could render it insolvent. To manage down this risk, OPEN asks the court to make a protective costs order (PCO), which limits the amount of legal costs that can be awarded against a litigant in the event that the case is lost. Until now, the courts have limited PCOs to cases with more than local significance. However, this is inconsistent with the Aarhus Convention as PCOs are essential to achieve 'equality of arms' between well-resourced local and national government authorities and not-for-profit community-based companies such as OPEN, which seek to challenge them via donations, fundraising and voluntary effort.

However, the remedy of judicial review has limited value. Parliament has conferred the discretion of whether or not to grant planning applications on the LPA and not the courts, and so the court's concern will primarily be with the form and not the content of the decision. The court will not substitute its own view of the merit of the scheme but can order that the application be reconsidered if the permission granted has the appearance of bias, inappropriate procedure or other error. Nevertheless the developer can require the planning application be reconsidered and the LPA may then grant permission lawfully, by a decision which corrects earlier errors. In view of this, OPEN's legal challenges are combined with campaigns to raise public awareness and apply political pressure – particularly where the public authority is in partnership with private developers or is itself the landowner.

In its campaigns, OPEN analyses and disseminates information regarding development proposals including Environmental Impact Assessments. It then:

· consults affected local communities and assists the formulation of objections
· forms alliances with local and national organisations and amenity societies and coordinates objections to LPAs
· convenes local election 'hustings' and develops communications with local political representatives, and
· makes representations to local, regional and national planning authorities.

The involvement of local people in OPEN, as company members and directors, strengthens contacts with the local creative communities. OPEN Dalston worked closely with documentary filmmaker Winstan Whitter and writer Michael Rosen to communicate complex issues in popular forms and broadcast these across the community and media networks to raise public awareness and understanding of events. In Shoreditch, local artist Brad Lochore worked with artists Tracey Emin, Rachel Whiteread and others to organise an Art Storm to lobby the Greater London Authority regarding its support of City expansion into the Bishopsgate Goodsyard. This had proposed sterile towers, without any community consultation or promised masterplanning, and prominent artists have helped to raise fighting funds by donating valuable works to an auction.

An emerging area of law that potentially offers assistance to environmental campaigners concerns the Aarhus Convention. Compliance with the Aarhus Convention of 1998 is an overarching requirement of states within the European Community. Aarhus provides that adequate protection of the environment is essential to human well–being and the enjoyment of basic human rights including the right to life itself. With this in mind, Aarhus recognises that to enjoy and assert these rights:

- citizens must have access to information affecting the environment in a transparent, timely and understandable form and free of charge
- be entitled to early participation in decision-making, while options remain open and effective public participation can take place, and
- have access to justice and legal remedies in environmental matters that are fair, timely and not prohibitively expensive so that legitimate interests of the current and future generations are protected and the law upheld.

Aarhus therefore requires national, regional and local authorities to take whatever steps are necessary to achieve compliance with these objectives and to ensure that members of the public, irrespective of their location, do not face discrimination or penalties in seeking to enforce such rights. In recent years, the UK courts have recognised that national amenity societies have a legitimate interest and expectation that the courts will entertain challenges of environmental decisions of wide public concern. Since Aarhus, however, judges increasingly recognise that local citizens' organisations should enjoy the same rights in relation to environmental issues that affect their local communities. The provisions for access to environmental justice in the UK risk beaching its convention obligations. We can expect to see increasing reliance upon the Aarhus Convention in challenges made to public authorities for environmental justice.

BIOGRAPHY

Bill Parry-Davies is a partner in the London solicitors' firm Dowse & Co., and a founder member of the community action company OPEN (Organisation for Promotion of Environmental Needs Limited).

Self-Organised Spatial Practices

and Desires in Conflictive Urban Developments

MARA FERRERI

This essay has been conceived as an integrated commentary to the screening of the video *Isola Nostra* (2007) at the TINAG festival and as a way of furthering the concerns that surfaced during the following discussion. Although the experiences of Isola Art Center and OUT constitute the main focus, the paper will open up to other critical practices in contexts of urban renewal and decay as sites of social, cultural and political struggles within contemporary cities. Between the representative and the performative, each of the practices discussed offers important perspectives on modes of action not only to exercise pressure on the power/knowledge dynamics behind urban conflicts, but also to produce alternative ways of inhabiting urban spaces.

Isola Nostra

To begin with, *Isola Nostra* is not a documentary proper. It was not shot coherently by one author and much of the visual material was part of a general and collective effort to document a practice in the process of becoming. The result is an edited assemblage of footage archived over several years, a patchwork narrative of eventful moments as well as periods of relative calm. The film is organised thematically in chapters,[1] each section attempting an overview of the simultaneous trajectories of the collective occupation of a vacant urban space in Milan, Italy, and of the struggle to keep its public existence. The chapter headings give glimpses of the elements that composed this experience: the neighbourhood and its inhabitants; the controversial need/desire for public spaces and the actions leading to its precarious constitution; the top-down imposition of an urban renewal plan with little or no public consultation; the inevitable clashes between the interested parties; the cultural and political role of contemporary art and curatorial practices; and the conflicts that led to its closure and demolition.

Beside hindsight considerations on its success or failure, the space that *Isola Nostra* attempts to sketch is a space of potentiality, built through gestures, tactics and strategies. Commonly known as the Stecca, the centre of this space was an abandoned factory in the Isola neighbourhood of Milan that had ceased to trade after bombings of the city in 1945, standing untouched for several decades, in stark contrast to the upmarket urban city-centre only a mile away. In time, neighbourhood associations were formed and in the 1990s they carried out a campaign to turn the vacant land of the ex-industrial site into public green areas, finally achieving their aim of turning a cumbersome ruin into a space for the neighbourhood.

Around the year 2000, the city council declared the intention to destroy the ex-factory and the parks to make space for an extensive urban development, a plan currently known as Milano Porta Nuova.[2] The threat of demolition and the opposition of the inhabitants to the development triggered an interest in the space. Several self-organised groups moved in and began projects to re-use the Stecca, which became a sort of catalyst for architectural, social and artistic experiments. Starting as a small curatorial experience within this context, Isola Art Center began to work with the local inhabitants, and later organised the Office for Urban Transformation (OUT) as a platform for research and action on the city.

As the complex story of this centre and its activities has already been summarised elsewhere,[3] this essay will focus on selected practices and experimental ideas tested by these two groups in the ongoing conflict between the city council and the neighbourhood. It is the interplay of desires, demands, tactics, urban planners' agendas and counter-proposals that make the experiences of Isola Art Center and OUT potentially important when thinking about critical urban practices.

Against representative monopolies

Urban spaces are never neutral containers in which social processes unfold, but are constantly produced on several different registers by changing social arrangements and power/knowledge dynamics. These processes of production are particularly visible in spaces left vacant or undergoing urban renewal, where economic and social conflicts can be publicly articulated by active inhabitants through forms of street protest and counter information, against a background of images of the city produced by councils and development agencies.

The result is often perceived by city inhabitants as constituting an 'imaginative monopoly' over the representation of possible urban futures, produced through performances of 'urban expertise' such as technical discussions on development plans in the press and glamorous renderings of buildings-to-come placed on the hoardings of construction sites. In contexts of conflictive urban development in particular, these representations are crucially connected to knowledge dynamics in which problems are formulated and solutions provided, setting a visual and technical language that draws a line around a field of knowledge which becomes the unquestionable prerogative of a small group of individuals, often reducing the rhetoric of public consultations and neighbourhood participation to skilful exercises in persuasion.

This controversially bleak and static perspective on power/knowledge urban dynamics, however, has been challenged both from within the group of so-called 'professional spatial practitioners' as well as from critically engaged actors and movements external to it, often through dialogue and co-operation. Historical experiments of participatory architecture and self-organised urbanism have in recent years regained importance in light of a growing proliferation of practices attempting to develop imaginative and practical counter-proposals to existing dynamics of spatial production. Under the name of 'critical spatial practices',[4] a wide array of experiments and interventions – between art, activism and architecture – have been gathered, and can be said to constitute temporal and spatial disruptions of the often simplified and biased representations of contemporary cities, as well as of the relationship between subjects and spaces.

In this framework, the work begun by the European Platform for Alternative Practice and Research on the City (PEPRAV) and its publication *Urban/Act: A handbook for alternative practice* (2007) constitute important attempts to formulate "a collective critical enquiry into contemporary alternatives to practice and research on the city".[5] The projects collected and investigated by PEPRAV, such as Park Fiction and ECObox, which will be analysed in this paper, are often characterised by small-scale forms of self-organisation that attempt to mobilise and connect inhabitants, activists and professionals to deal with specific problems through collective engagement.

These attempts at critical research have developed from a critique of traditional architecture towards a more participatory and collective approach,[6] as well as from a growing interest in the fields of performance and contemporary art practices by socio-spatial disciplines such as urban studies and cultural geography. The significance of these critical practices, and their relevance to the study of urban geographies, lie in what could be called a conjugation of oppositional and propositional tactics and modalities of action. In fact, what differentiates these practices from traditional political activism on urban issues is the combination of modes of action, such as marches, petitions and pickets, with forms of autonomous production and dissemination of different ways of inhabiting urban spaces, unfolded on a representative and a performative level.[7]

OUT and the Isola neighbourhood

An alternative way of thinking about urban spaces demands, first of all, a critical engagement with the existing power/knowledge dynamics that shape them. This begins with questioning the access to the specific knowledge required to comprehend the transformations occurring in the living environment and to produce informed counter-proposals. The video *Isola Nostra* describes how this need was addressed in the Isola by a heterogeneous combination of neighbourhood associations and local activists in conjunction with artists and architects who organised OUT as a platform to share knowledge on local and global urban issues. Professionals and local inhabitants created an archive of the transformations planned for the neighbourhood, and public discussions were held to understand and articulate the existing legal rights of the neighbourhood inhabitants. From this, legal proceedings were instituted against the city government, focusing on those aspects of the plans that did not comply with the council's regulations, for instance, in terms of the destruction of public green areas to make space for private developments.[8]

With these analytical skills, and deeply rooted in an open discussion of collective needs and desires, a counter-proposal was put to the council. The alternative plan would have enabled the developers to build the same volumes without destroying the parks and the former factory, which could have been renovated and turned into a common space for social and cultural purposes, following OUT's aim "to make possible a bottom-up urban process, based on three basic principles: to understand the city, to dream the city, to transform the city".[9]

These three different principles can be seen as different moments building on the opposition to the development plan, but going beyond it, developing a practice around a different vision, an alternative and collective production of space. In the first moment, the contingent urban situation has to be researched and analysed through an engagement with specific urban issues as well as with the constantly shifting needs, demands and desires articulated by the inhabitants. The second is "to imagine and dream about [the] transformations of these situations",[10] engaging with the representational aspect of urban life and thinking about the power of imagination as a force of change. The last – although the three feed into each other at different moments and in different combinations – consists in taking the initiative to activate these transformations and to support them in time.

To illustrate these propositions with a practical example, two drawings can be sampled as ways in which an understanding of the contingent situation lies at the basis of the production of alternative imaginings of the Isola neighbourhood. A written description of the first drawing (*fig.* 01) explains: "the master plan (left) called 'Garibaldi Repubblica' [now part of the larger Porta Nuova plan] would cut the district in two parts with a highway feeder road, that has the form of a Y. It would destroy two small parks and an old factory, and build high-rise towers and a shopping mall".[11] The drawing on the right shows the project of the neighbourhood associations, which "saves the existing green areas and the old factory building without preventing the construction of new buildings".[12]

The second drawing (*fig.* 02) goes a step further. Besides showing an alternative development, a counter-proposal is put forward to valorise the existing use of the space, to extend it, and to affirm the collective desire to keep its pluralistic and self-organised vision. In an interview released in 2003, Bert Theis from OUT explained the collective elaboration of this second drawing as follows:

> OUT *made a very elementary drawing and everybody added suggestions and proposals with drawings or text. The final version is a synthesis, a "collective dream" of urban transformation. This drawing was printed by the neighbourhood associations and put into [sic] the shops of the district in order to convince everybody of the possibility of a different project. The drawing was also given to all politicians together with a petition signed by all associations of the quarter [sic].*[13]

It is important to observe how both drawings operate on the level of representation by providing alternatives to the developer's projections on the space. The 'collective dream' of the second drawing, in fact, not only challenges the visual monopoly of the council's posters celebrating the development plans, but also promotes the alternatives elaborated by the neighbourhood associations. This form of counter-propaganda, paired with public discussions on technical aspects of the development, have become increasingly important in light of the changing marketing strategy of 'eco-gentrification'[14] devised by Milan's council and the development agencies. In a nutshell, a new 'eco-district' plan was presented – partly in response to the critique of the old 'Garibaldi Repubblica' development project – boasting two tree-covered towers called 'vertical forest', designed by Stefano Boeri Studio, in addition to the construction of luxury dwellings, underground parking lots, offices and a shopping centre.[15]

The 'green' marketing of the new development plan attempts to mystify the fact that the trees on the private terraces of these luxury skyscrapers will not replace the public green area that has been destroyed, and that the remaining small parks between the high-rise developments will be de-facto cut off from the existing neighbourhood by the new buildings. This representational strategy is the result of translating the inhabitants' demands to keep the green areas into eco-friendly designs, which do not engage with the controversial social and economic impact of these top-down transformations and with the demands for public spaces in the neighbourhood. Writing in the French journal *Urbanisme* about this development campaign, the philosopher Tiziana Villani has called it "a mass media's fairytale utilised to mask particularly aggressive techniques of governance".[16]

Save Our Heritage and possessive pronouns

Opening the discussion to similar practices of counter-representation in contexts of conflictive urban development, a parallel can be drawn between the experiences of OUT and those of OPEN Dalston (Dalston section of the not for profit Organisation for Promotion of Environmental Needs) in Hackney, as depicted in the film *Save Our Heritage* (2008) by Winstan Whitter screened during the This Is Not a Gateway Festival. The documentary was shot during the making of *Legacy in the Dust* (2008), a film that charts the history and untimely demise of the Four Aces Club, former Dalston Coliseum, one of London's most influential music venues.[17] However, while *Legacy in the Dust* recollects retrospectively the many lives of the club from its inception to its decay and demolition, *Save Our Heritage* develops from the filmmaker's encounter with the lawyer Bill Parry-Davies of OPEN, and his campaign to save the building from the plans of Hackney Council to destroy and replace it with a residential tower block.

As an independent organisation, the objects of OPEN Dalston are not restricted to fighting gentrification in East London. As their blog states, its aim is broadly "to

promote excellence in the quality of the built environment, the provision of transportation and the provision of amenities, and to ensure that changes to these have
proper regard to the needs of residents and businesses and the maintenance of a
sustainable residential and business community".[18] These aims and Parry-Davies'
interest in the Dalston Coliseum led to a series of actions against the development
plans proposed by the local council under pressure to construct new transport
infrastructures between the centre of the city and the 2012 Olympic site.

One of these actions consisted in the production of a poster that showed a different representation of the building, challenging its image of cumbersome decay
and triggering the possibility of a different renewal to turn the building – some
could argue *once again* – into a common space for the neighbourhood (*fig.03*).

Despite the smaller scale, a similar argument about counter-representational
practices can be applied to OPEN's image: an attempt to challenge the appeal of
architectural renderings – 'what they propose we have' – with a proposal based
on the desires of local inhabitants. It can be argued that OPEN's alternative depic-
tions of the future of the Dalston Coliseum were not just images for the movement
of opposition, but had already begun to initiate an imaginative action capable of
disrupting both the imaginary of an abandoned building and the polished renderings of the advertised developments. In the third phrase – 'what we could have'
– is contained the moment in which the inhabitants' demands gain independence
from the movement of resistance, and begin to elaborate a new, possible, city.

In this regard, an apparently trivial observation should be made on the use
of possessive adjectives in the titles of the two documentaries. Both *Save Our
Heritage* and *Isola Nostra* (*Our Isola*) narrate the story of neighbourhoods that
acknowledge an undesired urban change imposed from above and act in various
collective forms to give visibility to an alternative future for their living environment. In their actions, abandoned buildings were reclaimed as 'our', in a strong
statement on the relationship between inhabitants, on the one hand, and a space
they did not legally possess, on the other.

Both the Dalston Coliseum and the Stecca – however different in quantity of
participants, temporal scale and means of 'occupation' – are described through
these actions as spaces of common use, in contrast to the private projections of
real-estate developers. In this sense, it could be said that both films explore not
only the conflicts generated by top-down urban transformation and its possible
counter-practices, but also the collective desires that get ultimately fixed in the
adjective 'our' applied to the spaces cared and campaigned for.

Desire archives

How to think about these desires and their potential role in the collective production of alternative spaces? From OUT to the experiences collected by PEPRAV, the
use of the concept of desire echoes and refracts practices of self-organised urban
design through so-called 'desire archives'. The idea of constituting an archive of
desires, as the starting point for collective imaginations of urban spaces, finds
a direct and important referent in the practice of the urban collective Park Fiction in Hamburg's red light district since 1995. The project of producing a parallel
plan for a public park originated from the decision of a network of inhabitants to
propose an alternative to the economic and political interests of the developments
planned by the city council, and is grounded in the belief that "the production of
desire – as ideas and practice – should be the driving force behind the reshaping
of cities".[19]

What is the significance of thinking about critical spatial practices in terms of
production of desire? And how is it possible to see this production as the ground
for something radically different from the needs and demands of oppositional activism? These questions resonate strongly with a series of recent discussions in
the journal *Multitudes*[20] in relation to the experiences of Park Fiction and of the
ECObox by the atelier d'architecture autogérée (aaa) in Paris.[21]

aaa's project started with the acknowledgement of an under-used 'vacant'
space in the Parisian neighbourhood of La Chapelle, which a collective of inhabitants, artists, architects and students turned into a self-managed community garden. Doina Petrescu, one of its organisers and theorists, describes it as "a bricolage
project [that] resulted from an assemblage of desires".[22] Discussing the experience
of the ECObox, the French sociologist Anna Querrien has furthered this argument, offering an analysis of the heterogeneous assemblage of desires and forces
behind self-organised projects in urban spaces.[23]

The first desire, Querrien argues, is the 'anti-desire' of the inhabitants of districts or cities affected by urban renewal plans, who oppose the plans but lack the
time, the knowledge or the strength to elaborate an alternative project. The 'anti-
desire' of the oppositional moment prompts the collective efforts to share information, analyse legal implications and organise movements of protest on several
fronts. On this platform, the desires of the inhabitants can be said to have entered
into dialogue with what Querrien describes as a 'second' desire, which comes from
professionals who refuse to reproduce the system they have been trained in and

who seek alternative practices to gain a different knowledge and apply it to more socially and politically challenging projects. On the representative level, this 'second' desire might describe the force that moved artists and curators to constitute Isola Art Center as a centre for contemporary art and community activities.

In Milan, where public exhibition spaces are risible, the art centre provided a unique possibility for curators and emerging artists to organise and manage a public programme of critical conferences, events and exhibitions. At the same time, the creation of an open cultural space inside an abandoned building can be said to have actualised the 'collective dream' of the centre for art and the neighbourhood depicted in OUT's second drawing. In this sense, the site-specific art projects and exhibitions that took place over the four years of Isola Art Center's existence became tools for a theoretical and practical discourse on urban alternatives and for the exploration of critical cultural engagement in specific spatial contexts.

Within this logic, many artists produced site-specific and unmovable works that de facto gave rise to a permanent art collection.[24] One of the latest examples of this tactic was the realisation of a 10-metre long, neon sign that read 'New Museum' to be installed on the factory's roof,[25] which playfully sought "to legitimate the space and paradoxically render official the presence of a clandestine node".[26] These projects, quickly absorbed by the cultural world as creative uses of vacant space, were always critically inscribed into the contingent struggle of the neighbourhood through texts and statements on the parallel opposition campaign and legal cases against the development plans. The neon sign and many other non-ephemeral artworks constituted a collection that functioned both as a form of self-authorisation and as a symbolic and physical barrier to the demolition of the building.

Desire as intensification of relations

It is clear from these examples and from the discussion on counter-representations that in order to understand self-organised critical practices it is necessary to engage with notions of collective and individual desires. To further this argument, an important theoretical tool to approach the forces behind urban action can be found in the writings of Spinoza on the notion of affect.[27] Without undertaking an analysis of the subtleties of Spinoza's *Ethics* and their interpretations, suffice to say that desire is conceptualised as one of the three primary affects, together with sadness and joy, which are described as changes in the intensity of relations[28] by which "the body's power of acting is increased or diminished".[29]

By drawing a correlation between the power of acting and increased intensities, a critical perspective is offered to address urban practices and the intensities that they can potentially generate. In the case of the constitution of desire archives, for instance, the practice of producing different imaginings of the city can bring the inhabitants to alter their approach to the environment in which they live and to act upon this relationship. If this renewed interest in the urban environment of the everyday flourishes in the generation of new desires and more intense relationships, then these imaginative practices of counter-representation can be seen as the very basis for alternative action, in a way that cannot be brought back to the categories of needs and demands within which desires are commonly articulated in the arena of representative politics.

If the relation between subjects and spaces can be seen as a changing intensity, then affective register becomes a fundamental tool for urban practices that aim to be critical and transformative. In this framework, the modalities of these actions become decisive, and certain socio-spatial practices gain more relevance than others. Here the question of embodied practices becomes crucial. According to Spinoza, affects belong to the body and to the mind alike, and it is through empirical experience that body and mind are affected and moved towards action or inaction. Collective actions of tending and re-using abandoned spaces, for example, can therefore be understood as ways of practicing intensified socio-spatial relations.

In this perspective, the practice of the ECObox as collective gardening can be compared to the occupation and maintenance of the abandoned ex-factory and green area in the Isola neighbourhood. By transforming a wasteland into a garden and an abandoned building into a communal space, the very occupation of these spaces and the action of transforming them can trigger experiences of intensified receptivity to spaces and subjects. The empty space – or emptied, as often bearing the effect of calculated speculations – ceases to be the shell of an absence and can become a space of possibilities. Active affects such as desire or joy can be seen as the forces behind such self-organised 'inoperative' collective actions.[30]

The affective framework, introduced by the discussion on desire and alternative practices, is crucial to engage with the dynamics that shape contemporary cities, both in a positive and in a negative way. Theories of affect can provide an important framework within which to analyse processes of disinterest of inhabitants with the spaces in which they live. By acknowledging the ambivalence of affect, Spinoza defines sadness as a decrease in the ability of acting. And on this note, it is interesting to draw attention to the curious fact that in the French language a disused space is *désaffecté*, as if constituted by 'negative' affects as forces of detachment and subsiding intensity.

The economic and political implications of an affective approach to urban processes are particularly important in contexts of conflictive urban developments. It is in the interest of a certain type of real-estate speculation that some areas in a city become *désaffecté*, since the disinterest of the local inhabitants guarantees a swift and smooth transformation of spaces according to unquestioned blueprints of so-called 'regeneration'. The abandonment of dilapidated buildings and land in urban contexts would serve the scope of representing the area as insecure and worthless, and promote *any* urban intervention as inherently positive. In particular, the question of affective registers could be profitably explored in further research in relation to ex-industrial sites that were once places of social and political identity, as in the case of the Isola neighbourhood.

By way of conclusion

The conjugation of representational and embodied tactics in the practice of the Isola Art Center and OUT has enabled the development of a discussion on the potential of critical urban action to transform traditional forms of opposition to conflictive urban planning. Beyond the oppositional moment, the practices analysed have elaborated different forms of counter-proposals to the top-down shaping of contemporary cities. From forms of parallel planning to participatory imaginings, their actions attempt to challenge the privileged position of urban professionals in the creation of spaces, and to disrupt – through counter-representations – their visual and imaginative monopoly on possible-cities-to-be.

The local specificity of the experiences that have been taken into consideration in the course of this essay does not allow for a general 'grand theory' of self-organised critical spatial practices, but a few critical perspectives have been sketched in an attempt to articulate a discussion about tactics and practices as forms of research and production of a different knowledge about urban spaces and those who inhabit it. Conceiving desire as an affect and as an intensification of relations, in particular, enables the deployment of a critical angle from which to address the potential of these embodied practices to initiate different relations between subjects and urban spaces. Critical attempts to understand the challenges that they pose to power/knowledge dynamics in the context of urban development will have to stem from an understanding of the role played by desire, of its use and abuse, and of its potential as a transformative force.

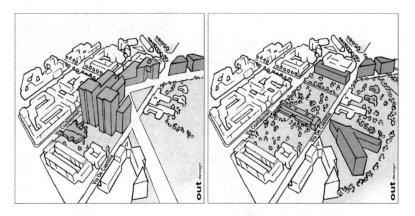

fig. 01: Counter-proposal to the Garibaldi
Republica development plan, OUT, 2002

fig. 02: Isola–Q'ART–Centre for art and the
neighbourhood, MARCO VAGLIERI and OUT, 2003

BIOGRAPHY

Mara Ferreri lives and works between London and Milan as a freelance writer and
researcher. She has been an active member of Isola Art Center since 2007.

Legalities of Space

WHAT WE HAVE

Dalston Theatre (More recently The 4 Aces & Labyrinth Clubs) and Georgian houses.

WHAT THEY WANT US TO HAVE

At least two 18 storey tower blocks on Dalston Lane.

WHAT WE COULD HAVE

Restored theatre entrance and Georgian town houses for small local shops and community and cultural uses.

dalston

www.opendalston.net

For more information contact
info@opendalston.net

or contact **OPEN c/o Dowse & Co. 23-25 Dalston Lane E8 3DF**

fig. 03 : Poster for OPEN Dalston campaign to save the Dalston Coliseum, "What We Have, What They Want Us To Have, What We Could Have"

1. The narrative unravels through the following chapters: *Isola Milano, Public Space, Top down, Disagreements, Art, Conflict.* The last chapter, *Uncertainty,* refers to the standstill created by the destruction of the building in April 2007, thus closing the film somewhat chronologically.

2. The development is now carried out by the real-estate development agency Hines, famous for high-rise office buildings and towers. Milan is a peculiarly low-rise city and the Porta Nuova development will have a drastic impact on its skyline. www.porta-nuova.com/ www.hines.com/development/office.aspx

3. Luis Miguel Selvelli, 'Representing Isola: Archaeology of an Art Center', 2008, http://transform.eipcp. net/correspondence/ (accessed: 24/02/09)

4. Jane Rendell, *Art and Architecture: A Place Between* (New York: IB Tauris, 2006).

5. aaa-PEPRAV (ed.), *Urban/Act: A handbook for alternative practice* (Paris: aaa-PEPRAV, 2007) p. 13.

6. See the essays collected in P. Blundell Jones,D. Petrescu and J. Till (eds), *Architecture and Participation* (London: Spon, 2005).

7. Alex Loftus, 'Intervening in the environment of the everyday', *Geoforum* 5, 2008.

8. The several legal battles of the neighbourhood began before the demolition of the Stecca and are still in the process of being judged. A verdict in July 2007 by the Lombardy regional court of justice (TAR) has ruled the suspension of the construction of the shopping centre on the parks. See 'Isola, stop al palazzo Ligresti', *Repubblica Milano,* 27 July 2007.

9. From the archive of the Isola Art Center, OUT, 2002, www.isolartcenter.org/

10. *ibid.*

11. *ibid.*

12. *ibid.*

13. Interview with Bert Theis by curator Noah Stolz at the presentation of OUT at Ciocca Contemporary Art, Milan, 2003, www.isolartcenter.org/

14. Definition coined by the curator and art critic Vasif Kortun.

15. See Stefano Boeri Studio and the Bosco Verticale project (Vertical Forest), www.stefanoboeri.net/

16. Tiziana Villani, 'Milan: Conflits autour de la requalification du quartier Isola Garibaldi', *Urbanisme,* 358 (January/February 2008), p. 38 (my translation).

17. thefouracesclub.com/

18. opendalston.blogspot.com/

19. Margit Czenki and Christopher Schäfer, 'Park Fiction', in *ibid.,* aaa-PEPRAV (2007) pp. 22-33.

20. Doina Petrescu, Anne Querrien and Constantin Petcou, 'Agir urbain', *Multitudes,* 31 (Winter) 2008, pp. 11-15(12).

21. aaa-PEPRAV (ed.), *Urban/Act: A handbook for alternative practice* (Paris: aaa-PEPRAV, 2007).

22. Doina Petrescu, 'Losing control, keeping desire', in P. Blundell Jones,D. Petrescu and J. Till (eds), *Architecture and Participation* (London: Spon, 2005) pp. 43-61(45).

23. Anne Querrien, 'Production of desires in the urban field', uncorrected, unedited manuscript of Anne Querrien's talk at Park Fiction, Umsonst & Draussen Symposium, 14 October 2006, www.parkfiction.org/2006/10/168.html

24. See Permanent Collection, www.isolartcenter.org/

25. Art project by KINGS, curated by Alessandra Poggianti.

26. Alessandra Poggianti, 'Isola. Tactics and Transition', 2008, in 'Who we are', www.isolartcenter.org/

27. Benedictus de Spinoza. Edwin Curley (ed. and trans.), *A Spinoza reader: the Ethics and other works* (Princeton: Princeton University Press, 1994).

28. Brian Massumi, 'The Autonomy of Affect', in *Parables for the Virtual: Movement, Affect, Sensation* (Durham: Duke University Press, 2002).

29. Spinoza, Ethics, III, def. 3. See also Don Garrett, *The Cambridge Companion to Spinoza* (New York: Cambridge University Press, 1996).

30. See Gillian Rose, 'Performing Inoperative Community: the Space and the Resistance of Some Community Arts Projects', in Steve Pile and Michael Keith (eds), *Geographies of Resistance* (London: Routledge, 1997).

A Guerrilla Greenbelt for London

A Connected Corridor of Reclaimed Spaces

HEATHER RING

"I thought this was a walk," an impatient man complained when I broke the news that our advertised 'Guerrilla Garden Walk' would, in fact, require a bus across town and a ride on the tube. It was an overcast afternoon in October and an unexpectedly large crowd had gathered to take part. I began to feel a little self-conscious as the leader of this organised tour of illicit activity.

The 'illicit' activity in question, guerrilla gardening, is simply the cultivation of land, without permission. A lucid, direct gesture, it bypasses the red tape of committees and the stifling procedures of planning permissions to bring life to challenged land. This walk was the first London expedition of the Wayward Land Stewards, a global group of guerrilla gardeners, landscape architects and geographers dedicated to exploring larger issues of land use and the politics of space. We consider wayward land to be both land that may be orphaned, neglected or abandoned, as well as land that is runaway, demonstrating a form of resilience, such as a vacant lot undergoing ecological succession and wild growth. In preparation for the tour, the Wayward Land Stewards attempted to map all the existing guerrilla gardens in London. Through this exercise we soon realised that while there are several clusters of guerrilla activity in neighbourhoods throughout the city, they are all quite spread out. As such, it soon became evident that any tour which attempted to capture the wide range of guerrilla garden practices in London would entail traversing the vast distances of the city. "And if anyone doesn't have Oyster cards," I apologetically explained, "we can help with that."

We started the tour in Dalston, a neighbourhood of diverse immigrant communities, including large Caribbean, Turkish and Vietnamese populations. Two miles north of the City, Dalston is undergoing rapid gentrification in part due to the regeneration schemes for East London in preparation for the 2012 Olympic Games. While this starting point for the tour made sense logistically, as we were gathering participants from the Dalston-based headquarters of the This is Not a Gateway Festival, it presented a challenge, as there were no known guerrilla gardens in the area. Despite appearances, we were hopeful: guerrilla gardening is a subtle, often anonymous activity. Most people just don't notice plants, whether cared for or neglected, and it's unlikely anyone, including ourselves, would be inclined to attribute a well-tended roadside median to a rogue landscaper when it's more logical (although perhaps no more likely) to assume that Hackney Council is just doing its job.

Occasionally we come across plantings in the city that are so unexpected, whimsical or incongruous with their surroundings that we suspect the hand of a guerrilla gardener. It's in these artful interventions – of large sunflowers shooting out from an otherwise bland carpet of turf, green shoots cracking through a concrete sidewalk to find the permeable ground underneath, ivy growing over billboard advertisements – that we appreciate guerrilla gardening's link to street art practices such as graffiti. Like these actions, which view the street as a platform for social change, guerrilla gardening often comes from a strong activist current, challenging the private ownership of public space. But unlike more overt forms of street art, few gardeners leave a recognisable mark or signature style: there hasn't yet been the gardening equivalent of a Banksy. Many guerrilla gardeners have stepped forward, encouraged by online social networks like www.guerrillagardening.org, but unless they've been explicit, either by blogging about it or highlighting their efforts with a sign, it's difficult to even begin cataloguing their gardens. While some planted actions have been radical enough to stand out, most guerrilla gardening remains anonymous, idiosyncratic and ephemeral – the tossing of seeds, the planting of bulbs – actions almost unmappable, but no less meaningful.

I figured we could overcome this obvious glitch in the guerrilla garden tour – the absence of any known guerrilla gardens – by adopting some wayward land of our own. But the lack of any gardening activity in Dalston might be explained by the fact that, along its main corridor, there really isn't much soft, fertile space, neglected or not. On the ride up Kingsland Road, which crosses through several East London neighbourhoods, the coverage of street trees thins out at Dalston, giving the area a hard, urban edge. When searching for areas of garden potential, the hardscape seemed relentless, from the stretch along Kingsland to the newly revamped public space, Gillett Square. Even the tree-pits were covered with grates to prevent any weeds from poking free. After much searching we eventually found an odd, exposed pile of dirt in the square across from Dalston Junction.

Facing three imposing cranes and a fence with billboards heralding the future of Dalston regeneration, the square is bordered on three sides by walls, one the Peace Carnival Mural, a vestige of Thatcher-era anti-capitalist resistance. The gentrification triggered by the current burst of regeneration seemed to neutralise what was once a radical mural: a colourful image of diversity which might yet survive while the small local businesses, markets and affordable housing which surround it are lost.

It was unclear whether the humble dirt pile we found on the back edge of the square was intentionally allocated by the council for planting, or whether it was merely wind-blown construction debris trapped in between these painted walls. While part of our tour group took shovels, or just pawed at the dirt with their hands to plant daffodil bulbs, some local Dalston residents on the tour explained that this square used to be part of a larger community gardening effort, one that has been undermined by the regeneration scheme.

"You should carry a sign on a post to corral people along," one woman quipped, as the large and now slightly soiled crowd worked its way back to the bus stop on Kingsland Road. As we boarded the bus it was already getting quite dark, and I worried we might lose people along the way. After a short trip, we arrived in Shoreditch, a gentrified neighbourhood in the inner city known for its concentration of hipsters and creative industries. Under the glow of billboards, at the intersection of Old Street and Great Eastern Street, I work with others to maintain a guerrilla garden. We now found it surrounded by bikes and revellers from the neighbouring bar, who looked on with interest as the tour group peered over the low iron fence that borders it on all sides.

It's unclear who actually owns this 4-metre wide, triangular piece of wayward land, but I walked by and scoped it out daily for a year before gaining the courage to organise a small group of friends to clean it up. On this first guerrilla garden dig, it was filled to the brim with rubbish from the surrounding nightlife. Whether the property of Hackney Council or the large private parking lot behind it, we'd argue that because it faces the street it's essentially a neglected public space, ready to be adopted.

The primary challenge of this particular garden was to make it visible as a place of value and meaning, so that people would be less inclined to toss their bottles over the fence. We introduced garden gnomes to the plot (knowing that Shoreditch hipsters tend to have a soft-spot for all things Amelie), and took in wayward plants of all sorts. On our first clean-up, we were quickly confronted by the bar owners, who were deeply concerned that our illicit activity brought attention to their illicit activity (the informal congregation of people outside with drinks). Both activities, ironically, serve to activate the public space and make it a safer and more social environment, while the neglect of this land seems to be met without consequence. 'Illicit' as our garden may be, we've found that the best times to maintain it are in broad daylight. Without the suspicion-raising cloak of nightfall and the complicit actions of the crowds, we are often mistaken for official volunteers, chatting with elderly people who stop to commend us on being such good Samaritans.

From Old Street, we took the Northern Line train and headed south across the Thames to Elephant & Castle, an ethnically diverse neighbourhood well-linked with public transport. Due to its close proximity to the City, Elephant & Castle, with its monolithic tower blocks flanking two menacing roundabouts, is undergoing one of the largest regeneration schemes in Europe. About 15 people made it this far on the tour and I was relieved to deliver them into the capable hands of Richard Reynolds, an outspoken leader in the guerrilla gardening movement. The gardens on this side of the river are all of Richard's instigation, ably assisted by 'troupes' mobilised via his website, and due to his know-how, dedication and initiative, each was of an impressive scale and ambition, by any gardening standards. Elephant & Castle is a system of disorientation for outsiders but, paradoxically, an area of strong local identification. Richard led us through this urban maze to unexpected sunflower fields and lavender beds that made an even greater impact when juxtaposed with this intense backdrop. Like Dalston, Elephant & Castle faces gentrification due to development schemes, and these gardens may yet play a role in asserting public will in the face of institutional change.

Guerrilla gardens vary in the level of commitment they require and may reflect a collaborative spirit or an individual's aesthetic view. The sense of ownership and responsibility guerrilla gardeners feel towards wayward land they adopt may be directly related to the amount of time and resources they invest in its care. The sense of empowerment, however, that new guerrilla gardeners feel from realising their capacity to transform neglected land, unimpeded by bureaucratic hassles, occurs – like an epiphany – at the very first act of transgression: planting a seed. The more communities begin to recognise their capacity to assert their agency and shift the public sphere through guerrilla gardening, the greater their resilience will be as their neighbourhoods undergo regeneration.

The proximity of stops south of the Thames gave a sense of continuity to the final part of our walk, but we recognised that these gardens were all primarily the expression of one local resident (despite the collective efforts of the local guerrilla gardening community to cultivate and maintain them). In order to conduct a tour that represented a wider range of guerrilla garden practices, we needed to cross into the territories of different gardeners. To fill in the gaps, and imagine a less fragmented journey for those who wished to walk, we recognised the potential for a large-scale interconnected strategy for the adoption of wayward land. A continuous tour achieved not through a revamped itinerary or a swifter means of transport, but through the process of shifting the urban landscape itself to allow for a continuous flow of guerrilla activity. A walk across the capital that trekked through appropriated spaces and reclaimed public land. Could we make a Guerrilla Greenbelt?

Greenbelts have been an essential element of UK planning policy for the past four decades, preserving open space in the face of development. Their benefits are many: from halting the onset of urban sprawl, creating wildlife corridors and enhancing bio-diversity, to encouraging landscape-driven sustainable urban development. The London Metropolitan Greenbelt, established in 1938, is both the oldest and largest green corridor in the UK at 486,000 hectares. Another 61 hectares have been designated as a green corridor along the Lea Valley, interlinking green space along the River Lea from Hertfordshire to the Thames, passing through the 2012 Olympic Park in Stratford. While the Lea Valley Green Corridor becomes a focus of an Olympic makeover, our Guerrilla Greenbelt will pass through East London neighbourhoods impacted by the larger scheme for London's Olympic future.

One might argue that attempts to connect guerrilla gardens risk compromising their autonomy and spontaneity. But unlike a traditional greenbelt strategy, which allows for a ribbon of anti-development from the onset, the Guerrilla Greenbelt would be a series of discreet moments, so intensified that one could jump from one to the other, like cracks on the pavement. This superimposition onto the city works, not within the planning structure, but on top of it, adding new layers and meaning to an already complex urban landscape. And as guerrilla appropriations of land vary from sustainable acts of stewardship to ephemeral flash-mob moments, the ways in which guerrilla gardening would manifest itself along the route would be flexible and ever changing. Each of these interventions, however transient, will create connections between acts of resistance and community initiatives, growing a movement of individuals that feel empowered to reclaim their local landscapes.

A Guerrilla Greenbelt would be initiated just as we planned the route of our walk – by linking known guerrilla gardens, both those physically existing and those that still live as histories of a place (like the gardening once done under the Peace Mural in Dalston). The gaps between these points would be addressed by mapping all wayward land and opportunities for intervention, such as neglected roadside medians, empty tree pits, the patchy and uninspired front lawns of council estates, empty cow troughs, and even stretches of hardscape that need to be softened with some green relief. Disseminating this map may be enough to instigate the first adoptions. After all, it does not take long for vacant buildings on the radar of squatter communities to be filled. Perhaps wayward land will be picked up as quickly, as more people experience the rush that comes with guerrilla gardening and other actions in taking back public space.

As guerrilla gardening is often social and collaborative, people may gain courage to adopt their own wayward land after participating in existing digs. But if they need a nudge, the Wayward Land Stewards could assist latent green vigilantes by giving them a 'licence' to landscape, like one of those enterprising astronomy outfits that sell the stars in the sky. By assuming this authoritative role, we would be simply encouraging the public to take ownership over their public spaces.

Alternately, we could facilitate the adoption of land by mapping the conditions along the greenbelt that best facilitate guerrilla practices. This infrastructure of resistance would allow for gardening without interference (charting a route of surveillance blind spots to enable gardening free from prying eyes), a strong set of guerrilla growing conditions (breaks in the hardscape, lines connecting the dappled pockets of sunlight that escape the shadow-cover of tall building blocks, a series of rest-stops from the wind tunnels), and an embrace of the elements to spread seeds through the circuit (whether through wind, or in the tyres of buses along road networks).

The Guerrilla Greenbelt would be a series of events, from political actions and space-hijack stunts to well-tended and loved local gardens, from high-impact plantings to soft-spoken and symbolic moments. In the hardscape areas, the Guerrilla Greenbelt will be no less lush. Hanging gardens along wrought iron fences of council estates will emerge, like the Olympic-resistance project in Hackney Wick where local residents planted soil and flowers in empty bags and milk bottles. Vacant lot allotments will be made from growbags filled with vegetable seeds, green moss will graffiti building walls, metered parking spaces will be turned into temporary parks, bus stops will be given 'green' roofs, and mobile gardens will be affixed to the back of bicycles, while seed bombs fly overhead.

We aspire to a connected corridor of anarchic actions. But while the Guerrilla Greenbelt proposes continuity in space, its temporality is flexible and ever changing. Each event along the route may fade after a season, last just a moment, or continue to grow, becoming ever more complex, beautiful and exciting as it matures. And while these ephemeral actions may not be simultaneous, their impact will be cumulative, enabling local residents to feel ownership over their neighbourhoods in the face of regeneration. When they express their resistance, their graffiti will be green.

BIOGRAPHY

Heather Ring is a landscape architect working in London. She is one of the founders of the Wayward Plant Registry, which provides halfway homes for unwanted plants, and the Wayward Land Stewards, a global group for neglected and rogue land.

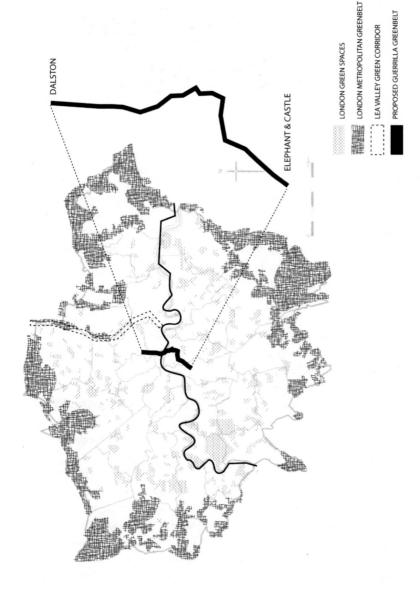

DALSTON

ELEPHANT & CASTLE

LONDON GREEN SPACES

LONDON METROPOLITAN GREENBELT

LEA VALLEY GREEN CORRIDOR

PROPOSED GUERRILLA GREENBELT

Proposal for Guerrilla Greenbelt,
2009, HEATHER RING

A Line Is There To Be Broken

CAROLINE KNOWLES, GESCHE WÜRFEL, TRISTAN FENNELL
AND DAVID KENDALL IN CONVERSATION

A Line Is There To Be Broken originated in 2008, bringing together individual photographic projects that
scrutinise struggles between transformations of 'place' and 'space'.
Tristan Fennell, David Kendall and
Gesche Würfel create photographic
works that explore social and spatial
disruptions in everyday life and
the urban landscape. This ongoing
curatorial project and group exhibition continues to question changes
in social-governmental policies,
spatial and economic developments,
and initiatives in cities throughout
the world.

The following conversation between
Professor Caroline Knowles, Gesche
Würfel, David Kendall and Tristan
Fennell took place at the Centre for
Urban and Community Research
(CUCR), Department of Sociology,
Goldsmiths, University of London,
during January 2009. The dialogue
explores the process of making urban landscape photography; social,
spatial and ethical conditions that
affect how we perceive and make
photographic images; and, as visual
practitioners, how we create images
that locate or reveal new or existing
spatial processes and cultural specificities that evolve in cities.

CK: Is A Line Is There To Be Broken
a collective project? Are you all
working on different aspects?

GW: Our interest in exploring and
developing micro-macro aesthetics
of urban landscape photography
has brought us together. My work is
concerned with London's desire to
remain a 'global city', the effects of
spatial and architectural development of the 2012 Olympic sites, and
how regeneration processes could

conflict with local needs. Tristan's project is based around temporary architectural structures built in park spaces spatially appropriated and re-used by homeless people in Tokyo, Japan. David's work explores how everyday activities of migrant construction workers in Dubai could produce new social spaces to meet, and re-orientate within, in the new architectural landscape.

DK: A Line Is There To Be Broken is a proposal that links it all together. Promoting ideas and debates about spatial and trans-global interconnection between people within cities, rather than just 'local' London-based urban issues.

CK: Yes definitely, I'm interested in the threads that run from London. Where do they go? Who are the people involved? What and where are the activities? What are the material objects? How do those things actually work?

GW: The global event?

CK: Yes, and how that ripples out

DK: My project, Always Let the Road Decide, was a starting point in Dubai, where new architectural sites and tourist attractions designed (or being designed) to direct visitors

on visual journeys are made visible and accessible by highways. Walking is discouraged; roads become walls, boundaries and lines to be navigated, alienating pedestrians. I focus on how migrant construction workers, who have limited social rights of use in the city, independently access these busy networks. Climbing onto the road allows participants to dictate the pace of their collective movements, subvert spatial dynamics, and create informal meeting points or spaces within a hostile environmental climate/cityscape. The photographic process was influenced by my experiences of working with architects employed by transport-planning companies in London and methods used to calculate and assess the circulation of people within architectural spaces. I was initially interested in how the micro aesthetics of the photographic 'snapshot' is used to collect this data and how this information disappears or reappears in macro models and planning proposals. What attracted me to Dubai as a location was my lack of knowledge about the city. Roads could act as photographic and spatial metaphors for 'distance' and 'proximity'. Being forced to walk long distances restricts access, yet wandering over a long period of time at particular times of day leads to the

"Basketball Arena",Go For Gold!, 2006, GESCHE WÜRFEL

"Olympic Village 1", Go For Gold!, 2006, GESCHE WÜRFEL

discovery of spatial scenarios that would have been overlooked if I had been in a car. Working with architects has made me question debates about the ethics of image-making in, for example, sociology and photojournalism. Should one be held back by these terms or attempt to generate a new set of visual conditions? Photographs could link consensual and conflicting territorial practices and challenge what constitutes segregation, revealing hidden maps and boundaries.

CK: No, I believe it's important not to be put off by those kinds of credentials. Who has the right to speak? Who has the right to know this? We all have a right to speak and know these things if we have due caution to other kinds of viewpoints, and the fact that we are outsiders and admit that, I think that works. But I think one needs to be quite careful of how you do those things.

TF: Yes, there's a flip side to your position as a practitioner. My project, Midori, is based in Tokyo. I lived there for three years, between 2003 and 2006. When I went back in 2007 it had changed. The government was attempting to move homeless people on, putting up barriers and other types of material objects to exclude

them from these spaces. The project wasn't really about the homeless communities as such, but indirectly about how these people utilise park space as a dwelling space rather than as a leisure space. As these spaces are at a premium in Tokyo, I see, like the authorities, this appropriation as a political act or a disjuncture in the fabric of the Japanese urban cityscape that has become a public platform. I became interested in how material objects can turn the park into a political tool. As a white Irish person, even though I lived there for a couple of years, I asked myself, how do I engage with this environment and produce a project like this? I want people to see these images because they reveal spatial and social concerns that shouldn't be hidden away. Surrounding, inadequate, social-welfare policies are framed by these types of spatial contestation between sections of the homeless community and the local Tokyo government. People aren't located elsewhere, they are just moved on, excluded to a less visible place. It's a way of exposing people to these issues as well. So it's that flip side of who is speaking, rather than ignoring the situation.

CK: I don't think we need to be shy about it. Anyone has the right to do it. It's submitting to the limits we know and what we have access to. That's a bit like the 'flip flop' project, Footwear and Social Fabrics, I travelled to China and just pitched up. (Footwear and Social Fabrics is an 'object biography' that follows the journey of a pair of flip-flop sandals from their production in China to consumption in Ethiopia.) I don't speak Chinese, so you're saying, look, I have come here to understand, to explore how you make this stuff, and to become involved in the process. As long as you're learning and establishing links with people...

TF: Yes, I think it's very much about making sure there's some kind of dialogue.

GW: I think it was the same for me. I came to the Olympics site in the Lower Lea Valley in East London in 2006, when people were still working and living there. My project, Go for Gold!, engages with the places and spaces of the Lower Lea Valley, a landscape that will be replaced by the structures of the 2012 Olympic project, which will attempt to eliminate traces of the past and impose an entirely new spatial reality on the area. London's success in winning the bid was primarily a result of its focus on urban regeneration in East London, as well as its emphasis on its multicultural character and the need to inspire young people in the area. The Olympic slogan 'Go for Gold!' primarily reflects London's desire to remain a 'global city' without consideration for the needs of locals. Regeneration, in this case, is not about the Lower Lea Valley or East London but about competing with other 'global cities'. This will make London even more unequal since de-industrialisation will be enforced, financial services will be privileged, employment will be re-located and many people displaced. My photography poses important questions about these developments. When photographing, I try to engage with the local people and understand their perspective.

CK: Yes, and how did you do that? It's how you open situations up that's important.

GW: People would tell me about their lives, their work, or about particular sites I was intending to photograph. This was valuable information. Even though I engaged with a lot of people, they're usually not visible in my images. My focus is on space. However, I think my images say a lot about the people who use the space and who work there.

Midori, 2007, TRISTAN FENNELL

Midori, 2007, TRISTAN FENNELL

CK: Yes, I think we underestimate that. It's not obvious how to do it and how to establish rapport with people. That's really important and it's difficult to do.

GW: I've been in touch with people who've helped me to access different places. For example, the Manor Garden Allotments were closed in September 2007 and demolished to construct a footpath for the 2012 Olympic Games. The plot holders allowed me to take photos of their shed interiors. The series entitled Farewell from the Garden Paradise captures the long period of eviction. The images present the small personal spaces of sheds that have no place in the ongoing Olympic development. I raise questions about which approach to regeneration is most appropriate. I seek to problematise the notion of the 2012 Olympics as 'green' – often cited in promotional literature – by documenting the destruction of allotments that are a rare example of sustainably managed green spaces in East London. David, you show some people from further away and the work is definitely about people though they are not the main focal point in the image. So all our projects connect to the spatial traces people leave behind.

DK: By returning to the same site, and re-tracing events, I wanted to discover how the space was being reused or adapted, how 'repetition' created a sense of 'place' for its users. It appears that both your projects involve returning to specific sites over periods of time and revealing hidden maps or events. All our work offers alternative spatial representations that contradict the 'public' image promoted by governmental authorities in each country. Was that your starting point, Gesche?

GW: My focus was on urban regeneration. I previously worked as an urban planner in Germany, where I was engaging the local population in participatory processes that were part of urban regeneration initiatives, especially in the Ruhr Valley. I was interested in the Olympics first from an athlete's point of view, but since I took up urban planning I have developed a critical perspective on mega events. My idea was to question why and how the Olympics have been transformed from a sporting to an economic event. I photographed the future sport venues in their present state, starting in 2006, but I have always had the politics and spatial developments in mind. The focus of Go for Gold!, therefore, is mainly on the politics behind this particular spatial development.

CK: So, not necessarily about people's lives but in a more removed way?

GW: Yes, more in a removed way. My critique is that the Olympics are neither about improving the situation of people living in the East End nor about the sports aspect, but about London competing with other cities for a position on the 'global cities' stage. I have photographed on a micro level but within a macro framework.

CK: You're asking questions about the whole city?

GW: Yes, I'm asking questions about the whole city and about the Olympics in general.

TF: There is a certain micro to macro scaling process in my work as well. The issue of the right to occupy a public space scales outwards and feeds into more global issues of homelessness that affect every city. I'm looking at who has the right to transform these park spaces, or who has the right to do certain types of things in these spaces. The fact that these are public spaces – everybody is allowed to use them. If somebody

comes along and actually uses it for a purpose that is a survival purpose, e.g. setting up a camp, the chance of survival increases. This is one of the most fundamental things that you can do when you're unemployed and homeless. They're seen as unemployed squatters or strangers avoiding employment. I'm not sure how conscious or subconscious it is: the fact that they use these very public spaces. The blue tents you can see, sometimes they hide them, and sometimes they are quite obvious. It's a visible thing. To me, it's saying: we should be looked after but we're not being looked after and we're not being helped. This is why they live there. There is little social support. There are very few agencies that help them to get houses. It's about who has the right to do that in that type of space.

CK: You make me think of Sea-wright Mills' public-private troubles in public issues, how those things are always connected, and also the aggregating of individuals to make a bigger protest. This is like the tent cities that were set up at the lakeside in Toronto as a protest against homelessness. That was very much a collective kind of protest. It matters on what scale these things are conducted. It's always interesting what

Always Let the Road Decide, 2008, DAVID KENDALL

the responses are when these things happen. What are the consequences socially and individually? Those things are always being interconnected somehow.

DK: It's interesting how these people are using or transforming these spaces. Focusing on the 'everyday' is useful in both challenging and grounding visual and spatial experiences in Dubai. The city attracts tourists and migrant construction workers, who could import or exchange cultural specificities, activities and spaces, establishing unique social and spatial imprints on the region's architectural ambitions. For example, I've witnessed informal cricket games played by migrants from the Indian subcontinent on vacant underdeveloped sites. Sporting activities such as cricket attract a diverse worldwide audience. State authorities in the UAE wish to attract and host major worldwide sporting events, and urban infrastructures are being built to publicise and accommodate this. Whilst working with architects from the region, a cricket league was proposed to bring together teams from the Indian subcontinent and European migrants and tourists who would not come together in existing social settings. Inserting this new

social dynamic could raise visitors' awareness of the hidden lives of construction workers, confront spatial separation in the wider population, and help to break down micro political divisions imposed by the city-state's societal regulations and architectural design.

CK: If you just think about the 75% migrants in Dubai, the commodification of land-property markets in the Middle East and especially Dubai has been really important, its expansion.

DK: They're all in transition. They're not going to be there forever, regardless of whatever level they're working at. The project has evolved from a small, micro-type project into a wider macro idea because I can see interconnections between how the city publicises itself to a worldwide audience and the visual and physical boundaries, put up by the authorities, that restrict visual and spatial access for certain social groups to some architectural sites within the city.

GW: It's a problem I had when I wanted to continue my project after the ODA (Olympic Delivery Authority) had erected the blue fence and I couldn't get on the site anymore.

It's created a huge border and it's become impossible to access the site now. I've started documenting other sports venues in London. A lot of competitions will be hosted in central London and I have not been allowed to access every site. I wanted to visit Wembley Stadium but was denied access. The authorities want to let the public have access to particular images; one is not allowed to express an opinion or say something critical.

CK: The most useful and engaging projects are the ones that you don't have access to. Breaching boundaries, getting in and bringing things back, seems to be essential. It's also about the social boundaries within people's minds that affect the whole process. They are all global projects; the challenge is how do you draw the links between the micro and macro levels. The most interesting work has to draw on both aspects. Drawing lines that connect to wider contexts, it's always overlooked. It's always assumed that we have access to start with and then we go on. My experience is that how you establish contact is vital, and how they think about you. How the project pans depends upon the social and spatial connections we form.

BIOGRAPHIES

Tristan Fennell is a photographer based in London. He has exhibited internationally in Dublin, Belfast, London and Tokyo. (www.tristanfennell.com)

David Kendall utilises biography, the 'archive', memory, mapping, architecture and the 'event' as conceptual devices to develop photographic, film and site-specific projects exploring spatial and social interconnection in cities. (www.david-kendall.co.uk)

Caroline Knowles is Professor of Sociology and current head of the Centre for Urban and Community Research (CUCR), Goldsmiths College, University of London. (www.goldsmiths.ac.uk/sociology/staff/knowles.php)

Gesche Würfel is a visual artist who focuses on changing spaces. Recently she has conducted several urban and landscape photography projects. (www.geschewuerfel.com)

Olympic Sports, Spirits and Stories

Small Stories and Miniscule Myths

HILARY POWELL

With every large-scale masterplanning exercise comes a grand narrative of regeneration, with every Olympics comes the weight of the 'Olympic story', and with every map or plan comes a legend. As 2012 approaches and the increasingly contentious issues and ideas of legacy come to the fore, enchanting tales of the future are woven and mapped onto the East London Olympic development site. Amid this spinning of stories, the aims of this article are to give voice to the smaller stories, miniscule myths and histories of the area that examine, intervene in and puncture the utopian myth of progress inherent in the Olympic development – counteracting tabula rasa urbanism and questioning the dystopian reality of such visionary projects.

With the vast scale of transformation bearing down fast, perhaps the best place to begin is by telling of one of these smaller Olympic stories – my own.

This tale begins in an artist's studio in the East London area of Hackney Wick – in a draughty, paint-daubed, breeze-block room without plumbing, overlooking the waterways that border what is now the Olympic construction site. The Wick, beginning life as a village on the edge of London, is now designated a new 'urban village' and focus of regeneration teams – then and now an outpost, an urban island bordered by road, river, rail, and now ridges of soil and rising architecture. In 2006, this frontier land became the focus of publicity and prospectors as

Critical Cities

London geared up to fight for its place on the world stage as an Olympic City. Day by day, landmarks of this territory were rapidly cleaned up and cleared out. The Hackney Wick Stadium, previously home to greyhound racing, speedway tracks and a vast informal market paradise for scavengers, was marked for demolition. The area that had been our source and resource as a place to roam and photograph, was infiltrated by fly-by-night news presenters and the surreal sight of bobbies on the beat strolling down Marshgate Lane, past the banners of protest, looming power lines and verdant riversides. These waterways featured prominently in St Etienne's 2006 film homage to the lower Lea Valley, *What Have you Done Today, Mervyn Day*, and the usual wanderers were joined by spiralling documentalists, official and unofficial media, artists and archivists.

Further shots exist in multiples, all capturing the last small etchings of protest: 'Fuck Seb Coe' on a rusting turquoise bridge; 'no bids', 'no games' 'no bids', 'no games' (the repetition interrupted by 'no parts' on a car yard's corrugated gates); and the rapid deletion of these voices of dissent by mobile graffiti-removal units, scrubbing and spraying on a mission to erase. The cries from the multiple sites and communities that make up what will be the Olympic Park reached varying pitches and resonances: from the shrieks of waterfowl, to the organised resistance of the businesses of Marshgate Lane industrial estate, residents of Clays Lane housing estate, travellers' sites on Waterden Road, and the community of Manor Garden Allotments.

The Games

Local photographer Stephen Gill's Archaeology in Reverse series attests to the traces of the future already present or inflicted upon the landscape: boarded windows spelling 'Good Bye and Good Luck', trees marked with an X. And indeed, an X had been drawn over this swathe of eastern land – a white land on the A-Z map; an 'empty' land in the rhetoric of erasure, dirt and renewal expounded by the development agencies and media. For myself and filmmaker Daniel Edelstyn, faced with the reality of the Olympic dream arriving on our doorstep, it became imperative to present a critical and creative vision of the area as full rather than empty, to mark this moment in London's political and urban fabric, and to celebrate the area as it was, at that point, in the present.

Over two cold weekends in February 2007, we made the film *The Games*, staging an alternative Olympics amid the diverse sites set to become the 2012 London

Olympic Park: a steeple chase through trapeze-training spaces, housing estates and allotments; hub-cap discus on demolition rubble; and synchronised swimming on dirt-slope traffic islands. The production base, shared with construction workers, was at Rosie's 'Griddler's Café' in a portacabin in Hackney Wick. In both its aesthetic and ethos, the film took inspiration from the last time the Games were in town in 1948, when the Olympics were dubbed the 'Austerity Games' and DIY ruled. This application of another era to the 2012 sites questioned the need for the global promenade of stadium construction, positing an alternative 'make do and get by' scenario, working creatively with existing spaces, places and people – a vision that, to some, may now be redolent of an Olympics 'after the crash'.

Photograph taken during production of
Hilary Powell's *The Games*, 2007,
FEDERICO FIGA TALAMANCA

As the leotard clad figure of the 'Olympic Spirit' jumps out of a tree, leapfrogs bollards, and swings on Hackney Marshes' football posts, *The Games* is a poignant swansong of an area on the brink of dramatic transformation. The Olympic wreath is a crown of wild brambles, and the final 'thank you' goes to "All the streets and sites of the future Olympic Park".

That was then. Those street names are now memories, and a view into the site from the vantage point of the Greenway (aka the Northern Outfall Sewer) provides no points of reference to this old world of old names, but rather a new city where construction workers wait at bus stops marked 'Aquatics' and 'Zone b'. Photographer Gesche Würfel's ongoing project Go for Gold! resonates; in 2006, she patrolled the area using the masterplan as a guide to target the sites of future sporting venues, labelling what existed (shed cafés, waste lots, billboards) with their future titles of 'Media Centre', 'Velodrome', 'Olympic Village'. Making *The Games* was itself a lesson in disappearances, as roads closed the next day and guerrilla shots were snatched through red and white barriers and security fencing. In July 2007, the vivid blue fences rose quickly around the site and this area of East London was closed to the public for good – to re-emerge, re-constructed, and repackaged as an urban park for the 21st century, in 2012.

In the meantime...

As the work of the archaeological teams on the Olympic site affirms, the city expands and contracts; buildings and legends fall, rise and are buried again. Stephen Gill quite literally buried his photographs in this land, and the Museum of London Archaeological Services Standing Buildings team documents the former uses and subversions (e.g. pylons used as boxing rings in *The Games*) of the industrial icons that no longer grace the skyline of the valley as power itself goes underground. Just as the stories of the hands (the labourers and skilled migrants), that are at this moment building this Olympic dream, remain largely untold (transcripts of recordings selected and censored for official promotional material), much that has happened and continues to happen around the edge of this site remains below the radar – ephemeral, eventful and illusive.

The aim within my work and the TINAG salon is to illuminate and engage with the hidden histories and processes behind this Olympian production, making a place for multiple projects that create a heterogeneous vision of the layered past, present and future of this zone. To cluster, witness, document and tell the variegated stories of the events and incidents that happen along the way, and create a panoramic and choreographic view of the site's 'before', 'after' and most importantly, its 'in-between', i.e the ever evolving now. For if, to use their own phrases, the ODA (Olympic Development Agency) are building the stage and setting the scene for LOCOG (London Organising Committee for the Olympic Games) to put on the show, then there are also numerous other players involved as this drama unfolds: crucial parts, performing the fringe in the fringe-lands.

Salon de Refuses Olympique – an alternative Cultural Olympiad?

Originating out of [space]'s Olympic Artist Forum and subsequently inspired by TINAG's regular salon series, the event I organised was a discussion called Salon de Refuses Olympique for TINAG's October 2008 festival. Such a name takes its inspiration from the original Salon des Refusés of the 19TH-century Parisian art world where, beginning as an 'exhibition of rejects', the Salon des Refusés came to represent and hold an avant-garde of sorts – a counter exhibition and site of experimentation and innovation. Here, in the context of wider 'official' Cultural Olympiad programming, the salon gives voice to those operating alongside and offering a more critical stance – from outright rejection of the 'Olympic story' to ironic creative critique and adaptive actions. Primarily, this salon aims to address practices that attempt to engage audiences and participants with the Olympic-led regeneration happening in East London in the run-up to 2012, in a thought provoking and creative way. Does it stand in opposition to the overall 'official' vision for arts and culture in the Olympic Park? As with the first Parisian Salon des Refusés and other forms of 'fringe' or 'alternative' programming, the relationship is more complex and symbiotic.

The ODA advocates an arts and culture project that "honours the history of the past, captures the imagination of the present, and leaves space for aspirations of the future". Such aims resonate with both the reasoning behind the salon and the works gathered within it, but how much of this is rhetoric? How much actual engagement with the real changes happening does this allow for in the context of the blinkered positivity and top-down political force of the Olympic movement? An element that it is easy to suspect is lacking from the reality of this cultural agenda is freedom – the freedom to present diverse understandings of, and direct interventions in, landscape on the brink of change. This attachment to place and site are critical here, as the salon focuses on projects, at a literal 'grassroots' level, operating in the territories bordering the Olympic Park. It is not about debating 'culture' but about exploring diverse forms of cultural agency operating on the ground in a celebration of change that can encompass critique, as opposed to oblique and one dimensional celebratory projects. It posits a freedom of expression when engaging with political and urban change – one freedom that is increasingly challenged. If each Olympics responds to, or reflects, the international zeitgeist or geo-political climate (from the Nazi Olympics of 1936 to post-war Britain's 1948 'Austerity Games' and the recent and current Beijing and Vancouver human rights' infringements), then the 2012 Games may be christened the 'Copyright Olympics' as Orwellian corporate control and surveillance, under the misplaced excuse of 'brand protection', extends to possession of words and words in combination – another reason for the salon's own 're-brand'.

But that's another story to be told. For even before freedom, the f word on most artists' and cultural organisations' lips is funding. At the October 2008 salon, artist Tessa Garland presented a polemic slow-motion video of a run around the borders of the Olympic Park in which Vangelis' 'Chariots of Fire' provides the soundtrack to funding cuts and disillusion. In her journey through the 2012 website, the 'inspire' mark figures prominently as a means of gaining support and of 'getting involved' in the Cultural Olympiad. In reality, this involves a branding exercise in which chosen events or projects are bestowed with the 'mark'. This mark comes with no financial support, raises complex issues of co-option, and potentially alienates participants – issues faced in the first Hackney Wick Festival in September 2008, which, based as it is in the community most directly impacted upon by the large-scale construction site on its boundaries, contains many local residents far from inspired by their situation.

Creative clustering

Paradoxically, however, the salon and the projects *are* 'inspired by' 2012. If 'inspired by' means to affect or call to action, then the Olympics' site, brand propaganda machine and media circus have become a rich source for creative appropriation. Without needing to be stamped and approved, the impetus for the operation of the salon remains somewhat outside of debates on cultural funding, inspired as it is by its beginnings in my film *The Games* and the DIY ethos of making do and getting by, keeping calm and carrying on. A salon is in essence a gathering of people, ideas and opinions. This particular salon is a place for curios, collections and alternative visions of the past and future – as far away from a masterplan as you can travel – in which snippets and stories, not grand narratives, abound. This is where the Wick Curiosity Shop comes in.

[space] commissioned the public works art and architecture collective to produce a project for the first Hackney Wick Festival centred on an under-used green space amid the housing estates of the Wick along the Eastway, which forms just one

of the outer boundaries of this urban-island site. Throughout summer 2008, they were out and about in Hackney Wick, hosting music bingo, organising walks, finding out more about the area, and encouraging people to show and share recollections, facts and finds. On the inaugural day of the festival, a shop – a moveable and adaptable structure called the Mobile Porch – hosted an eclectic mix of local curiosities, acting as museum, cinema, stage and meeting place. Online, the shop exists as a living archive of local ephemera, from objects (Bovril bottles excavated from the Manor Garden Allotments site) to songs (from rocking Wick band Hackney Boots to Trowbridge Senior Citizens' Club singing 'Dear Old Hackney Wick'). Such collections grow organically, prompted by conversations, chance meetings and organised outings of the 'shop' into this Olympic fringe area. But the curious stories and spaces it stumbles upon are now becoming prized commodities within a wider institutional impulse to collect the Olympics and map the change.

Off to a late start, these Saatchis of the edge-lands and colonisers of community history are in overdrive. And this drive is indeed important – a need to record and give voice, and to do this within a culture of exchange and not plunder. However, plunder and erasure are built deep into the foundations of exploration, discovery

Image from Trespassing the Olympic Site, 2007, STEPHEN CORNFORD

and collection, which paradoxically thrive on destruction – in an archaeological context, 'finds' (from Bovril bottles to Roman roads) only become unearthed through excavation and disruption. As such, their collection is a removal from both site and context. Whilst this mass collecting impulse continues full-speed ahead, the word and practice I am drawn to is 'gleaning'. Literally understood as 'to gather after the harvest', gleaning is a creative political model and mental activity – knowledge obtained through experience and interaction with everyday minutiae and me-ta-narratives. It is a process in which the practice itself can influence the story, in which accidents and anecdotes have key roles, and footnotes and scribbles in the margins counteract and navigate a variegated way through the dominant narrative of progress. For amid the glory of history that emerges through excavation, there is its dirt – a history of landfill, radio-active waste and soil contamination now exposed to the present, floating on the winds of East London – inhaled (but absolutely not collected) by institutions, and appropriated and critiqued by others: dust from the Olympic site sold in souvenir packets like the canned air of 'the last breath of communism'.

The blue period

Two weeks after publishing the image online the already made-to-fit gate had been extended further, lengths of steel welded to within an inch of the tarmac on every other fencepost. A month later still and unwanted eyes were excluded too; the whole thing had been clad in the now ubiquitous blue plywood.

Stephen Cornford

Whilst playing around with the art historical referencing of the salon, perhaps much of the work so far is part of a wider 'blue period', dominated as it has been by the big blue fence that surrounds the Olympic Park. Erected on the ODA's pos-session of the Olympic site in East London in July 2007, this blue fence has become a potent symbol of privatisation and exclusion. As blue-fence painters patrolled the site ready to erase the everyday evidence of dissent, this East London border paradoxically acted as a trigger for debate and communication, and as a focus for creative interventions and critiques of this emblem and reality of enclosure: tres-passing, adapting and exploiting the comedy value of this unnatural blue jutting into the void over closed green waterways.

From attempted and achieved incursions into the park (Stephen Gill and Iain Sinclair on the waterways, Stephen Cornford's trespassing), numerous psycho-geographical walks and tours around it, and reconstructions and interpretations of it (Penny Cliff and Immediate Theatre's interactive *Big Blue Fence*), this painted fence has certainly been inspiring activity. It has played host to expressions of dissent and ridicule, from graffiti to the We Are Bad collective's anti-Olympic sloganeering; and, contrary to hiding what goes on behind its perimeters (for health and safety reasons), the fence has prompted increased determination to see beyond it – evidenced in the sprouting of unofficial monitoring and webcams on local vantage points such as Gainsborough school, and Forman & Son's 'Fish Eye Lens' keeping a beady eye on goings-on in the land once owned in part by them.

Tessa Garland's playful film, *Park Life*, explores this fascination, adapting footage of demolition and construction to create a site in which cranes break, the d falls of the word 'design' and the ground shakes with the promise (or threat) of its future in classic Jurassic Park style. This deep bass rumble of change emitted from the construction site makes up part one of Jem Finer's sonic map, *The Rise and Fall of the Olympic State*, accompanied by helicopters overhead and trains passing. Part two takes the listener on an ever so slightly subverted Olympic bus tour sampling some of the more exemplary sights or sounds of the park, such as 'digger school', before being joined by the distant sound of trumpet and saxophone building to a discordant crescendo as a brass band attempts to blow the fence 'a tumbling down' in reference to other cities and other divides across the ages.

The fence is a literal barrier, but the largest border is the future park itself, which, in its making, inevitably closes down route ways and forms a divide between the London boroughs that surround its edges. Within the salon, the link to this 'other side' (from our Hackney base to Stratford) was made through the work of Julika Gittner and John Purnell and their project, From the Picturesque to the Demolished – a group show that functioned as protest and mourning for the illegally demolished Georgian Angel Cottage on the park's Stratford edge. An angel's viewpoint can now be had from above its former site, i.e. from the speculative towers that rise in the East and most specifically from Holden Point, a residential tower with a top floor commandeered as the official viewing platform for the Olympic site and host to the Queen, Blair, Livingstone and the International Olympic Committee. In November 2007, this became the venue for another provocative artist-organised project, London 2012 Never Took Place, in which Mark Wayman performed his own *East London Border*, playing with the dichotomy between plan view and the idiosyncrasies of the edge-lands.

Down on the ground, the blue continued to cast its spell, and whereas most describe its hue as arbitrary, unnatural and chemical, artist Jem Finer sees beauty in it – the colour of a leap into the void, the colour of freedom and possibility or emptiness – issues that resonate with current discussion of legacy. Jim Thorp's photographs of the blue fence in varying light conditions capture this essential duality, as the barrier appears to shimmer and reflect – an illusive mirage on the horizon of East London, but a mirage that on closer inspection remains a solid barrier. As artist in residence at [space] in 2007, Jean-Francois Prost shunned studio for urban space and most specifically this blue barrier, getting to know the patrolling blue-fence painters. On discovering a discarded paint can, he acquired the code for this strange hue and, finding it was called 'All Aboard', set about extending the Olympic wall by painting practically everything else in the vicinity blue too. This blue was also put to good use by the Office for Subversive Architecture in their blue fence intervention (in collaboration with Blueprint), Point of View, criticising the lack of corporate transparency and physical absence of viewing opportunities into a major construction site. A simple blue staircase led up the fence, instantly bringing to mind the final scene of the film *The Truman Show* in which Jim Carey's character sails off across a seemingly vast ocean only to crash into the wall of solid blue sky that borders the world constructed around him.

As the ODA's phased plan of 'demolish dig design' met targets behind the fence, parallel reactions to this from the outside have been disbelief, disillusion, dejection. With eviction and betrayals raw in adjacent communities, the blue period has been inflected with an overload of nostalgia. But now the page is closing on a specific era, the projects above can be archived in a blue-bound volume and filed as history or myth. Following this analogy of a set of encyclopaedic Olympic volumes collating creative reaction to the change, and in line with the onslaught of militant urbanism (in the form of a 4-metre high, high-voltage, replacement barrier), the next volume will, by association, be electric, with each turn of the page inducing a shock – a jolt to the system and perception. The blues are over. Get ready to rock and roll!

Adaptation

As time rolls on and earth shifts on the site, new arrivals rock up for a piece of the Olympic action. But one leftover project from the 'blue epoch' remains of increasing resonance. Jean-Francois Prost's Adaptive Actions involves found and made alterations in the urban landscape as an expression of collective imagination. This idea of adaptive action is key as a model for not only the Olympic fringes but our city and our world, as spaces and places evolve, and tiny actions and everyday revolutions may intervene in our expectations and imaginings of how we are able to shape now and the future, creating alternative legacies to those imposed from outside or above.

This writing has been an exercise in weaving tales of craft and craftiness – webs of connections in which fact and fiction combine. I began with my small story – someone who came to know and love the Lower Lea Valley and subsequently develop a deep interest and concern with the changes taking place, both those within and those inflicted upon it. However, I am also something of a newcomer in comparison to the local company Pudding Mill River: Purveyors of Sporting Spirits and Foodstuffs, which has regularly sponsored salons on the Olympics. The firm has been based in this area for generations, harvesting local wild fruits to manufacturer products from blackberry jam to perfume. Adaptive action is part of their everyday survival. Just as the evicted salmon-smoking business H. Forman & Son now prosper in a brand new, state-of-the-art factory in a prime position on the edge of the Olympic site, Pudding Mill River have relocated and adapted. Their company ethos is grounded in nature's bounty and the seasons, and they have certainly lived through many. They have seen the valley's greenhouses erected and dismantled, industrialisation prosper and decline, been caught up in the stories of evictions and upheaval, and are now witness to the clamour descending on the edge–lands.

They are reliant on the gaps in planning for survival – the overlooked spaces where the impacts of development are starting to be felt – but are also very aware that their's is both a resilient and an abundant harvest. In the privacy of their factory they may imagine the stadium's skeleton decked with hanging bows of wild rose and bramble, the scent of elderflower floating in the air and the Pudding Mill River, after which they are named, infiltrating and rising again in the stadium site. With more than a lifetime's experience in the Lea Valley they have learned what development agencies should also pay heed to – that even before the birth of plastic and the manufacturing of soap and matchbox cars in the area, the balance between human settlement and nature has been a precarious one. The gods of commerce may do well to offer gifts to appease the river gods, as their ancestors did centuries ago. Working in the shadow of the rising stadium, Pudding Mill River's own agenda, their very foundation, is in gathering (from blackberries to elderflowers) and, as such, they are proud to support gatherings of people and ideas and events erupting around this ever-changing East London site.

BIOGRAPHY

Hilary Powell is an artist and partner in the film practice Optimistic Productions. Her interdisciplinary practice and research focuses on sites in the urban landscape on the brink of dramatic change. She is currently working on projects exploring the fringes and impacts of the London 2012 Park. (www.optimisticproductions. co.uk) (hilaryspowell.googlepages.com)

Pudding Mill River scientists
in harvesting action, Greenway, 2007,
OPTIMISTIC PRODUCTIONS

Public Air Space

*Planning and Accessing Tall
Buildings in London*

LÉA AYOUB

In the last five years Central London has changed dramatically. Its skyline has gone up in height with the appearance of new tall buildings (ten buildings between 15 and 40 storeys since 2000), some with very distinct and innovative architectural shapes, such as the Swiss Re tower (commonly referred to as 'the Gherkin'). At the moment, these very tall buildings are mostly located in the City of London. So many new buildings have been constructed in this area that it is now known in the planning sphere as the Eastern Cluster, to be distinguished from the cluster of the Isle of Dogs.[1] Until recently, apart from national monuments and rare exceptions like the BT Tower or the Barbican's residential towers, tall buildings have remained a rather alien typology in central London, whether for office or residential use. Before this building boom, the main local experience and reference for tall buildings were those of the 1960s and 70s, which have mostly been relegated to the periphery and generally convey an enduring image of housing and planning policy failure and social exclusion.

Today's renewed and overt enthusiasm and support for very tall buildings is not uncontested, especially by conservationists concerned with the preservation of urban historical heritage. Without endorsing the cause of any party, these rapid and radical changes urge questions about the implications of skyscrapers for the public and civic experience of the city, the heart of which is in public spaces, i.e. spaces accessible to all, at all times and under no conditions besides general law. It is often said that usage, openness and quality of public spaces reflect the degree of democracy and freedom in a given society. Enrique Peñalosa, ex-Mayor of Bogota, Colombia, states that public space is not a luxury but a strong indicator of a democratic society and an issue of human dignity. Talking of cities in developing countries, he says: "Cars parked on pavements and parking bays carved where there should be pavements are symbols of a democratic deficit and a lack of respect for human dignity. It shows that the needs of citizens with a car are considered more carefully than those of people who walk. A quality pavement shows respect for pedestrians who make up the majority of the population."[2] In an analogous sense, what are the merits of very tall buildings for improving urban experience? Seeing the city – or indeed the ground – from the sky is always thrilling. By building higher, do we get access to these elevated positions? Who commands these spaces and who has access to them?

The purpose of this short essay is to briefly describe the processes behind the construction of skyscrapers in London and to explore the role of these buildings in the urban experience and in providing public (air) spaces.

Tall buildings in London: negotiating the global city

Tall buildings are clearly objects of desire nowadays, in London as well as in many cities around the world. In England, this desire is present at national and regional government levels and, sometimes, at the local authority level. During his two consecutive terms as Mayor of London (2000-08), Ken Livingstone was a key promoter of tall buildings, integrating their desirability and urban merits in the various versions of *The London Plan* – a spatial development strategy produced by the Mayor's office. The driving forces are aesthetic and market factors. According to Igal Charney,[3] Ken Livingstone has been instrumental in narrowly framing the debate about tall buildings in terms of the links between iconic architecture and famous architects, on one hand, and the global status of London, on the other, as well as the role of these developments in regenerating areas of London. Although the current financial climate is affecting the development of tall buildings, so far the sustained demand for space in high value locations has created a lucrative market for them. In this respect, the City of London is probably the most coveted location for skyscrapers' clients because of its historical role as the centre of trade, business and finance – a position the City is eager to capitalise upon. The City has sought to maintain a position that counters Canary Wharf's competitive offer by supporting the development of very tall buildings. "The financial boom of the late 1990s has seen the Corporation of London planners and property developers exploring the potential for expanding and consolidating the Eastern Cluster",[4] with buildings such as CityPoint by Sheppard Robson or the consented Leadenhall (dubbed 'the Cheese Grater') by Lord Richard Rogers, the Bishopsgate Tower ('the Pinnacle') by KPF or 20 Fenchurch Street ('the Walkie-Talkie') by Rafael Viñoly. The latter, for instance, provides 639,000 square feet (59,348 square metres) of floor space, of which 600,000 square feet will be dedicated to "premier office space".[5] The rental value of office space in the City continues to vary because of the interplay of various factors: the availability of office space which fluctuates depending on the undergoing developments, the quality of the space, the occupancy rate, and now, because of the US subprime crisis, prices are pushed downwards – already losing 9% of their value at the beginning of 2008.[6]

In an essay exploring the history of the visual experience of London, Robert Tavernor explains that "the precise character of this particular assembly of tall buildings will not last for long".[7] It is expected that we will begin to see a spill-over effect, in which tall buildings will be constructed outside the City's boundaries, in its fringes, such as the adjacent boroughs of Hackney and Tower Hamlets, and to the south of the Thames with the upcoming 1 Blackfriars Road and 'the Shard of Glass' (officially London Bridge Tower) in the boroughs of Lambeth and Southwark. This radiating effect is due to two mutually reinforcing factors. First of all, the very compact, albeit magnetic, geography of the City of London: the scarcity of land in this borough makes sites in its close proximity very attractive for property firms. Second, the increased acceptance of the new typology of tall buildings promotes their geographical spread across London. Until recently, skyscrapers were seen as an essentially US typology.[8] In Europe, they were perceived with suspicion and thought to be incompatible with the historically older urban fabric of European cities. This perception was later reinforced by the failure of modernist architecture and planning ideology. As Susan Fainstein puts it: "Seen as the application of science to nature and society, the high modernism that was embodied in the planning principles of most of the last century represented a certain form of idealism ... But seen from below, the effort to create brave new cities represented an undemocratic imposition of a particularist vision masquerading as the public interest".[9] Indeed, modernist planning was implemented at the expense of historic urban fabric, multiple ownership and uses, and was qualified by Jane Jacobs as the "rape of cities" and by Sir Peter Hall as one of the "great planning disasters".[10] Today, the inter-city economic competition has contributed to architectural competition translated by the regain of tall building popularity worldwide, as if they were a "sine qua non condition" for a global position.[11]

Whether tall buildings are actually needed to improve the way cities function is a contested matter. Debates about the containment of urban sprawl, the reduction of the carbon footprint of cities, the necessity to build skyscrapers to maintain an international economic position and where to locate them, or how tall they should be, have not yet reached a consensus. The idea of a compact and dense city was supported by the Urban Task Force – a research initiative lead by Lord Rogers and developed with the Department of Environment Transport and Regions (DETR) that sought to identify ways of creating urban areas in a direct response to people's needs and aspirations.[12] However, many, like Richard Sennett,[13] believe that the higher a building, the higher its needs in energy and thus its carbon footprint will be. Similarly, others, like Geoff Marsh,[14] argue that the same economic and global performance of London could be achieved with better use of the existing built stock and not necessarily with more tall buildings. As a matter of fact, none of these questions is really answered in policy and planning documents, and it is probably a specific characteristic of national and regional policy for England and Wales to avoid being prescriptive, indicating instead what is desirable in specific situations and arguing why. *Policy and Planning Guidance 15* (PPG15) aims to protect the distinctive character of conservation areas as well as listed buildings and their settings. As its name indicates, the document only provides guidance and as such is less regulatory than a policy and planning statement. *The London View Management Framework SPG* (adopted in July 2007)[15] to *The London Plan* (2004[16] and 2008[17]) is probably the most restrictive planning policy for the development of tall buildings. It sets the framework to visually protect the dome of St Paul's Cathedral, the Tower of London and the Palace of Westminster from 26 viewpoints across London – from locations as far as Primrose Hill or Richmond Park to closer ones along the South Bank or in St James's Park. At the local level, policies regarding tall buildings vary for each borough, but rarely adopt radical positions either for or against tall buildings. The Borough of Hackney, for example, accepts tall buildings as a fatality and prefers to have them located to the south of its territory, close to the City. By contrast, the City of Westminster is rather opposed to tall buildings and makes it difficult to build them within its boundaries.

In this policy and development context, building skyscrapers in London is ultimately a process of negotiation between different stakeholders. The latter are: on the one hand, the developers, clients, architects, various consultants and planners, and on the other hand, the local and regional authorities, at times the national government, and state organisations like CABE (Commission for Architecture and the Built Environment), English Heritage or Design for London. Depending on how contentious a development is, there is sometimes a third sphere that comes into play: civil society, represented by NGOs and/or local associations that articulate concerns about local matters, heritage protection, neighbourhood and social wellbeing. They usually try to oppose the development or to alter one or many aspects of it, such as the height, the architectural style, etc. They often contest the benefits of a tall development for the local community and perceive it as an instrument of gentrification, fearing that local inhabitants would be gradually pushed out of their neighbourhood because of higher real-estate prices.

Given the current taste and desire for tall buildings, the process of negotiation actually starts with the developer consulting other stakeholders prior to the submission of the planning application. Very early on, developers (especially those that own the sites) touch base with the local and regional authorities to share their visions and ambitions for a site. They then regularly meet with them to inform them of progress and get feedback on the proposed scheme(s). For large developments, they are informally expected to do so and mechanisms, though not fully institutionalised, are rather established. Discussions revolve around the conception and design of the scheme and how it conforms to the various local and regional policies. A more precise example is 'scoping', which consists of sending the contents of the Environmental Statement to the local authority for review before the planning application is submitted. Developers also sometimes meet and consult with members of the local community to promote their scheme. This means that the scheme that is submitted for planning permission already takes into account the local and regional authorities' feedback and therefore generally represents a compromise solution.

Changes can also be made to a development scheme after it has been granted planning consent. One famous case is that of the Minerva Tower (also known as St Botolph's House) in the City of London, which was originally proposed as a 53-storey building and was finally reduced to 14 storeys. The reason was the failure of the company to find a tenant who would occupy 50% of 100,000 square metres, or later, even 70,000 square metres, which is much more space than single companies generally require. "Minerva designed the tower to cater for a single major client, and more importantly they missed the boat with a business plan several years behind the market with all the leading players already decamped to Canary

Wharf. The current demand for towers in the city comes from companies wanting smaller amounts of space creating the need for multi-let buildings, something British Land, Heron and Land Securities are all addressing so confidently they plan speculative builds ...The final nail in the coffin is the change of chairmen at Minerva Plc."[18] This was a dramatic turn, as other prospective developments were then being designed according to this building's height and presence in the Square Mile.

Tall buildings and the role of public space in a democratic society

In 2002, a 'prestigious tall building' cost, on average, £3,000 per square metre, against £2,000 per square metre for a low to medium rise building.[19] Today this figure is much higher due of the significant increase in the price of steel – about 35% since 2005.[20] Given the huge investment required in terms of capital and time to build a skyscraper, real-estate companies or developers must make sure that they get value for their money and only pursue these projects with the perspective of large profits, rather than poor margins. One way to do that is to create different land-uses within a skyscraper, including offices, residential areas, retail, hotels, etc. This is very different from previous generations of tall buildings worldwide, which were mono-functional and mostly poorly integrated into their environment. In the new vertical mixed-use developments, every function is meant to generate revenue and all of the building must be made attractive and innovative in order to draw the potential clientele.

This marketing effort works better with features that capitalise on the spectacular heights of the building and enable the user to enjoy those heights in the most spectacular way. Proposals for tall buildings therefore incorporate the creation of spaces that supposedly offer similar characteristics and activities as public space on the ground. In marketing documentation, as well as in architects' design and access statements, one finds all sorts of names to designate these spaces: sky lobbies, sky gardens, viewing galleries, rooftop restaurants, etc., and they are portrayed like a street scene but with a view. In these representations, there are allusions to the open and free character of public spaces. However, when considering the enclosed character of these spaces and the meaning of public space as defined in the introduction, are these air spaces truly public or semi-public? How will they be accessible? Will everyone have access to them?

There are reasons inherent in this typology of building that make access a delicate issue. The sheer verticality of skyscrapers means that there are complex organisational, logistic and circulation issues to solve and then to maintain to ensure the smooth operation of the building. This means managing the flow of people within the building, ensuring that the needs/desiderata of the various tenants (be they residents or businesses) are met. Another issue is making sure that the different functions (offices, hotels, restaurants, leisure spaces, apartments, etc.) can occur simultaneously without clashes in terms of circulation of goods and people or in infrastructural requirements. These issues are directly linked to security which, especially since 11 September 2001, has become a major concern in these increasingly complex environments. In the Square Mile or Canary Wharf, access to tall buildings is always severely restricted and monitored. People, whether regular users or punctual visitors, are registered and then always under observation. The occupants/owners of the building also have a right to exclude whoever is deemed or perceived as 'unconforming' or indeed 'unconformist' or dangerous to the (infra)structure and its users. The complexity and large number of storeys in tall buildings make them more difficult to evacuate in case of emergency. The paranoia generated by 9/11 motivates a lot of this behaviour, as well as the establishment of these hyper-surveilled environments. Talking about the "most highly valued spaces in global city cores", Graham and Martin explain that, as clusters, "they are increasingly organised carefully to filter out unwanted connections with the surrounding metropolis – those that are judged to be 'threatening' or deemed to be irrelevant to the direct needs of the glocal enclave".[21] This statement applies to individual tall buildings operating in isolation from their local environment or choosing to interact in a strict and unilaterally controlled manner.

This endows the term 'public' with degrees of meanings. Many proposals make room for viewing galleries or sky gardens, which feature in the communication documents, but developers remain generally ambiguous about issues of access and intended use and users for the provided public air space. One reason for this is the likelihood that management and ownership may change once the building is constructed and therefore those submitting the planning application cannot pledge that the sky lobby or viewing gallery will indeed be accessible to all. Another reason is simply the actual willingness to make air spaces public. Tall buildings are expensive and are made for a type of clientele that appreciates their restricted access and exclusive character, including that of the air spaces. Spectacular because of the heights and views of the city they offer, the air spaces are undoubtedly attractive as leisure areas and are therefore seen as an asset to valorise the proposed building and its functions, especially the retail, entertainment, and perhaps residential functions. However, the ambition is not to recreate an urban public space, i.e. a civic space where citizens can spend leisure time but also exercise their right to express opposing beliefs. Instead the ambition is to provide an extension of the private sphere within the tall building, be it for offices or apartments. However, the extent to which the security of a skyscraper is insurmountable can be questioned. Ensuring the provision of separate and secure ways for the public to directly access the sky lobbies is an easy means of protecting the privacy of regular building users and residents. Overcrowding (not filtering!) can also be monitored at the entrance.

Conclusions

Tall buildings affect our visual and civic experience of the city and will increasingly do so – with an expected 18-20 tall buildings by 2015, many of which will be in Central London.[22] They are expensive to build and their construction is driven by the market and by the private sector. They represent a certain type of culture and image, linked to the idea of a strong economy and a strong position for London amongst global cities, according to Ken Livingstone, who spurred their construction, as well as many people working in urban planning, design and development. At present, among local authorities and citizens, there is a kind of resignation about skyscrapers as something inevitable, with impacts mitigated through policies and negotiation. It would perhaps be more encouraging and proactive if we urbanists, planners, architects, urban designers, developers, etc., start thinking and imagining ways in which very tall buildings can contribute more positively to public urban experience.

Finally, just as *The London View Management Framework* (July 2007) protects the skyline of London and its landmarks for the enjoyment of all citizens, this right should be reciprocated by the possibility of enjoying the city from the skies. The following few words in *The London Plan (consolidated with Alterations since 2004)* (2008) – still under Ken Livingstone's mayoral mandate – have not really changed the role of public air space in the urban and civic experience of London: "In considering applications for tall buildings, the Mayor will take into account the potential benefit of public access to the upper floors and may require such access" (Policy 4B.9 Tall buildings – location).[23]

Before the 2008 mayoral election, Boris Johnson, the Conservative candidate for the post, made the subject of tall buildings one his campaign themes.[24] His position was clearly more conservative in that he generally deplored the effects of skyscrapers on London's skyline and intended to adopt a different attitude towards them than that of his predecessors. Shortly after being elected, he made the following statement at the London Architecture Festival: "I am not opposed to all tall buildings … But if I think a tall building is simply out of keeping with the area, if the proposal is just gigantism for the sake of gigantism, then I will not hesitate to direct refusal. We will be in favour of creating high density without necessarily creating high rises."[25]

After a year under Boris Johnson's mayoral authority, the situation on tall buildings and the Mayor's position are, at best, puzzling. As Sir Simon Jenkins puts it: "London towers policy is in chaos".[26] On the one hand, the Mayor has been very vocal against certain schemes, such as the Beetham Tower to the south of Blackfriars (which has been granted consent after an enquiry) or Rafael Viñoly's highly ambitious plans for Battersea power station (which was altered to the point of completely removing the tower element from the plans). He is also proposing to widen the viewing corridors to further limit tall buildings and their visual impacts on Central London. A new document is currently being drafted to that effect.[27] On the other hand, Johnson supports the erection of three buildings of 33, 27 and 22 storeys to be built over Waterloo Station. Similarly, by allowing a 25-storey tower in a conservation area in Ealing and a 42-storey tower in Wandsworth,[28] he seems to have shattered the concept of clusters, which has so far confined tall buildings to a rather specific, albeit expanding, perimeter within Central London and Canary Wharf. In this confused political and policy context, it seems that the issue of public air space has been completely sidelined. The provision of Policy 4B.9 on public air space – and sadly, with it, some of the issues of public interest and democracy in city-making and urban experience – has become no more than a red herring.

BIOGRAPHY

Léa Ayoub studied political science in Beirut and subsequently urban design and social policy in London. After working for UNESCO, as a consultant in the management and economics of cultural heritage, and with the Professor Robert Tavernor Consultancy, she has joined Alan Baxter & Associates where she is pursuing her career as an urbanist.

1. Isle of Dogs is an area in South East London that has undergone extensive re-development since the late 1980s. It has the highest concentration of social housing in England but is best known as the site of Canary Wharf – a business district that rivals London's traditional financial centre, the Square Mile. It is also the location of the UK's three tallest buildings: One Canada Square at 771 feet (235.1 metres), followed by HSBC Tower and the Citigroup Centre, both at 654 feet (199.5 metres).

2. E. Peñalosa, 'Politics, Power, Cities' in R. Burdett and D. Sudjic (eds), *The Endless City* (London: Phaidon, 2007) pp. 307-319.

3. Lecturer at the University of Haifa, Israel. I. Charney, 'The Politics of Design: Architecture, Tall Buildings and the Skyline of Central London', *Area* Vol 29, 2007, pp. 195-205.

4. R. Tavernor (2006), 'Composing London Visually', in A. Marcus and D. Neumann (eds), *Visualizing the City* (London: Routledge, 2008) p. 21.

5. www.20fenchurchstreet.co.uk

6. T. Macalister, 'The dire state of real estate: credit crunch marks end of boom', *The Guardian*, 3 January 2008. www.guardian.co.uk/business/2008/jan/03/creditcrunch.realestate

7. R. Tavernor (2006), 'Composing London Visually', in A. Marcus and D. Neumann (eds), *Visualizing the City* (London: Routledge, 2008) p. 22.

8. L. Nicolaou, 'Viewing Tall Buildings in London', *Urban Design Quarterly*, Issue 90, 2004, pp. 28-31 and I. Charney, 'The Politics of Design: Architecture, Tall Buildings and the Skyline of Central London', *Area* Vol 29, 2007, pp. 195-205.

9. S. Fainstein, 'Cities and Diversity: Should We Want It? Can We Plan for It?', Leverhume International Symposium: The Resurgent City, London School of Economics, 19-21 April 2004, www.lse.ac.uk/collections/resurgentCity/Papers/susanfainstein.pdf, p. 5.

10. P. Hall, *Great Planning Disasters* (New York: Basic Books, 1982).

11. S. Zukin in I. Charney, 'The Politics of Design: Architecture, Tall Buildings and the Skyline of Central London', *Area* Vol 29, 2007, pp. 195-205.

12. Urban Task Force, 'Towards a Strong Urban Renaissance', 2005, urbantaskforce.org/UTF_final_report.pdf

13. Professor of Sociology at the Massachusetts Institute of Technology, USA.

14. Co-author of *High Buildings and Strategic Views in London* (1998) for the London Planning Advisory Committee. G. Marsh, 'Do We Need Tall Buildings?', *Urban Design Quarterly*, Issue 90, 2004, pp. 22-24.

15. Greater London Authority, *The London View Management Framework SPG* (London: Greater London Authority, 2007).

16. Greater London Authority, *The London Plan: Spatial Development Strategy for Greater London* (London: Greater London Authority, 2004).

17. Greater London Authority, *The London Plan (consolidated with Alterations since 2004)* (London: Greater London Authority, 2008).

18. Skyscrapernews.com, 'Minerva Skyscraper Faces Dumping', 2006, www.skyscrapernews.com/news.php?ref=679

19. G. Cox, H. Girardet and W. Pank, *Tall Buildings and Sustainability*, (London: Corporation of London and Faber Maunsell, 2002) p.12.

20. www.steelonthenet.com/commodity_prices.html

21. S. Graham and S. Martin, *Splintering Urbanism* (London: Routledge, 2001) p. 313.

22. I. Charney, 'The Politics of Design: Architecture, Tall Buildings and the Skyline of Central London', *Area* Vol 29, 2007, pp. 195-205.

23. Greater London Authority, *The London Plan (consolidated with Alterations since 2004)* (London: Greater London Authority, 2008) p. 252.

24. K. Shaps, 'Boris Johnson pledges to protect London's views from tall buildings', *Building*, 17 March 2008, www.building.co.uk/story.asp?storycode=3108999

25. BDonline.com, 'Boris set to keep Rogers as advisor', 2008, www.bdonline.co.uk/story.asp?storycode=3116499

26. S. Jenkins, 'Spare London's skyline yet another episode of these faulty towers', *London Evening Standard*, 24 February 2009.

27. W. Hurst, 'Mayor's proposals to increase London's viewing corridors would further restrict tall buildings', 5 June 2009, BDonline.com, www.bdonline.co.uk/story.asp?storycode=3142173

28. S. Jenkins, 'Spare London's skyline yet another episode of these faulty towers', *London Evening Standard*, 24 February 2009.

Land Quality in Urban Design

How Does A Lack of Standards Affect
Sustainable Brownfield Development in England?

Current legislation and guidance in England regarding contaminated land does not operate, contrary to EU ethos, on the precautionary principle. This is of particular concern in the redevelopment of brownfield sites and may have a detrimental impact on land quality in previously industrial urban settings and the wider environment.

The regulation of contaminated land is still in a fledgling state and there is a current lack of standards in England to determine the risk of contaminants in soil and how they affect human health and the wider environment. This has led to inconsistencies in land quality enforcement throughout the country and impacts on a wide range of topics including public perception, liability and the sustainability of developments.

What is contaminated land?

Past and present industrial uses are ubiquitous throughout urban settings. Power plants, smithies, gas works, oil distribution depots and similar operations were all necessary on and near to city centres to ensure their prosperity and to promote productivity and advancement. There are other common non-industrial sources of contamination in urban settings, such as landfills, former brickfields and former quarries. Brickfields were utilised to source brick in the development of cities and were then often filled with municipal waste and built over as development sprawled; the same holds true for some landfills. Farmland, meadowland

and marshes along rivers also required the importation of waste materials to build up and level them for development to occur. Areas of concern do not exist solely within the boundary of these previous land uses. Activities such as those related to large industry, such as power stations, utilised adjacent plots of land for storing vast quantities of coal, as well as pumping coal slurry through a network of pipes around and within these plants. These activities, as well as from any leaks in the distribution pipes, would therefore contaminate storage areas away from the plant. In addition to this, the smoke stacks from power stations would deposit particulate matter downwind at large distances. There is also the matter of mobile contaminants, such as liquid petrol products, which, when spilled, may enter surface or ground water sources and be transported down gradient hence diluting, but also potentially spreading, the pollution. Due to the compact nature of cities, it is common that sensitive end uses such as homes, schools and parks are developed on land previously used or effected by industry, landfills or other excavations, or even bomb sites – collectively known as potentially contaminated land.

Perception

Although most people are aware of issues regarding air and water pollution, the topic of land quality tends to go unnoticed. It is known that air emissions must be regulated and controlled by polluters, and that water quality is ensured by the supplier. The public is not generally aware, however, of who enforces land quality. When land quality issues are highlighted it often results in heightened concern most likely due to a lack of familiarity. A further exacerbating factor is its potential impact on land value.

Most people would not think to drink water from their local canal, stream or river in an urban setting, but do they give the same consideration to planting edible crops in urban soils? This issue was highlighted recently when *River Cottage* on Channel 4 broadcast an episode in October 2008 featuring a grassroots movement to sidestep long allotment waiting lists and utilise urban green space, which is considered derelict land, for planting edible crops. Contaminated land specialists and governing bodies reacted to the airing of this programme with concern. Although they all support regeneration and the environmental benefits of producing and consuming locally grown crops, they were concerned that at no point was the quality of the soil discussed. The organisation Environmental Protection UK wrote to Hugh Fearnley-Whittingstall to highlight this issue and asking him to consider making his viewers aware of these concerns in future programmes, so that they check with their local authority or a soil scientist to ensure that the soil does not pose a risk and potentially to remediate it themselves before use. Mr Fearnley-Whittingstall's reply was positive and stated that future episodes would emphasise the need to consider contaminated land.

Guidance and legislation: progress and pitfalls

The issue of contaminated land is not one that many people think of when listing common concerns regarding urban design and development. When considering environmental aspects of construction, most people think of dust and noise, and in design, concerns generally revolve around light, space and noise abatement. In England, legislation regarding these aspects of development stretches back to before the turn of the last century, whereas legislation regarding land quality is a relatively recent consideration.

The identification of contaminated land as a material planning consideration did not take place until this century. A duty of care by developers to deal with potential contamination was required by legislation from 1988. However, this re-quirement was not widely known and was not overseen by any outside governing body to ensure that relevant issues were being addressed. In 1994, *Planning Policy Guidance (Planning and Pollution Control PPG 23)* was produced. This provided planners with guidance on planning conditions addressing contaminated land concerns. However, at this time, the subject was still not widely known or under-stood, and local authorities lacked the expertise to ensure that these issues were properly addressed. Finally in 2001, Part IIA of the Environmental Protection Act 1990 (EPA) came into force, requiring local authorities to identify areas of potentially contaminated land and prioritise them for future investigation, risk assessment and remediation as required.

The EU recently promulgated the Environmental Liability Directive, which was implemented in England as of 1 March 2009 through the Environmental Damages (Prevention and Remediation) Regulations 2009. This legislation does not cover any contamination that took place prior to its implementation; however, it does enforce the 'polluter pays' principle for pollution incidents from this date forward. It stipulates that any pollution incident to a controlled water source or which may affect bio-diversity must be remediated to its original state, or if this is not possible, that the polluter must monetarily compensate for the residual contamination.

Unfortunately, once again the issue of land contamination is given a lesser priority than that of pollution of controlled water sources or even bio-diversity in that the polluter is only required to remediate land if the contamination is considered a risk to current site users. This would mean that if the pollution occurred on an industrial site where site users will not have significant contact with the contaminants, then it does not need to be remediated. As stated above, contaminants are sometimes mobile and therefore a pollution incident on one site may affect off-site land uses. Determining the fate and transport of a substance in the environment from the point of pollution to any sensitive receptors is a complex process of supposition and theory. Modern mathematical modelling programmes endeavour to provide us with the most likely fate and transport pathways, however, there is always an element of uncertainty. It follows that, in order to apply the precautionary principle and ensure that the polluter does indeed pay, they are required to remediate any pollution they cause regardless of where it occurs and at least to the exacting standards required for controlled water and bio-diversity.

The local authority's role

Part IIA of the EPA changed the face of land quality enforcement in England. Finally, a governing body was charged with overseeing the state of contaminated land and ensuring that developers are taking all necessary measures to ensure that future site users are safe from contamination. Unfortunately, a set of standards by which to measure the quality of land and determine risk has left individual local authorities with a great deal of autonomy, which has led to a lack of homogeneity in the way contaminated land is determined and addressed across the country.

Under Part IIA, the investigation and remediation of sites is undertaken by the local authority (LA) when addressing existing potentially contaminated land sites. However, in the case of redevelopments, the burden is placed upon the developer via contaminated land conditions placed upon their planning permission. These require that the developer ensures the safety of the site and submits all relevant reports to the LA for approval.

Therefore, issues regarding contaminated land are dealt with by individual LAs, who must ensure these sites are properly assessed. For most authorities, this is a task for one or two officers whose specialty is often not in relevant fields, such as environmental science/engineering, hydrogeology or geosciences, but in broad environmental fields such as environmental health. As a result, the expertise employed by developers through environmental consultants can often not be refuted, nor often understood, by these authorities. This issue is diminishing in urban authorities that have the knowledge and resources to employ the appropriate staff, but is still prevalent in more rural authorities. This is but one of many issues negatively affecting the state of land quality in England.

Another major concern, mentioned above, is the autonomy given to these authorities. Knowledgeable and experienced officers are able to utilise this to ensure that a site is properly assessed. However, some sites cross authority boundaries and this can result in conflict. An example is that of a site in a London borough (LA1), which had no previous contaminative use but was, however, heavily polluted by fuel. It was determined that this contamination was coming from an adjacent petrol station, which is situated in another London borough (LA2). At the time, the contaminated land officer in LA2 was inexperienced in such issues. Unfortunately, because the source of pollution was outside LA1's jurisdiction, they could not require that this petrol station remediate its contamination as well as that of the property within LA1, and the LA2 officer did not have the knowledge to ensure that this took place. This resulted in the developer in LA1 having to pay for the remediation of his own site and independently endeavour to recuperate costs.

The need for land quality standards

It is not unusual for 25% of land in an urban setting to be considered contaminated. This may sound alarmist, however, when you couple this with the fact that there are many known ways by which these contaminants can be detected, and even further, how they may be remediated, these concerns are obviated. Unfortunately, holes in current guidance and legislation mean that there are no set levels to indicate at what concentrations contaminants are to be considered a risk to human health and the environment.

This is one of the issues of greatest concern regarding contaminated land. Currently, there are no statutory, or even non-statutory, limits for any known contaminants in soil in England. This stands in stark contrast to other countries such as the US where there are over 500. This comparison may not be considered fair as the US has a more than 20-year head start in relevant legislation. However, other countries whose land quality legislation is more current than England's, such as Spain, have over 50 such limits.

England's Department for Environment, Food and Rural Affairs (Defra) may argue this point and say it is not the quantity but the quality. Their argument against using data from more experienced countries like the US is that they cannot be sure of the robust nature of the data. They also believe that the data is not comparable considering differences in geology and flood patterns, not to mention human epidemiology. It should be noted that the land area of England could fit into the US more than 70 times, and that the variation in geological strata in the US is much more diverse.

Considering the lack of guideline values, this is a difficult task for all parties involved. What toxicological data can be considered robust: World Health Organisation data, UK-only data, other nations' more comprehensive data? What risk assessment tools should be used: bespoke tools created by frustrated environmental consultants, US Environmental Protection Agency tools? The risk assessment tool published by Defra – *Contaminated Land Exposure Assessment* (CLEA) – has been published many times and then soon after removed from use, making it a much less reliable tool. This has resulted in environmental consultants working for developers having to apply different standards, depending on which LA their property lies within. Also, as highlighted above, if a development crosses LA boundaries, there may be large differences in the way the relevant councils regulate contaminated land.

Damage and liability

An example of how this lack of standards may lead to the detriment of human health and the liability of those responsible for ensuring these risks are abated is currently being debated in the High Court. The families of 18 people, between the ages of 9 and 21, have brought a multi-million pound compensation claim against Corby Borough Council, alleging that defects were caused by toxic substances released when the Corby steel works in Northamptonshire was redeveloped. Demolition, excavation and redevelopment of this site took place between 1984 and 1999 and therefore before Part IIA, but a current lack of standards means that remediation methodologies have not greatly progressed and there is still potential for this type of situation to arise.

Remediation

Due to all of this confusion, a great majority of time used addressing contaminated land is spent in the realm of immuno-toxicology. This is a field in which no

LA officer should have to become an expert. The role of determining such limits should be left to specialists. Unfortunately, this means that very little time or effort is spent in designing and enforcing the sustainable remediation of sites. Most often, remediation consists of the digging up of contaminated soils, which are placed onto lorries and transported for large distances to be placed in landfills. The great pity in this is that there are many innovative remediation technologies that enable soils to be left in place and actually cleaned, reducing the follow-on environmental impacts such as the expending of fuels and production of greenhouse gases through soil transport or the concentration of contaminated soils in landfills for future generations to deal with.

A couple of 'soil hospitals' have opened in England. These are large areas to which contaminated land may be transported and remediated for re-use. Whilst this is an improvement on the practice of digging and dumping good soil, this still requires the movement of soil over great distances and a cost to the environment.

The future of urban land quality

The government has announced its intention to remove the landfill tax exemption for waste from contaminated land disposed of by landfill from 1 April 2012. This will mean that the option to dig and dump contaminated land will no longer be an economical solution for developers and could encourage developers to start considering in-situ methods of remediation. There is, however, the possibility that developers will take advantage of the change and the lack of standards to allow unnecessary risks to remain at potentially contaminated land sites.

Hopefully, Defra will recognise the need for a conclusive set of standards that will help LAs to implement the precautionary principle, concentrate on ensuring sustainable remediation solutions, and educate the public about land quality, so that we can live safely on England's brown and pleasant land.

BIOGRAPHY

Elizabeth Fonseca is an environmental engineer and the Environmental Quality Manager for the London Borough of Hammersmith and Fulham.

The
Medical City

...A Story of Venus and Mercury

ALAN THOMPSON

This essay was prepared in response to an urban salon organised by This is Not a Gateway and hosted by public works' Shoreditch offices on the evening of 14 July 2008. At this meeting we were offered four very different perspectives, each dealing with the relationship between the city and medicine. This tiny piece of writing is a foolhardy attempt not only to respond to the four presentations, but also to muse on the history of medicine, architecture and urban design in relation to each other: a task which, at the outset, seems prone to absolute failure. Nevertheless, let's hope that what I have written here will, at least, be a little provocative and somewhat entertaining.

I begin by referring to some ideas originating in antiquity; these concepts relate architecture and the city to the human body. I follow this with a hectic history of the emergence of modern hospitals, which leads to a consideration of how concepts emanating from medicine have impacted on the development of the city. It would seem to be a one-way street: medical necessities have significantly affected the design of our cities, whereas urban theories have rarely had any impact on the practice of medicine.

Into this narrative, I weave remarks from our speakers. In his talk 'Paradoxical Frogs', the theorist Phil Gusak spoke of how visions of the utopian city, especially those concerning medicine, have been shrinking somewhat in recent years. Conversely, Mary Whittaker, from the healthcare team at London architects YRM, spoke of ways in which hospitals are being designed with evermore subtlety and consideration. Elizabeth Fonseca approached the subject from ground level as a practitioner who is responsible for the administration of public health in

Legalities of Space

Hammersmith and Fulham. Finally, the urban software designer Chris Sharp, director of Holistic City, mused on what cities could learn from medicine in the future.

Architecture

As any first-year undergraduate in design will tell you, around 20BC the Roman military engineer Vitruvius defined architecture using three essential categories: *firmitas, utilitas, venustas*. *Firmitas* speaks of how buildings must be strong and solid; *utilitas* allows them to offer comfort and attend to their function; and, *venustas* is their ability to give us joy.

By the use of *venustas*, Vitruvius had a very special sort of pleasure in mind. The obvious alternative to *venustas* would have been *pulchritudo*; yet Vitriuius neither uses this, nor the adjective *pulcher* (beautiful) anywhere in his *Ten Books*. *Pulchritudo* is equivalent to the Greek *kallos*, a distant platonic beauty, whereas *venustas* parallels the Greek *charis*, a more direct grace or charm. *Venustas* is, of course, the adjective pertaining to Venus, the Roman goddess of love; and according to Vitruvius, *venustas* is responsible for producing *voluptas*, a direct, sensual kind of pleasure; a pleasure that is very much 'of the body'.[1]

It is also significant to remember that Venus was the mother of Aeneas; Aeneas being the Trojan hero who, according to myth, founded Rome. So, it's not too far fetched to imagine that there could be some sort of quasi-genealogical reasons for, at very least, the city of Rome wanting to be beautiful in this way? Nevertheless, Vitruvius seems keen to extend this sort of beauty to all forms of architecture, wherever we find them and however they are made.

Finally, let's not forget that the author of the *Ten Books* was responsible for the 'Vitruvian Man'. The happy proportions of this perfect, healthy, human frame show a body in harmony with the whole universe. Vitruvian architecture was to strive after this ideal: pursuing the beauty of the body, not the beauty of the mind.

Medicine

So much for architecture, what about medicine? Of course, medicine is another animal altogether; in Vitruvian terms, its concerns are diametrically opposed to those of architecture. Medicine has to minister to members of society that are infirm, useless and unsightly: there isn't much room here for *firmitas, utilitas* and *venustas*. The sick are distinctly not Vitruvian men.

In the world of symbols, medicine is often represented by the caduceus, the emblem of the Roman god Mercury. The motif is always the same: two serpents entwined around a winged magic wand. The adjective 'mercurial' – quite contrary to Vitruvian *firmitas* – means volatile, fickle, flighty and erratic. Therefore, it seems that Mercury would not be the obvious choice for the medical profession to adopt? He is, of course, the messenger god, as well as the Roman god of commerce and profit; but he is, quite worryingly, also the patron of liars and gamblers. Nevertheless, perhaps there is a clue in Mercury's function as the Roman psychopomp: after all, it was Mercury who was responsible for accompanying souls into the afterlife. Belonging neither to the world of men, nor to the underworld, he could effortlessly traverse between life and death. This is a tempting interpretation, but unfortunately it is a totally incorrect one. All associations between Mercury and medicine are, in fact, the result of a 19TH-century error.[2] The correct symbol for medicine is the rod of Asclepius: one serpent wound around a simple staff. Asclepius was the Greek god of medicine (specifically healing), and his many daughters – Hygieia, Meditrina, Laso, Aceso, Aglaea and Panacea – aided him with this task, each having a defined medical role. The temples of Asclepius (Asclepieions) were the home of ancient medicine. They commonly offered two forms of cure: a trip to the spa, or a trip to the gym. The Asclepieion on Kos is thought to have been home to Hippocrates; Galen practiced at the Asclepieion in Pergamon.

The Asclepieion

The famed Asclepieion in Rome, like all things Roman, comes with several accompanying myths. This temple once stood on Tiber Island, a landmass that was believed to have sprung up soon after the body of the much hated tyrant Tarquinius Superbus had been cast into the river by an angry mob in 510 BC. Given these mythical beginnings, the place was best avoided. Subsequently, it became the preserve of criminals and carriers of contagious diseases. Since it was the only island in the Roman Tiber, tenuously linked to the rest of the city by only two bridges, it made the ideal spot to group such undesirables. After the great plague of 293 BC, as an offering to the gods, it was decided to found a temple to medicine in Rome. A delegation was dispatched to Epidauros in order to procure a statue of Asclepius; they also, very thoughtfully, bought back a sacred snake (these animals were commonly let loose on the floors of Asclepieion dormitories). On the return voyage, the snake compliantly curled itself around the mast of the ship, thereby making the sign of Asclepius: a very good omen! Once back in Rome, as luck would have it, the snake slithered ashore on Tiber Island, indicating that this filthy mud bank would soon become the centre of Roman medicine. The temple was promptly built. Much later, the Roman Asclepieion was buried under the foundations of the Christian Basilica of San Bartolomeo all'Isola (998 AD); however, the island still boasts a fully functioning hospital, the Ospedale Fatebenefratelli, founded by the Hospitaller Order of St John in 1584.

One can't help thinking that the snake had a pretty beady eye for the founding of a large medical institution. Given the contagious nature of many diseases, an easily isolated spot was an extremely good choice. And what could be more isolated than an island? Of course, the etymology of the word 'isolated' (1763) derives from *isolato* (Italian) and *insulatus* (Latin), meaning 'made into an island'; originally from *insula* the Latin word for 'island'.

The rise of surgery

The first comprehensive anthropomorphism of the city is found in Plato's *Republic*. The cantankerous old aristocrat compares functional parts of society with parallel parts of the body. He asserts that the head, the heart and the stomach all have their own specialisations. Of course, they all co-operate, yet they also attend to their own very particular business; each knows its place in the order of things. Similarly, the philosopher king, the guardians and the auxiliaries all have their place in Plato's body politic. Plato's argument is deployed against democracy: he declares that it's only natural that each sector of society also has its own specialism and consequently has its rightful place too. Needless to say, in Plato's pecking order, the belly is well below the brain![3]

In his book *Flesh And Stone*, Richard Sennett relates two, slightly more sophisticated anthropomorphisms of the Middle Ages: one from a political scientist commenting on the body; the other from a surgeon speaking about politics. John of Salisbury believed, much as Plato had, that the city should be compared to a healthy body, where everything is in equilibrium: "If people rebel against their place in the hierarchy, a ruler knows what to do: expel or kill the unruly, just as a surgeon cuts out diseased organs." Conversely, the surgeon Henri de Mondeville thought that the healthy human body necessarily had its various parts perpetually operating within the constant flux of heats and stresses. He had witnessed, at first hand, the phenomenon of syncope; where, under extreme trauma, organs of the body appear to rally to each other's support. His model of the human anatomy was one of sympathy and co-operation; he thought that rigid discriminations and stasis were antithetical to vitality and ultimately led to death. His contemporaries would extend this thinking to the city: we should not recoil from "the knife wound" caused to the city by the appearance of foreign exiles, rather we ought to extend mercy. As Sennett would have it, "there is a biological foundation for altruism".[4]

City of God

Medieval medicine was, for the most part, administered by the church. Monasteries had infirmaries attached and, although intended for sick monks, their services were charitably extended to the surrounding community. Such institutions strived to bring about Saint Augustine's 'City of God': a proto-utopian vision in sharp contrast to the brutal and dirty 'City of Man'. Augustine's ideal was very much of, and indeed for, the medieval mind. It was not at all for the pleasures or convenience of the medieval body. In fact, it was not for bodies of any kind, particularly not Vitruvian bodies. No, especially not them! It was, indeed, a New Jerusalem, but not yet on England's green and pleasant land. We ought to remember that, before the biblical fall, paradise was once a garden,[5] and many would imagine it as a garden again. The only surviving architectural drawing from the Middle Ages is a plan of the Monastery at Saint Gall (Switzerland), which clearly shows an infirmary with courtyards and ancillary gardens. These green spaces not only functioned as a therapeutic retreat for the convalescing patient, but also propagated the medicinal plants needed for their treatment. The drying of such plants to produce healing compounds gave rise to our contemporary word 'drug'; from *drouge*, Old French for 'to dry' (1327 AD). Unfortunately, this very direct connection between patient, landscape and medicine has, long since, been lost – partly as a result of the modern mind's proclivity for compartmentalisation. The patients now belong in the wards; the medicine belongs at the pharmacy; and the landscape belongs somewhere else, far beyond the city. A patient's connection with nature, although proven to be beneficial,[6] is often very limited. Saint Augustine's dream was of building the all-inclusive 'City of God'. At Saint Gall, within a microcosm of a real city, the infirmary gathered together a community of the sick into a diminutive, green, urban district. Unfortunately, despite such high Christian ideals, the first modern in-patient facilities were devised to set patients apart from society, rather than incorporating them into it.

Contamination

In 651 AD, a hospital was founded on the Ile de la Cité, an island in the Seine. Although constructed on an island, the Hotel-Dieu was by no means isolated; for this site, directly beside the Cathedral of Notre Dame de Paris, was at the very heart of Paris. Medicine in medieval France had not progressed that much from the time of imperial Rome; a visit to the Hotel-Dieu was to be avoided at all possible costs. It was thought to be one of the most dangerous places in the medieval world and incarceration there was tantamount to a death sentence. During the plague of 1584, the hospital requested the use of municipal houses built along the Petit Pont, a bridge linking the Ile de la Cité to the mainland. The city flatly refused. They objected that the hospital was "like a heart in the middle of a man, such that bad air within it can infect the rest of the body, and all the parts and places of the city." This expansion would be like "adding wood to fire, poison to poison". However, by the late 18TH century, heedless of such warnings, the institution had not only occupied the opposite bank of the Seine, it had straddled the river with a shanty town of piers and cantilevered projections. Conditions were dire: "the walls are dirtied with spittle, the floor soiled with filth oozing from the mattresses and from the commodes where they are emptied, with pus and blood from wounds or venesections." There were beds that accommodated as many as eight patients!

When the Hotel-Dieu finally burnt to the ground in December 1772, over 200 proposals were made for its replacement. Oddly, all of the final schemes owed their inspiration to military architecture. The advisor to the committee of the Academie des Sciences, surgeon Jacques Tenon, had been dispatched to England to report on emerging hospital design in 1787 and he had taken a keen interest in the new naval hospitals at Haslar and Plymouth. These vast new buildings had replaced a more traditional method of naval medicine: the lazarette.[7]

Landfall

The lazarette, named after the biblical leper Lazarus, was, very simply, a plague boat. 'Lazarette' is still a commonly used nautical term, which describes a locker in the stern of a vessel. This compartment is always to be found below the weather deck, always has a lockable hatch or door, and is, uncontroversially, a place for the containment of equipment – we can only speculate about its other historical uses.

Such lazarette boats were set up in ports for quarantine – literally the 40 days needed to be sure that there was no chance of suspicious visitors infecting the town with alien disease. The first built example, or *lazaretto*, was established in the Venetian lagoon in 1403, on the island of Santa Maria di Nazareth; although the Lazaretto Vecchio barely counts as being part of the city since it occupies a tiny, far-flung island, close to the Lido. In 15TH-century Venice, medicine, or rather sickness, was not to be entertained as being 'of the city'; rather, it was held firmly at arm's length from it.[8] This tradition of offshore exclusion for the sick was to endure until quite recently. The HMS Dreadnought, a 98-gun ship of the line, launched in 1801, was little different from the early lazarettes. After many years of active service, including early action at the battle of Trafalgar, the HMS Dreadnought ended its days as a hospital ship, moored at Milford-on-Sea (Hampshire), becoming the headquarters of the Seamen's Hospital Society. In 1870, this infirmary finally transferred to terra firma as the Dreadnought Seamen's Hospital at Greenwich,[9] later becoming the Dreadnought Unit at Saint Thomas' Hospital in 1986.

For his report on the rebuilding of the Hotel-Dieu in 1789, Tenon's colleague Le Roy encapsulated his ideas on medical architecture: "think of the wards entirely isolated from one another, like tents in an army encampment". Although originating in England, these ideas would not return there for quite some time.[10]

The Great Stink

The 19TH century was the century of public health. With industrialisation giving rise to ever increasing densities of population within modern cities, state intervention had become a necessary development. Public health reforms were not, strictly speaking, altruistic: density meant that the well-to-do could no longer isolate themselves from contagious diseases spawned by the more wretched elements of society. To do nothing was simply not an option. The Booth *Maps Descriptive of London Poverty*,[11] shown in two of the salon presentations, were an illustration of the growing unease concerning 'proximity'. The turning point came with the 1854 Broad Street cholera outbreak. Famously, the physician John Snow observed the grouping of deaths around one particular public water pump in Soho, London, and as a result, proved that polluted water was to blame for this blight, and not 'bad air' as miasma theory had always maintained. Although Snow's findings were initially rejected, the Great Stink of 1858 was soon to apply more than adequate pressure on the government. In that year, an enabling act, which was needed to push ahead with Joeseph Bazaljette's proposals for the de facto rebuilding of London's sewage system, was passed. At the TINAG salon, this important episode was alluded to by a number of our speakers. Phil Gusak pointed out that many cities from antiquity seem to have been laid out with the geometry of public health in mind, whereas modern cities were healthy only as an afterthought. His point was that the design and evolution of cities seem not to be generated by concerns about health at all. Jane Jacobs' points out that many cities were established in comparatively blighted spots, despite excellent alternatives being available in abundance in close proximity.[12] What could account for such apparent foolishness? Cities, of course, are not generally built by philanthropists; they are built by the greedy, out of self-interest. Mercury is more at work here than Asclepius? Perhaps the 19TH-century confusion over the symbol for medicine may be more revealing than we first thought?

Cleaning up

The 20TH century consolidated the state's jurisdiction over the health of the city. Statute after statute enshrined new codes and directives, making it possible to intervene against unhealthy, unregulated self-interest. Elizabeth Fonseca, Environmental Quality Manager at Hammersmith and Fulham Council, necessarily operates under numerous statutory instruments. In her day-to-day job, she deals mainly with urban land quality, confronting either historical contamination (industrial or infill) or current considerations (new potentials for contaminating activity or changes of use.)

European guidance urges the precautionary principle: "scientific uncertainty shall not be used to postpone cost effective measures to prevent environmental degradation",[13] and UK directives not only require a proactive approach considering the source, the pathway and the receptor in any remediation of land,[14] but ask for planning and pollution control.[15] Unfortunately, such strategic thinking tends to falter when it comes to practical application. Elizabeth presented us with a case study: a development straddled by a local authority boundary. On one side of this boundary was the proposed community centre and nursery; on the other side, a disused petrol station with leaking oil pipes. Confusions of jurisdiction often lead to a lack of joined-up thinking. In another case, lack of connection between successor and existing contamination meant that there was no ongoing knowledge of the liability. So it seems that lack of communication and ghettoisation is problematic in this area? Elizabeth was wary of the UK habit of containment rather than remediation. She finally observed that the allocation of finite resources allows day-to-day enforcement to shape the development of our environment. There is never enough time or money to be properly proactive or strategic! In a way, we are taking a bit of a gamble with our future? Still, let the dice roll ... let's see how it all turns out. Mercury, the god of gambling, would be proud of us!

Towards utopia

The state's control over public health finally confronted the regulation of the individual body on 5 July 1948. With the introduction of the National Health Service, one would hope that mercurial flightiness and volatility were coming to an end? For too long, basic healthcare had been beyond the reach of too many. And surely the private market in medicine was antithetical to the notion of healing? Returning to an unfinished story: Asclepius' damnation at the hand of Zeus came by way of a thunderbolt. It is significant to note that he was not punished for raising the dead, something that he had done many times before without condemnation. No, his transgression was more serious: he had accepted gold in exchange for his services! The NHS was, indeed, somewhat utopian; there would be no exchange of gold from now on. Phil Gusak treated us to a presentation on the history of utopias, both of the city and for the provision of health. In passing, he mentioned the 'Garden City' of Ebenezer Howard;[16] it's nice to see that visions of paradise were still offering fresh air and a backyard, a reconnection with nature. Closer to earthly concerns, the 1970s saw a government drive for 70 new 1,000-bed hospitals: the ultimate industrialisation of healthcare. The patient was to be processed, becoming subject to a medicine that was all about the body, but the body as mere object? Meanwhile, architecture was flirting with the loss of *venustas*: there would be little room for the pleasures of the body, little room for any pleasures at all! Since a couple of the salon speakers noted the significance of Northwick Park Hospital,[17] it's worth taking a closer look. This huge medical establishment was devised by John Weeks in 1962. The scheme epitomises the concept of indeterminate design: "The conceptual solution ... simply depicted an entrance area with an extendable corridor leading from it and extensible departments plugged into this 'street'. By creating a communications system independent of the plug-in departments, growth and change in the overall hospital could occur without detriment to the comprehensibility of the street."[18]

Paradoxical frogs

Northwick Park was a seminal piece of mercurial thinking: it resisted built-in obsolescence by embracing the possibility of change; it engaged with the shanty-town approach to town planning; volatility was at the heart of this enterprise. The inspiration for Northwick Park was Alison and Peter Smithson's University of Sheffield project faculty buildings: "their shape must not only be able to 'take' change but should imply change".[19] It was a profound move to admit that the only certainty that we can have about the future is that we have no idea what the future will actually be like! In some ways, this was an abandonment of utopian thinking in favour of the real politick of medical planning. It was also an abandonment of beauty! Ironically, as it turned out, this became yet another failed vision of utopia. In 2007, only 45 years from its inception, Northwick Park was being prepared for demolition, in favour of a new, purpose-built facility; the cost of refurbishment being more than that of new build. Phil Gusak argues that, like his paradoxical frogs and despite all of our utopian hopes, "the frog always turns out to be small-er than the tadpole".[20] We are living in an age of contracting dreams. Should we downsize our dreams even more? Before the 1973 oil crisis, there seemed to be a time of abundance, offering the chance of health, comfort and leisure for all. In 1958, President Nixon optimistically urged the American people to prepare for the 14-hour working week. Fifty years later, what we have really been preparing ourselves for, as any young design graduate will tell you, is the 14-hour working day! And finally perhaps, thanks to the swift hand of Mercury, benevolent god of commerce, our routine will soon be commuted to the 14-hour working month? At last, here is all of that leisure that we were once promised, only this time without the accompanying comfort, security and salubrity of the 1950s. Volatility, chance, mendacity! Surely this is not a healthy way to arrange our lives? As we suspected, Mercury was always an impostor? He was never the god of medicine! Why did we ever agree to trust him?

Reasons to be cheerful

So many visions of utopia seem to have led us nowhere?[21] However, it can't be correct to believe that we have made no progress at all in this long journey? Surely we are overlooking the obvious benefits that have emerged in recent times? Mary Whittaker, senior healthcare architect at YRM suggests that we are. In her presentation, Mary offered many compelling reasons why we ought to feel good about the current state of hospital design.

Since the great fire of London in 1666, urban development has been fiercely policed, ranging from the broad-brush government building regulations to very specific Health Building Notes (HBN) documents, each relating to specialist areas of hospital design. More recent concerns about sustainability have led to new guidance: BRE Environment Assessment Modes (BREEAM) and Leadership in Energy and Environmental Design (LEED) prescribe energy conservation, reduced carbon footprint and efficient use of water. Phil Gusak argues that, with respect to architectural design, "there is currently, only one game in town ... and it isn't health". Sustainability is a pressing issue. Without concern for the future of our planet there would be no need for healthcare of any kind? But do the proposed new eco-towns offer anything for our physical and mental wellbeing, or is the public health agenda now simply a subsidiary issue? Architects are currently striving to maximise the use of natural ventilation and daylight, which provide well-documented health benefits.[22] A notable exemplar is Arup Associates' Druk White Lotus School in Ladakh.[23] In many contemporary projects, choice of setting and integration with landscape are very carefully considered. There are clear health advantages emanating from 'welcoming design' too. Unlike the days of Northwick Park, beauty is back on the agenda. Mary argues that it is healthy for people to have a welcoming and respectful environment; and patient expectations are very important! Robustness and durability not only make for sustainable, long lasting buildings, but also give a feeling of well–being. The Evelina Children's Hospital is a clear example of this.[24]

Leeches or laudanum

Yet, even if it is true that our healthcare facilities are experiencing a renaissance, given the renewed boom in hospital building, what of the city itself? Chris Sharp casts some light on this. He considers whether contemporary trends in medical thinking have anything to offer the urban designer.

Modernist thinking, both in medicine and in urban design, historically tended towards specialisation and compartmentalised thinking. For example, a multi-lane elevated road junction, although the perfect solution for a traffic engineer, offers very little to the pedestrian. Disciplines have been allowed to work independently for far too long? Contemporary thought in medicine encourages a more holistic approach: treating not just the disease but the whole person. This thinking is a wise prescription for the urban designer. Recently, reforms in the NHS have attempted to tailor medicine to the wishes of the patient: so-called patient-centred medicine. If we provide patients with enough information, they can make decisions about their preferred course of treatment. In the past there were far fewer options available: antiquity offered the spa or the gym; the 18TH century gave us leeches or laudanum; today there is much more choice. Does this have parallels in urban theory? To make a medical analogy, there is no longer a panacea to our urban problems; public consultation is a necessity in 21ST-century design. Finally, evidence-based medicine has been very much in the news – although it does beg the question: what on earth were we doing before? It seems that many of our preconceptions about medicine were just dogma or habit. Therefore, there is need to conduct experiments into the most effective courses of action. In medicine, one would have hoped that this was already de rigueur, but in urban design, we are far less willing to allow experiments to take place. Not only have we had a stomachful of utopian experimentation in the 20TH century, but we are reminded that, unlike the surgeon, the architect cannot bury his mistakes!

Conclusion

As far back as John of Salisbury's *Policraticus* (1159 AD), the merchant class was already characterised as the "greedy belly" of the body politic: "If these men have been stuffed through excessive greed and if they hold their contents too obstinately, [they] give rise to countless and incurable illnesses and, through their vices, can bring about the ruin of the body as a whole."[25] When looking for somebody to blame in our present uncertain economic times, there are many who would gladly rally to echo his sentiment. Perhaps a greedy and retentive sector of our society is to blame for the ill health of our political life and, by extension, for the sickness we find in the fabric of our cities. Ultimately, are they not the cause, too, of the malaise and mortality of our citizens? Was Gusak right to conflate the comparative health of the city and that of the citizen?

It seems obvious that we ought to rehabilitate rather than contain contamination? Our short-termism has been led by an all-too-human greediness: we are only prepared to spend enough to bury a problem, and no more. We reject good sense in the same way as Victorian politicians rejected John Snow's observations on cholera: they only reacted to public outrage in the face of the Great Stink?

117

Unfortunately, our climatic problems are not quite as malodorous as those of the 19th century so we need to learn to be more strategic.

It is still an open question as to whether Asclepius ever wrested his jurisdiction over health back from the pretender Mercury? Is there reason for hope, as Chris and Mary would offer it? Or is there more reason to be fearful?

Much has been said about how medicine has affected the development of the city. Yet does our theorising about the city have anything to offer medical thinking? It's not immediately clear to see how this might be done; but, in any case, it is a story for another day?

BIOGRAPHY

Alan Thompson is chairman of the cultural organisation, Art & Architecture, and director of the architectural design and animation company, 3DWG. (www.apthompson.com)

1. Indra Kagis McEwen, *Vitruvius: Writing the Body of Architecture* (Cambridge, Massachusetts: MIT, 2003). Discussion of Vitruvius' idea of beauty, pp. 198–212.
2. The rod of Asclepius is often confused with the winged caduceus, a magical wand invariably depicted alongside the Roman god Mercury. Such confusion has been exacerbated by the use of the caduceus on the uniforms of medical officers and stewards of the American Army and as a printer's mark for many medical textbooks. In the UK, the Royal College of Physicians also wrongly refer to their own president's symbol of office as a caduceus (it is clearly the rod of Asclepius.) The American Medical Association rejected the use of the caduceus in 1912 and have used the rod of Asclepius ever since.
3. Plato's discourse on the three parts of the soul (Book II Justice in the City and Soul. 434D-441C) in *The Collected Dialogues: The Republic* (Princeton: University Press, 1961).
4. Richard Sennett refers to the ideas in John of Salisbury's book *Policraticus* and Henri de Mondeville's work *Arts de la Medecine et de la Chirurgie* (1314) in *Flesh and Stone: The Body and the City in Western Civilization* (New York & London: WWNorton, 1994) pp. 164-168.
5. The word 'paradise' came from the French *paradis*, inherited from the Latin *paradisus*, taken from Greek *parádeisos*, and ultimately from Avestan, an archaic Iranian language, *pairi.daêza* literally meaning 'walled' (enclosure), from *pairi*, 'around' and *–diz*, 'to make or create'. The Old Iranian word described walled estates. Ancient Greek used *ho parádeisos* to mean 'an animal park'. This term is found in the *Anabasis* by Xenophon, 4TH century BC (Wikipedia).
6. Particularly the work of Professor Roger Ulrich. See R.S. Ulrich, 'Effects of Gardens on Health Outcomes: Theory and Research', in C. Cooper-Marcus and M. Barnes (eds), *Healing Gardens: Therapeutic Benefits and Design Recommendations* (New York: John Wiley, 1999).
7. See Chapter 8 Island Hospitals, in Christine Stephenson, *Medicine and Magnificence: British Hospital and Asylum Architecture, 1660-1815* (New Haven & London: Yale University Press 2000) pp. 172-194.
8. Medieval Venice also gave us the first ghetto. In medieval Venice, Jews were segregated together onto one tiny island in the district of Cannaregio; movement on and off the island was carefully policed. Before the Jews arrived, this site was formerly an iron foundry; in Venetian dialect, *ghetto* simply means 'iron foundry'. Of course, 'ghetto' came to mean much more, as the segregation principle took hold around the globe; but perhaps it makes some sense that this concept emerged from a city composed entirely of islands?

9. After the atrocities of the Crimean War, the campaigning of Florence Nightingale led to the establishment of the first British 'pavilion hospitals'. She pointed to the new Hotel-Dieu (1785) as a paradigm for modern medicine. The Dreadnought Seamen's Hospital at Greenwich (1870) was the first proper example of the isolation of wards in British hospital design.

10. Ironically, the Hotel-Dieu was actually based on the earlier British naval hospitals at Plymouth and Haslar (1750s). It seems to have taken the British a very long time to rediscover their own tradition in hospital design?

11. Booth *Maps Descriptive of London Poverty* (1898-1899) are very detailed coloured maps that chart relative affluence across the entire Greater London area. Street by street, from the black (lowest class, vicious, semi-criminal) through the blues of the poor and the reds of the well-to-do, we finally arrive at the yellows of the upper-middle and upper classes, the wealthy.

12. Jane Jacobs, *Economy of Cities* (London: Jonathan Cape, 1970).

13. 1992 Rio Declaration on Environment and Development.

14. Part IIA of the Environmental Protection Act.

15. Planning Policy Statement 23.

16. Ebenezer Howard, *Garden Cities of To-Morrow* (London: 1902).

17. Northwick Park Hospital (1962), Llewelyn-Davies Weeks.

18. Jonathan Hughes and Simon Sadler (eds), *Non-Plan: Essays on Freedom, Participation and Change in Modern Architecture and Urbanism* (London: Architectural Press, 2002) p. 99.

19. *ibid.* Jonathan Hughes quotes Alison and Peter Smithson from 'The Aesthetics of Change', in *Architects' Yearbook 8* (London: Paul Elek, 1957).

20. Phil Gusak's conclusion to his presentation 'Paradoxical Frogs', TINAG Medical City Salon, July 2008.

21. Thomas More coined the term in his classic book, *Utopia* (1516). 'Utopia' literally means 'nowhere'.

22. R. Ulrich and C. Zimring, The Role of the Physical Environment in the Hospital of the 21ST Century: A Once-in-a-Lifetime Opportunity (Concord, CA: Center for Health Design, 2004). www.healthdesign.org/research/reports/pdfs/role_physical_env.pdf

23. White Druk Lotus School (Phase 1, 2001), Arup Associates.

24. Evelina Children's Hospital (2005), Hopkins Architects.

25. John of Salisbury's *Policraticus* (1159 AD), as quoted in Richard Sennett, *Flesh and Stone*, p. 156.

CLOCKWISE FROM TOP RIGHT

Urban elevated highway junction, Tokyo, 2008, CHRIS SHARP

Anatomical representation from Henri de Mondeville's work *Arts de la Medecine et de la Chirurgie*, 1314 (Bibliotheque nationale de France, Paris)

Contextual drawing of hospital development within landscape, 2008, YRM ARCHITECTS

Demolition of Northwick Park Hospital, 2005 (Permission Phil Gusack)

Sculpture of the Roman god Mercury 17TH-century, ARTUS QUELLINUS (Bureau Monumentenzorg, Amsterdam)

MIGRATION AND HOME

Introduction

DEEPA NAIK & TRENTON OLDFIELD

What does it mean to create a home in an 'alien' city? How do the inter-linked processes of movement and settling shape new subjectivities and what is contributed to the form and function of space? This section explores issues of migration and home in relation to the production of urban space, architecture and its representations.

Fields such as cultural studies, critical theory, visual cultures, anthropology and geography have contributed much to understandings of the multiple layers and impacts of migration in a rapidly globalising world. Inter-disciplinary discourses have destabilised notions of space, place and identity as fixed or bounded constructs. Instead subjectivities and location have been re-imagined as multifaceted, contingent and continually shifting zones of contact. Terms such as 'intersecting regions', 'translocal/global/national' and 'nomadic identities' have allowed for an expanded discussion about the politics of space and conditions of migrancy. The following papers, visual essays and conversations investigate how 'subjects-on-the-move' create a sense of home. More specifically, they explore the way heterogeneous notions of dwelling are being translated into the urban environment.

'Migration and Home', unsurprisingly given the ferocious nature and scale of global migratory flows, was an ever-present theme at both the festival and the salons. Much of the material for this book was generated in London, a city where, in 2007 alone, an estimated 167,000 (2%) people immigrated, while 248,000 (3%) left.[1] These massive movements of people, and the processes of removing or establishing themselves in new places, have considerable consequences for how dwellings are conceptualised. The contributors to this section look at the ways numerous actors are challenging homogenous notions of 'home' and how cities are being re-proposed to reflect the changing desires of their inhabitants.

The opening text by architect John Oduroe and curator Paul Goodwin was produced as a result of the salon Re-Visioning Black Urbanism and the Production of Space.[2] The discussion they record is an ambitious attempt to explore how discourses of difference could influence the built environment. Initially born out of the African diaspora, 'blackness', they argue, has been synonymous with a certain notion of urbanism – a cultural signifier connected to jazz, break dancing, fashion and language. How can these types of cultural agency be translated into architectural spaces? How can 'black urbanism' draw on a spectrum of cultural influences, without fixing or essentialising ethnicity? What spatial possibilities emerge when theoretical projects converge with architectural practices? Provocative, interesting and at times tense, the salon brought together a considerable number of people interested in sharing their experiences and knowledge, and launched John Oduroe and Paul Goodwin's initiative the Office for Metropolitan Alternatives', a platform dedicated to investigating these very questions.

Joanna Zawieja uses cinema as a starting point to investigate the relationship between the production of spatial narratives and built environments. She argues that cities are increasingly mediated through images that aim to appeal to mass audiences and global markets, resulting in a flattening out of spatial difference. Woody Allen's film *Vicky Christina Barcelona* is cited as an example of the way representations of a city can be institutionalised as a consequence of cultural policies and financing. Importantly, the paper goes on to detail how omissions, such as that of the growing migrant communities in Barcelona, will not be limited to the space of the imaginary and will traverse into the built environment. As an architect, the author asks: Where in this mediated landscape are our architectural desires and needs formulated? Whose imagination are we materialising? What are the social, cultural and gendered constructs inherent in these foundational narratives? Are we building stages for already performed stories?

The embedded relationship between visual narratives and built spaces is further explored in the sound transcript from Zawieja's film *Imagine A House*. Screened at the festival,[3] it uncovers experiences of home and homemaking at one site in East London. It pieces together fragments of the lives of 'fallen' women who were housed at 195 Mare Street in the early 19TH century – a space of refuge and second chances, where they were taught 'homemaking skills' and codes of respectability. Later the space became a working-men's club where men were able to escape home and garner political consciousness. A third layer chronicles the arrival of a newcomer to an area of the city where multiple cultures and histories converge, interweaving present-day notions of belonging and creating a home for oneself.

Sites of worship play an important role in forming a sense of 'being home'. Rehan Jamil's photographic series, *East End of Islam: 1997–2007,* draws on a decade-long study of the East London Mosque and Muslim community in Tower Hamlets where two (and soon to be three) buildings on Whitechapel Road accommodate one of the largest congregations of Muslim worshippers in Western Europe. The mosque has a fascinating history of community-led action, dating back to 1910, when the London Mosque Fund was established to procure a permanent place of worship for the many visiting merchants, diplomats and sailors coming into local ports. For 30 years various rooms were hired for Friday prayers and in 1940 three houses were purchased on Commercial Road, becoming the first rooted site of worship. In 1975 the local authority bought the properties on a compulsory purchase order and in return provided a site where the current mosque now stands. After several years of raising funds from the local and international Muslim community, a purpose-built mosque was constructed. In the late 1990s, the community, which had grown to include people from Bangladesh, Pakistan, Somalia, Algeria, Morocco and Indonesia, rallied together to canvas for the vacant land adjacent to the mosque in order to meet their changing needs. Rehan Jamil, a member of the congregation, offers an intimate insight into this stage of the building's expansion. The images – shown and discussed during the Re-Visioning Black Urbanism salon – reveal the way a sense of 'home' takes form when people set out to articulate their own needs and desires, in this instance through establishing spaces for rituals, within the built environment.

Not unlike London and its population of South Asian seamen, in recent years Dubai has been a magnet for guest workers attracted by the prospect of being able to send money back home to support their families. The dialogue between Omair Barkatulla and Matthew Lee explores how Dubai's economic boom coupled with a cheap labour market in the early part of the new millennium produced a sense that anything was possible in the built environment. They question the spatial implications of seemingly unlimited (and imported) architectural possibilities. What results when floods of people from different parts of the world converge in one place? How do people navigate a terrain where there are no public spaces to gather; a city designed to reinforce the temporary nature of its workers? The conversation draws on Omair Barkatulla's film *Do Buy,* screened at the festival,[4] which reveals the gaps between the promise of the city and the lived experience of migrant workers.

Ania Dabrowska's two photographic series *You And I In Flux* and *I Used To Skate On Frozen Lakes* explore 'home' as always being connected to an 'elsewhere'. The artist has created portraits of people who, like herself, had migrated to London. She asked the sitters to consider what it meant to belong or to be 'at home' and to select the places they wanted to be photographed; later she created the landscape series in response to their conversations and memories of belonging to another place. The photographs give no indication of the individual circumstances, reasons for their journeys or places of origin. Instead, the viewer is given the space to reflect on his or her own notions of 'home'. During the festival, the images were shown in an underground bunker,[5] lit only by candles and torches, and accompanied by *Conversations* – an installation of passport books containing transcripts of her discussions with the sitters. By inserting their narratives within the symbolic official documents, Dabrowska suggests that contemporary identities are formed by complex, personal stories, and not bound by political borders.

In recent years, government agencies, educational institutes and not-for-profit organisations have mapped the considerable increase in the volume and the diversity of the forms of migration. How can one grasp the remarkable statistics and their effects on people and place? What does it mean to speak about new transnational/local social environments? For contributors to the festival and salons, an exploration of the individual notions and processes of creating a home (whether it be for a few months or years) offers an avenue to understand the wider spatial and social implications of recent migratory patterns. No doubt, 'home' is a preoccupation for millions of people across the globe. Concepts and experiences of 'home', like that of cities, are incessantly undergoing processes of change and this section shows how people continually strive to articulate their own desires within the built environment.

1. London's poverty profile, Migration into and out of London, londonspovertyprofile.org.uk/london/migration (accessed 10/08/09).
2. Held at the Institute of Contemporary Arts in London on 24 February 2008.
3. Screened at Space 1 Studio on 25 and 26 October 2008.
4. Screened at Space 1 Studio on 25 and 26 October 2008.
5. Exhibited in an underground bunker, Dalston 24–26 October 2008.

Re-Visioning Black Urbanism

and the Production of Space

PAUL GOODWIN & JOHN ODUROE IN CONVERSATION

JO: The first question we should probably deal with, the question we're probably asked most often …

PG: What exactly is Black Urbanism[1]?

JO: Exactly. I guess in my mind, I believe that Black Urbanism is an emerging discourse on how notions of 'blackness' or difference can offer new and perhaps overlooked understandings of the form and function of the contemporary city. Blackness in its various forms is a cultural formation that was initially born out of the African diaspora, but through time and travel, it has expanded to signify more than simply racial or ethnic boundaries. Blackness, in many ways, has come to represent an alternative to mainstream modes of living within cities. Whether through hip-hop culture, or the sensibilities typified by the jazz age, many individuals worldwide identify with blackness in order to find new ways of exploring and experiencing urban life.

PG: I agree. Blackness has come to be a meta-signifier for difference in the urban environment. There has been a long history of the appropriation of black culture by other cultures. At this current phase of appropriation, taking place in the age of international media and globalisation, this means that blackness as a cultural signifier is refracted across many different surfaces: music, dance, food, fashion, art, language. We want to explore the ways in which blackness is in dialogue with architecture and urbanism in this theoretical context.

JO: The relationship of ethnicity and race to the development of urbanism seems to be an under-researched topic. Much of the work exploring the impact of minorities on the production of urban space has generally been framed by racism/anti-racism discourses. While this is incredibly important research, it's not the whole of the story. There is a lot to be learned from the subjective experiences of people productively occupying the margins of urban space. I thought Munira Murza made a very relevant point during the salon discussion when she asked: 'If Black Urbanism exists, then what is 'white urbanism'? I think that 'white urbanism' is urbanism as we generally understand the discipline, as it is taught and discussed in universities the world over. What I believe to be crucially important is that this knowledge is generally based on white western male cultural subjectivities that have been rendered invisible. We accept most of this knowledge as rational and universally applicable while rarely interrogating the hidden biases and cultural assumptions that may exist. It's kind of a hegemonic form of urbanism.

PG: Modernist architects, such as Le Corbusier, have long been obsessed with the literal and figurative aesthetic qualities of whiteness. Whiteness has long been associated in the architectural imagination with qualities of purity, cleanliness and order. By contrast, blackness has been associated with the opposite: disorder, and danger. Arguably, this was played out in the colonial context, where colonial spaces were literally designed with gleaming white buildings to alienate the non-white natives. Whiteness, and its relationship with blackness, has always been just under the surface of thinking, writing and making architecture. It forms a large part of the architectural unconscious. Black Urbanism can be a way of beginning to explore those unnamed territories.

JO: And this is where Office MA comes into play.

PG: Exactly. Office MA will serve as a platform for exploring the relationships between minority cultural groups and the form and function of urban space. We are interested in the multiplicity of cultural formations existing within the African diaspora and how these groups are in dialogue with the other peoples and cultures co-existing within the western city. With Office MA, we are trying to move from theory to practice. Or rather, we're trying to set up a space where theories or ideas regarding Black Urbanism can be tested, considered and researched within the context of real world spaces.

JO: We're kind of a cross between a think tank, design practice, and artists collaborative. The hub of our activity will occur on our website, www.officema.org. It will serve as a space for debate, a site to showcase new ideas, and home to a kind of online archive of data of visual, audio and written materials that, in our minds, exemplify aspects of Black Urbanism. We hope architects and urbanists interested in these kinds of issues might use the site as a resource in their design work.

PG: I began the TINAG salon by tracing the evolution of my thinking on Black Urbanism. I discussed my involvement with the housing protests movement of West African immigrants in Paris during the early 1990s. These immigrants became politicised through a number of brutal expulsions from gentrified housing in the eastern part of Paris. In response to these actions, they occupied public spaces – set up tent cities and recreations of African villages in public space in the heart of Paris. These protests galvanised a number of other movements and started a national homeless awareness movement that has since become international.

The dominant mode of understanding what was happening in those movements was that this was the emergence of a new ghetto. The sight of black African families occupying public space in Paris caused mass panic and provoked a public debate about the fear of importing the American-style black ghetto into France.

JO: I found this very interesting, but I kept asking myself: What makes this special? There are tent cities and refugee situations all over the world. Was there something special about this one beyond the ethnicity of the occupants?

PG: This wasn't simply a collection of homeless protesters or anarchist squatters; these were Africans living their life as if they were in a village back home. What astounded me was the reaction of the media to what was described as a non-French alien presence. The only lens they seemed to be able to view these events through was the framework of the negative ghetto. But for me, I saw these movements as a way of re-framing the image of Paris. They revealed the existence of alternative ways of living or inhabiting the city that were previously invisible, and they challenged French social and spatial norms regarding housing and cultural assimilation.

Fast-forward: 15 years later, in New Orleans, and the tragic situation that occurred in the aftermath of Hurricane Katrina. This event revealed a similar dialectic of invisibility and the struggle for survival in black urban communities. I attended a conference in New York that discussed how we might rebuild New Orleans. What was significant about the conference was that it was organised by the Department of Jazz Studies. The idea was to have the input of jazz artists, bluesmen, architects, etc… to find solutions drawing on aspects of black creativity. I found this to be a powerful way of thinking urbanism.

JO: In my own work as an architect, I'd been thinking about similar questions, i.e. the link between black creativity and the production of space, well before I knew you, Paul, or had heard the term Black Urbanism.
As a student in architecture school, I often found design inspiration by

exploring the culture of minority groups and marginalised people. My presentation at the salon focused on one example of this practice: the design of a performing arts centre in Tennessee that was heavily influenced by an exploration into the form and culture of break dancing. By mapping the movement of a break dancer (b-boy) captured on 30 seconds of video, I sought to diagram the shape of the space he occupied through time. I was hoping to find a form that might spatially express the kind of tension created by the break-dancer's movement. The b-boy is continually re-assigning which parts of his body come in contact with the ground, and in the process, constantly inventing relationships between his body and the landscape beneath him. He scrambles on his feet, jumps on his hands, spins on his head, bounces on his bottom. Sometimes he physically lifts himself off the ground and tenuously freezes himself in mid air.

PG: I imagine that, in the midst of one these freezes, the viewer is afforded a rare moment of stillness – a 'pause' allowing him to comprehend exactly how the break dancer arrived at this position, while simultaneously anticipating when the moment will end and what the dancer might do next.

JO: Yes. I've been enthralled by this playful manipulation of the viewer's sense of time and space. Could my performing arts centre offer a similar experience I wondered? This question led me into a broader exploration of the 'performance tactics' used by the break dancer. I became particularly interested in how the break dancer appropriates, utilises, public space; in particular the use of a flattened cardboard box to delimit the space upon which the b-boy performed. In addition to the practical benefit of protecting the b-boy from the pavement, the box, more importantly, ensures that the b-boy can occupy just about any space, at any time. This flexibility allows the b-boy to again, constantly improvise new relationships to the city.

PG: So in a way, these initial explorations into break dancing lead you to broader issues regarding public space?

JO: Right. What can the tactics used by the break dancer (and others like him) tell us about public space? Perhaps more importantly, this initial exploration drew out several key questions that continue to stay with me now. How do I translate this kind of experience, which may not immediately appear to be architec-tural, into a spatial language that uses mass, light, texture, surface quality, function and construction as its vocabulary? How important is it that people see the original references to break dancing in my final design? Or more generally, what are the implications when the legibility of the object's initial source of inspiration, or its 'blackness' begins to disappear?

PG: This is a crucial question – this idea of where 'blackness' begins and ends in the process of design – that I think we are both still working through. It relates also to the broader question, which came up several times in the course of the salon, of exactly what do we mean by 'blackness' and to what extent are we speaking about a form of architecture and urbanism that is based exclusively on the black or African diasporic experience or something that is more universal. On reflection, I think that this tension that runs through the very idea of Black Urbanism can be a fertile source of ideas, reflection and research. In my opinion, blackness is a much more flexible and elastic concept than the way it is usually deployed in urban discourse. For example, there is a very specific history of blackness here in the UK that has been politically articulated to include the Asian experience. This is one of the reasons why we wanted to invite Rehan Jamil to the salon so that the dynamics of what is happening in so-called 'Muslim' or 'Asian' urban spaces are also brought into the discussion.

Rehan Jamil

JO: Rehan presented his 10-year photographic study of the East London Mosque Project. The development of the mosque has a fascinating 80-year history and demonstrates a prime example of a minority-community-led initiative within the built environment. In the 1990s, as the final phase of the mosque began, a developer also set its eyes on an adjacent property and a stand-off with the London Borough of Hackney began. Eventually, the Muslim community was given planning permission and the construction of the extension proceeded. It was around this time that Rehan began his photographic study, with the aim of documenting the complexity within the Muslim community. During the salon debate, Rehan characterised the architecture of the mosque as an imposing island in the heart of East London. He wondered how open the mosque presented itself as a public space. Could it have

included a coffee shop or other public facilities open to all members of the local community to congregate in its concourses? He sited a similar space in the West London mosque as a functioning example of a mosque that used open public space to draw in and engage with non-Muslim members of the population. Rehan also expressed disappointment in the mosque's extremely conservative design, claiming that a mosque does not require a minaret, nor a dome, in order to be a functioning religious space. Why wasn't there an international design competition, he asks, citing this failure as another missed opportunity to open up the space of the mosque to a wider audience.

PG: Rehan's point ties in very well with one of the most important aspects of Black Urbanism that needs to be discussed: the relation between ethnicity, culture and urban space. There is a danger that Black Urbanism can be interpreted as advocating an 'ethnicised' conception of architecture – in other words, black buildings for black people and Muslim buildings for Muslim people – a kind of closing of public spaces around essentialist notions of culture. I think a clear consensus emerged from the discussion that Black Urbanism is a much more complex formulation that is about opening up the city and its public spaces to cross-cultural and global dialogue. After all, places like Whitechapel, Peckham or Southall are extremely diverse, contrary to their image as 'ghettos' in the media. These spaces are shaped by the logics of global diasporas. Diasporic spaces tend to be characterised by multiple flows of different cultures, dialects and regions.

David Ubaka

JO: The next presentation of the evening came from David Ubaka, an architect and assistant director of Design for London, the architecture and planning office for the Greater London Authority.

PG: We selected David to offer a policy-oriented perspective on Black Urbanism. We wanted someone with practical experience to engage with our more experimental ideas. We wondered how receptive a public official dealing with regeneration in London might be to the alternative perspectives we've been developing.

JO: David gave a sense of what this official response might be in the preface to his presentation, when he stated that the Greater London

Authority believes that whatever is done in the development of London spaces must be done for the people who pay their council tax. He demonstrated the commitment to this principle by describing a series of projects being pushed forward by Design for London.

I found myself particularly interested in his description of the Tate Gardens/Windrush Square Redevelopment Project in Brixton, a neighbourhood long regarded as a centre of Afro-Caribbean culture in London. The project, as David described, aims to unite two existing public spaces – Tate Gardens and Windrush Square – which are currently disconnected by a road. This project has not only been met with practical concerns for the safety and comfort of its users in regards to adjacent vehicular traffic and the ongoing struggle to root out 'anti-social' behaviour; it also has received much criticism from local community members seeking a design that will acknowledge the historic and symbolic significance associated with these spaces: Tate Gardens being associated with the colonial sugar magnate, Henry Tate, and Windrush Square named in commemoration of the famous ship whose arrival in the UK after World War II signalled the beginning of a great wave of Caribbean immigration to the UK. David suggested that these concerns were acknowledged in the selection of Scottish landscape architects Gross Max over several other high-profile design firms. Gross Max refused to begin without engaging in, what David described as, 'major community workshops'. The proposal that was subsequently produced, according to David, offered an 'open' public space that could accommodate a variety of uses by the area's diverse population. At the same time, the design integrated elements inspired by the historical and symbolic significance of the site; most notably, the use of sugarcane as a key landscape element.

To David, it appears that this project serves as an example of how Black Urbanism is actively being revised today. Diversity and equality initiatives are increasingly introduced into public development processes, for example, in the process of contract bidding and selection, and in the use of community design consultation.

PG: In a way, he was normalising Black Urbanism within the discourse of public consultation and traditional planning practice within the west. I can understand this neutral line in a way: Design for London must be seen as representative

of all Londoners, or as David stated: "There is a requirement in government to make this country belong to its people and not its politicians." David's stance represents a common misconception about our mobilisation of the word 'blackness': in other words, as a form of identity politics that is only relevant to a small minority of the population. This is not our intention at all. In fact, we believe blackness can be more open and complex than this limited understanding allows.

Public consultation is something I've been thinking about for a long time; in particular, the role that art and artists can play to improve these processes. For example, there is a group called General Public Agency. They're a group of architects and designers who are often hired by governmental bodies to 'creatively manage' development projects. They serve as a kind of interface between the public and the state. They employ a curatorial logic in dealing with public consultation; that is to say, they treat the generation of space like a site-specific work of art. They're in the process of developing a masterplan for the Thurrock area in the Thames Gateway.

Andrea Philips

PG: Andrea is the assistant director of the MFA in Curating at Goldsmiths.

She is a theorist who works on spatial practices in public art. In the past I've discussed ideas about Black Urbanism with Andrea and she was quite sceptical about any ethnicised notions of architecture or space. We wanted to invite someone with a specifically critical or hostile perspective on Black Urbanism to balance the debate.

JO: She certainly did offer this by contemplating what the results might be if Black Urbanism was successfully pursued. With the statement: "I want to talk about money. Cash," Philips hypothesises into a discussion exploring the potential commoditisation of black culture as it becomes packaged under the name Black Urbanism. Philips comments: "As soon as [black culture] begins to take on a recognisable shape as a culture form, the appellation 'black' is slapped on it and [businesses can] market it as a commodity." Andrea used the example of Saadyiat Island (The Island of Happiness), a $2.7 billion development just off the coast of Abu Dhabi, to illustrate her argument. Fuelled by complex layers of money, principally oil money, the development has been organised as a culturally distinctive tourist capital of the UAE and will become home to projects developed by many of

today's most celebrated international architects, including Frank Gehry, Zaha Hadid and Jean Nouvel.

PG: I found this a very interesting example as Andrea is interpreting blackness as an expanded field, beyond ethnicity. She took the debate internationally, and explored how similar issues are playing out in Abu Dhabi.

JO: She concluded her argument by describing the intention of Saadiyat's developers that the project serves as a kind of new model for urban culture in the Middle East, and drew a comparison between this goal and what she perceived as similar intentions motivating the Re-Visioning Black Urbanism project. In Philip's view, Saadiyat Island represents a kind of "limit, or the horizon, of a certain version of Black Urbanism": a place where the modern architectural discourse, a social agenda, and the financing needed to achieve this agenda, have come together in a 'perfect storm' of sorts. While she doesn't see this as immediately negative, or even possible in London's intensely developed context, she thought it an interesting way of reformulating the questions we are asking.

Karin Woodley

PG: Karin serves as Chief Executive of the Stephen Lawrence Charitable Trust, which fosters employment skills in ethnic minorities and black youth to take up active roles in design-related professions. Karin has worked for many years within the voluntary sector specialising in community development work and arts projects. The Steven Lawrence Centre in Deptford is housed in a building designed by architect David Adjaye. It is the first purpose-built centre for inner-city youth to train in the practices involved in urban design and regeneration. The centre was named after the young black teenager from South East London who was brutally murdered by five white racist youth. The most poignant aspect of this tragedy was that Stephen very much wanted to be an architect. His death and the subsequent controversy brought increased awareness to the issue of black people engaging with urbanism.

JO: We selected Karin hoping she could bring a kind of grassroots-organiser perspective to the debate. We didn't want to hold a purely theoretical discussion; we were interested in the perspectives of people who were dealing with some of the questions proposed by Black Urbanism in real world contexts.

PG: Karin defines blackness as a political term, as a framework for mobilising people. For it is more than just a kind of by-product of diversity or multicultural policies. Karin argued that Black Urbanism should be produced from the bottom up; meaning, not as a top-down dictate of bureaucratic policy. Karin sees education as the key to democratising the regeneration processes that have historically excluded minorities and disadvantaged communities because of the highly specialised language that defines the discourse. As an antidote to this alienation, the Stephen Lawrence Trust aims to develop black and minority-ethnic shapers of urban space. In this model, education as a non-prescriptive approach to Black Urbanism is the key. In other words, young people are educated as design professionals and encouraged to grow and mature within the profession.

JO: For Karin, it's all about investing in young people. Regardless of the theory, moving minorities into the design professions is contingent upon getting youth critically interested in the idea of space, and early.

PG: Karin emphasised this point when discussing the David Adjaye designed Stephen Lawrence building. The building itself acts as an exemplar, a 'model' of what an architect with a global, cross-cultural perspective can achieve. Adjaye himself is also an interesting example in this instance. He's black, from Ghana, but grew up in Tanzania and Japan.

JO: And has practice sites in Portugal and the modernist work of David Chipperfield as influential to his work. At the same time, he references the spaces, places and objects of Africa as key design influences.

PG: Exactly! He folds all these signifiers into his work. Adjaye represents the kind of open and fluid sense of blackness that we're interested in exploring. Here you have this black architect who, in reality, represents a certain kind of globality, a kind of African modernity. Kids may initially relate to him or his work through his blackness, but they are exposed to a broader global palette of spatial experiences. Zaha Hadid, as an Arab woman who in many ways is the face of contemporary architecture, serves a similar function.

JO: We have to say though, part of what enables Adjaye do this is his class status. Should class, rather than ethnicity, really be our object of study? Should we be exploring how class plays out in contemporary urbanism, rather than blackness?

PG: While class is definitely important, and affords Adjaye a certain access to international circuits of architectural prestige, it's not a sufficient explanation. Adjaye is constantly classified as a 'black architect'. His blackness is seen as part of what makes him stand out.

JO: But at the same time critics ask 'what' makes his work distinctive in comparison to the host of other contemporary international architects? It's almost as if they're begging to see evidence of his blackness in his buildings.

PG: Adjaye refuses to be contained by any single cultural aesthetic. He makes references to African objects and spatial practices, but he refuses to be defined by a singular notion of blackness. Thus what becomes important is how he translates blackness into more open spatial and architectural languages.

In conclusion

PG: For me, the salon opened up as many questions as it answered. This is not necessarily a bad thing in my opinion. In fact, this was the very purpose of the salon: to work with an organisation such as This Is Not A Gateway and to lay out the questions in the context of an institution like the ICA. It was an opportunity to question the very possibility of Black Urbanism: its viability as an intellectual project; its role as a resource for designers; its economic viability; its applicability to public policy; and its importance as a tool to inform education that emerges from a history of struggle.

JO: During the next phase of this project we'd like to focus on Peckham as a case study to begin to address some of these points. Peckham is a disadvantaged neighbourhood in South London, undergoing rapid urban transformation and regeneration. The local authority has spent over £10 million on a number of high-profile regeneration projects in this area alone. At the same time, there is an incredibly diverse local population, a large portion of which are from Africa and the Caribbean. Focusing on themes of future visions, networks, migration, branding space and commodification, we intend to do research in Peckham and stage a number of interventions in order to open up its potential as a

site where a new form of urbanism is emerging.

BIOGRAPHIES

Paul Goodwin is an urban theorist and curator. He is an Associate Fellow at the Centre for Urban and Community Research (CUCR), Goldsmiths College, where he is director of the Re-Visioning Black Urbanism project. Recently appointed Curator of Cross-Cultural Programmes at Tate Britain, he is the Director of the Office for Metropolitan Alternatives (Office/MA) an urban think tank and creative intervention office based in London. (www.officema.org)

John Oduroe, a graduate of Carnegie Mellon University's School of Architecture, came to London in 2005 as a Fulbright Scholar and studied at UCL's Department of Geography. He is the Associate Director of Office/MA, an architectural designer for Orbit Architects Ltd., and lead environment and installation designer for the New York-based performance company Echo: System.

*The authors would like to thank Alison McDougal-Weil for her contribution to this work.

Building Stories

Cinematic Places and Architectural Narratives

JOANNA ZAWIEJA

The construction of places through representation is highly institutionalised nowadays. Cities are launched and landscapes formed with the help of regional cultural policies and mediated narratives. Municipalities and commercial operators wish to produce competitive and attractive local identities in relation to the economy of images.

The degree of institutionalisation was exemplified when the city of Barcelona some years ago contacted Woody Allen with an offer to part-finance his forthcoming film. Allen accepted, the production was located to Barcelona, and Barcelona city, in turn, paid 10% of the production costs (about $1,3 million).[1] The film *Vicky Christina Barcelona* is, in Allen's own words, "a love letter to Barcelona".[2] Picturesque alleyways, charming restaurants, spontaneous romance, neurotic Spanish women and, of course, Gaudi.

How can this relation between locality and representation be understood? Where do media production, planning policies and the spatial professions intersect? Where in this mediated landscape are our architectural desires and needs formulated?

The British geographer Doreen Massey has addressed these issues in a broad sense by pointing out how our geographical imaginations shape and maintain spatial relations. In her book *For Space*,[3] Massey shows how the narratives of globalisation legitimise certain political strategies and policies. Questioning an essentialised, static and a-political understanding of place, Massey argues for the importance to consider each place in relation to a larger system. She recognises places as constituted through interrelations with a diversity of co-existing trajectories, and points to how each locality is linked to places beyond. Always under construction, never final enclosures. Massey emphasises the importance of making spatial imaginations and conceptualisations explicit. To better understand our construction and practice of space, she claims that certain hegemonic imaginations should be challenged and the assumptions they lead to problematised:

> To challenge the class politics of London the city itself has to be
> reimagined as a clash of trajectories.[4]

As the local authorities in Barcelona were well aware, the film industry is a powerful producer of the spatial imaginary, although all too often unable, or unwilling, to *re-imagine* spatial narratives outside of hegemonic norms. Is it for the sake of narrative consistency, or to promote mass-market identification, that box-office success means portraying places as homogenous and stereotypical? Whatever the reasons, my proposal is that these exclusions from representation will not be contained within the space of the imaginary but intersect with, and impose themselves on, the built environment.

What does it imply for the gentrified area of Notting Hill that the Caribbean and Portuguese communities, who have deeply influenced that neighbourhood, were left out of its cinematic representation? In the film, the neighbourhood is white and the well-known Notting Hill Carnival, once instigated as a reaction to racist tendencies, is not mentioned.

In the case of the Catholic conservative 'Pope's city', Cracow, there are even clearer traces of the 'cinematic effects' on city life. Or how else can we understand that, after decades of taboo and a practising Jewish population estimated at about 150 people, there has been such a surge in 'Jewish' cafés following on the box-office success of *Schindler's List*?

As an architect, these are crucial questions. Whose imagination are we materialising? And what are the social, cultural and gendered constructs inherent in these foundational narratives? Are we building stages for already performed stories?

Architectural theoretician Beatriz Colomina discusses some of these issues when looking at the relationship between modern architecture and photography. In her book *In Privacy and Publicity: Modern Architecture as Mass Media*,[5] Colomina explores mass media as the site of architectural production. She points out that many of the major works that shaped the modernist canon were immaterial pieces.

140

Mies van der Rohe's Glass Skyscraper and Brick Country House were, for example, never built, while his main modernistic icon, the Barcelona Pavilion, was a temporary building that between 1929 and 1986 only existed in print.

The major currency in contemporary architecture is the image, the photograph not the building.[6]

Colomina's thoughts have their historical equivalence in Charles Rice's[7] research on the emergence of the bourgeois interior in the 19TH century and its image-based condition. Through Rice, we can conclude that image-driven narratives influencing the built environment is hardly something new.

In the video *Imagine a House* (2007), I explore cinematic storytelling as an architectural tool. Taking the 19TH-century mass-mediated cult of domesticity[8] and the separation of spheres (public-private, male-female, etc.) as a starting point, *Imagine a House* looks into the making of the modern home during the early days of British industrialisation. A story of Victorian domesticity is played out in the empty house on 195 Mare Street, East London, where 'fallen women' are trained in the art of homemaking and working-class men are taught political consciousness.

The episodes housed in this building reflect questions of belonging and assimilation central to an area like the East End, since long ago the entrance for immigrants to London. As a refuge, it offered women 'a way back' to domestic life and female respectability; as a working-men's club, it encouraged transgression of the house and the male claiming of a political space beyond, while the future Vietnamese art centre (in the making) celebrates place-based identities of distant locations. In working with this video, it became clear how many of the assumptions that inform residential building to this day have their ideological and culturally gendered roots in the Victorian concepts of privacy and respectability.

The Hackney Council Planning Department has done a survey where they state that the windows and the four stairs up to the entrance of 195 Mare Street should be saved as cultural and historical elements. I propose to save the housed stories. I propose a total makeover: *Imagine a House* as an attempt to narrate a monument into being. The video as a construction and an addition, by each repetition slightly transforming the abandoned house. If we rid ourselves of the distinction between building and storytelling, *Imagine a House* presents an act of rebuilding. If the viewer can be moved, architecture is altered.

Imagine a House: *Transcript*

JOANNA ZAWIEJA

2006. London. When I arrive it is September.

I find myself a room on Mare Street, in a house in the Vietnamese area. Mare Street cuts through East London like a diagram. In a straight line from north to south one smell follows another. Fried chicken, sweet potatoes, salt fish pie, banana cake. Spring rolls, lemon grass, soy sauce, fish sauce. Cummin, ginger, dal, coriander, cinnamon, saffron. Lamb, yogurt, sesame, mint, hummus, thyme.

In my room there's a sink and a wardrobe. On top of the wardrobe, shelves perfectly made for fitting suitcases. The estate agent tells me this was an Indian area not so long ago. He tells me about keeping suitcases full of Indian paraphernalia on the shelves. Like shrines.

Opposite my room there's an empty house. On its gate there's the name of a woman. The same name as on the £5 note in my wallet. People pass it by without notice.

'City Borough of Hackney
The Elizabeth Fry Refuge
To help women in need.'

I find Elizabeth Fry in a book. During a visit to the notorious Newgate Prison she was horrified with the prisoners' conditions and decided to fight for prison reforms. She managed to introduce segregation of sexes, education, employment and religious instruction. Bible study and needlework. She died in 1845. The refuge opened four years after her death. I read: "To make provision for a portion of the most helpless and pitiable class of human beings. Restoring her to the blessings of society, and the comforts of a home."

1885. Charles Booth, a wealthy businessman, decided to undertake an inquiry into London's poverty. During 17 years, Booth and his investigators mapped every street in the city through interviews. The research project resulted in the *Maps Descriptive of London Poverty* where each street in London was given a colour according to its poverty level.

I find Mare Street. It's red. Red as in "Lower middle class. Shopkeepers and small employers, clerks and subordinate professional men. A hardworking sober, energetic class." Further down the road there are some "vicious semi criminals". But no sign of the Refuge.

At the estate agent I'm shown a webpage, a postcode search for local area information. The country divided into 32,482 areas. All of them measured and ranked according to their deprivation level. Apparently my new home is ranked 1,595 in general deprivation.

1849. Four years after the death of Elizabeth Fry. Over a decade into the Victorian era. This city was the world's largest, and industrialisation was in full bloom. The will to classify was just about to embrace everything. Everything would be given a name.

Mare Street. Mare like a female horse.

Or Mare like the large dark areas on the moon.

Or like in Nightmare, the female demon that afflicts sleeping people.

New social problems followed the Industrial Revolution. Threatened in their position, the middle class began the grand project of separation. Their main concern: the pre-modern city's lack of boundaries. Their goal: social order. Segregation of classes, separation of sexes, and isolation of homes.

When production moved outside the home, home was given a new content. A decorated and private family home became a personal virtue. While the public was seen as the space of the progressive and the modern, home was defined as its opposite: as the escape, the eternal and authentic. And in that moment, woman became positioned at home.

New tools were needed for this process of domestication. Ornamental and symbolic objects. Corridors, systems of room divisions, walls, gates, hedges, spaces between buildings. Houses were rigorously planned after specific uses, whether there was room for it or not. Kitchen, scullery, pantry, larder, storeroom, butler's pantry, safe, beer store, cleaning place, wine cellar, housekeeper's room, stillroom, laundry, servant's hall, men's room, parlour, coals, dining room, study, hall, porch, drawing room, wc, bathroom, bedroom, master's bedroom, passage, dressing room…

Also time needed separation; every hour of the day had its proper duty.

1856. *The Enquire Within Upon Everything* was published and sold in more than one million copies. In this domestic manual there are 2,775 rules on cooking, playing, socialising, writing, talking, counting, washing and cleaning.

"Rule 426. To take Stains of Wine out of Linen:
Hold the articles in milk while it is boiling on the fire."

I start collecting documents on the Elizabeth Fry Refuge.
In a plan I find a big laundry on the ground floor. In the basement, there's a girls' dining room, and in the garden, lavatories seen from the matron's room.
On the other floors, there are bedrooms.
By each bed, there's a set of cloths in different shapes and sizes.

"Rule 437. To take Writing Ink out of Paper:
Solution of tin and water. To be applied with camel-hair brush. After the writing has disappeared, the paper should be passed through water, and dried."

In a meeting summary from 1851, the committee of the Refuge decides to forbid talk in the bedrooms and discusses a bell arrangement on the bedroom doors to detect movement. They also express concern about heartless mothers removing their daughters from the institution, and therefore ask for assistance to send some suitable girls from the Refuge to the colonies as emigrants.

"Rule 2441. To Remove Freckles:
Apply a mixture of lemon juice, Venice soap and bitter almonds to the face and hands. In the morning cleanse the skin by washing it copiously in rosewater."

I find the Refuge Regulations from 1879. Girls were received from the Metropolitan Prisons. Young hopeful cases were preferred. Cases remained in the Refuge for 3-12 months until a suitable situation could be found for them. Those cases who then could bring a statement of good conduct from their mistress received a dress as a reward.

"Rule 217. The Woman who wishes her conversation to be agreeable:
Her language will be easy and unstudied, marked by a graceful carelessness, which, at the same time, never oversteps the limits of propriety. Her lips will smile, she will not love to hear herself talk and her eyes will kindle with animation as she speaks. The art of pleasing is, in truth, the very soul of good breeding."

1884. The Refuge provided a home for up to 30 women at one time. All together there were 98 of them that year.
Their reasons for getting into the Refuge were: 61 for theft, 2 for breaking glass, 1 for disorder, 2 for assault, 4 for attempted suicide, 6 for illegal pledging, 3 for uttering bad money, 5 for disturbance at Unions, 14 for offences.
That year 6 dresses were given.
That year 92 of the women did not get a dress. 92 of them did not agree with privacy and comfort as a solution.
So what did they do? They were there obviously, for months. They must have washed, and cooked, and cleaned, and polished. Maybe they spoke in the bedroom, maybe they walked the wrong staircases, maybe they used the wrong doors.

Maybe they'd thought that things were changing.

Maybe they saw the park behind the house. It should be visible from the bedrooms. They might have seen the meetings being held. They might have seen that Victoria Park on a Sunday transformed into an open-air debating society. That riots were planned. That there were over a million trade union members. That the Married Women's Property Act passed two years earlier, now ensuring all women the rights to own houses.

And then, ironic as it might seem: In 1913, the constant need for repairs forces the Refuge to sell the house.
It is bought by a friendly society and turned into a working-men's club. The Landsdowne Liberal and Radical Club, later The New Landsdowne Club. "… to afford to its members the means of social intercourse, mutual helpfulness, mental

and moral improvement, and rational recreation."
A working-men's club.
With a library and a reading room that took left-wing papers. Pool and beer.
"Restricted for women."
The house that had taught them to clean, could not teach them to read.

After a week in my room they find me. First it looks as a mistake. A daily paper
with a home furnishing insert. Then I find "Gracious Domestics" and "Excellent living" in my mailbox. The next day *Better Homes and Gardens* lies outside
my door. "100 days of holiday, all new every day." "Great Bathroom Inspiration."
"Selecting the perfect bed pillow." "Restoring her to the comforts of a home."

Four years ago The New Landsdowne Club closed. The house was bought by
the Vietnamese shop by the side. It is now waiting to become a Vietnamese
art centre.

BIOGRAPHY

Joanna Zawieja is an architect based in Stockholm. Her work focuses on the
construction of place through storytelling; specifically examining narratives
of the domestic. Through writing, video and temporal interventions, Zawieja
locates her architectural practice in the social constructs that determine the built
environment.

1. www.time.com/time/arts/article/0,8599,1648406,00.html (accessed 27/02/09).
2. www.cbc.ca/news/story/2007/07/03/allen-woody-movie.html (accessed 27/02/09).
3. Doreen Massey, *For Space* (London, Thousand Oaks, New Dehli: Sage, 2005).
4. *ibid.*, Massey (2005) p. 158.
5. Beatriz Colomina, *Privacy and Publicity: Modern Architecture as Mass Media*, (Cambridge and London: MIT Press, 1996).
6. *ibid.*, Colomina (1996) p. 137.
7. Charles Rice, 'Rethinking histories of the interior', *The Journal of Architecture*, 9(3), 2004, pp. 275–287.
8. James Curran, *Media and Power* (New York and London: Routledge, 2002) p. 9.

East End of Islam

1997 -2007

Rehan Jamil is a humanistic photographer concerned with communities in transition and urban regeneration. His work has been exhibited in ZEROZEROZERO (Whitechapel Gallery, London 1999); Station Gallery (Frankfurt 2000); Common Ground (British Council tour 2003); Changing Faces 02 (2003) and PSP Beautiful Script exhibition (2005).

All images are from the series East End Of
Islam: 1997–2007, REHAN JAMIL

Do Buy!

A Dubai Documentary

OMAIR BARKATULLA & MATTHEW LEE IN CONVERSATION

ML: Why did you make this film?

OB: It was for an MA in Visual Anthropology at Goldsmiths. Usually this would be a film about a people, a tribe or a culture, or things that people deem anthropological. I was focusing on the material culture that sprang from Dubai. Buildings are visual and provoke debate; they incite emotion and can make people care about a place. People's voices come into the film but I also let the architecture do some speaking.

ML: Why Dubai?

OB: The city was being talked about a lot in 2005. I wanted to see what a place with a large influx of money focused on the built environment would look like visually. I went to explore its visual culture and architectural results. The city was getting a lot of media attention about its spectacular 'wonders', such as hi-tech buildings by famous architects and the use of vast wealth to create green gardens in an arid place. So it was asking to be filmed. The fabricated dream of Dubai created a kind of utopia in many people's minds, without ever having been there.

ML: What was your take on the architecture?

OB: I loved the malls for being so unashamedly huge and vibrant. Many people used the clichés 'plastic' or 'artificial'. I wanted to know what they meant by that. You lived there. What was your take?

ML: There's an obsession with everything being shiny and clean, and there's some UAE history in older parts of town that city planners keep getting rid of. That's why people say the leaders of Dubai ignore history and it's artificial. Also it's socially artificial, as you show with the amusing radio clips, showing the confusion of different people from all over speaking slightly different versions of the same language.

OB: Yes, and one thing that struck me was that Europeans, Indians and Arabs don't interact much. There aren't any places meant for everyone, except maybe shopping malls. I read that they are the equivalent of high streets, designed solely to encourage grazing and to build a desire for things you can buy. It is the plight of many cities designed around cars.

ML: The beach is the only other really public place where people can congregate.

OB: Yes. At malls I saw mainly single men, probably guest workers who go there in their spare time – they look really bored. It's an anonymous place where you can disappear, listen to some music, and look at shiny things while away from family.

ML: The sprawl of Dubai adds to anonymity, from east to west it's the width of London I think.

OB: American cities are idolised in the Gulf because they're seen as

world leaders, therefore it turned out that their style of cars, roads and buildings are admired.

ML: The documentary is called *Do Buy!* so your focus is on this passion for consumption and shopping.

OB: Buying into the city as a utopia also. I say: a documentary about Disney creating a town. It's like, why visit Disneyland sometimes? Why not move in? The perfect town is an interesting concept. People from poorer Arab countries think it's the perfect Arabic country; freer, cleaner and more jobs than at home.

ML: How much filming was involved?

OB: Ten days of shooting. I was going to show certain themes visually that are basically the film's chapters. I was really inspired by Jacques Tati's film *Playtime* (1967). It's a masterpiece, poking fun at the slick modern parts of Paris. The jokes are created out of the experiences in the machine-like city: transparency, repetition, mechanisation, and not knowing where you are. I was interested in the differences of heights in the city; getting to places in cars, lifts and planes; the inside and outside world being so separate. The widespread

Film still, *Do Buy!*, 2006, OMAIR BARKATULLA

international style, air-conned and cool, when outside is so dry, sandy and vast.

ML: I think architects would rationalise about how some skyscrapers are built with an Islamic influence and, although often they look amazing, the Islamic-ness is probably very token. I don't think the buildings will be that memorable, except the world's tallest or biggest obviously. You had a few interviews with people. Did you try to take your attention towards people and off buildings?

OB: I was trying to show quirks, and when I asked people about Dubai, they turned out to be very verbal. I met people at the hostel where I was staying. People were there to work, and not for shopping and a good time. It was usually people scouting for opportunities, young people and backpackers. I got the perspective of outsiders, who were not rich enough to live the Dubai dream, and were also unsure about what job or career they would get in Dubai.

ML: Of course now they're in recession and a lot of the mood of optimism captured in your film is no more. People have been leaving in the last couple of months. Rent is too high so people want to go home to their families.

OB: People feel everything is imported, I mean knowledge, skilled people and architectural styles.

ML: When I moved there, there was the idea of being caught up in a gold rush. Culture, art, cuisine and media weren't there in 2000, or 2005 even, and there were opportunities to start a business, to make money really quickly. You could reinvent yourself as an astronaut, model, artist or anything, if you could find demand for your services. The worry is Dubai is just consuming and not producing anything of its own. Every Gordon Ramsay plate of food is flown in. Most of the talent there is foreign. There could be a real brain drain if many people had to leave. And labourers too, if they went, there could be serious problems.

OB: So the criticisms about fakeness are not so important anymore?

ML: It is what it is. It's an airport transit lounge. A bunch of people stopping on their way to somewhere else. You can't complain about authenticity. It's a harsh desert climate. It's a very unusual place to build a metropolis, and they've done very well in attracting people in the past ten years.

OB: Maybe the airport analogy is good. The only activity available is shopping.

BIOGRAPHIES

Omair Barkatulla is a graphic designer and documentary filmmaker, and a graduate of the London College of Communication and Goldsmiths. He currently designs Gulf Air's in-flight magazine and has some film projects in development.

Matthew Lee is the editor of *J Magazine*, the in-flight magazine of Jazeera Airways, and has written guides to Dubai for Time Out and Lonely Planet.

"Eileen", 2007, You and I in Flux, ANIA DABROWSKA

OVER: "Beata", 2006, You and I in Flux, ANIA DABROWSKA

You and
I in Flux
&
I Used to
Skate on
Frozen Lakes

ANIA DABROWSKA

Ania Dabrowska is a visiting lecturer at Gold–
smiths (London) and the Ruskin School of
Drawing and Fine Art (Oxford). Her work
has been exhibited in I Palestine (Palestine
Gallery, London 2008); Into the Open (Four
Corners Gallery, London 2008); NoBody's
Perfect (Roncalliplatz, Cologne 2007); and NPG
Photography Prize (National Portrait Gallery,
London 2007).

"Ulyana", 2007, You and I in Flux, ANIA DABROWSKA

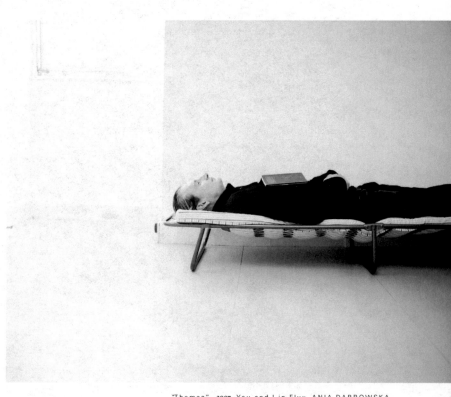

"Thomas", 2007, You and I in Flux, ANIA DABROWSKA

OVER: "Angel June 2003 For Eileen",
I Used to Skate on Frozen Lakes, ANIA DABROWSKA

"Morskie Oko 2003 For Ulyana",I Used to Skate
on Frozen Lakes,ANIA DABROWSKA

"Marzanna 2005 For Thomas",I Used to Skate
on Frozen Lakes,ANIA DABROWSKA

PUBLIC MEMORY

4

Introduction

DEEPA NAIK & TRENTON OLDFIELD

The marking and manifestation of shared memories in city spaces have recently entered a new and expansive realm. On the one hand, cities attempt to position themselves as brands – increasingly thought through and packaged as cultural events and destinations. This has been accelerated by cultural policies that support the construction of regional identities often through recurring activities – art biennales, music fairs and theatre festivals. A recent example is the Manchester International Festival, which "celebrates the city's pivotal role in music, culture, innovation and the arts".[1] Each year, the city's history – contributions to popular culture, music and the arts – is re-enacted and remembered through performances, concerts and exhibitions in the city's streets and public spaces, inviting local, national and international acknowledgement.

And, on the other hand, groups and individuals are using new technologies – digital cameras, websites, print-on-demand publishing – to examine, produce, circulate and archive their own memories of place. Often working at an informal and personal level, they unearth recollections and reconfigure significant shared histories that have been frequently misunderstood or excluded from dominant narratives. The shift towards focusing on localised or individual experiences allows for a reframing of prevailing accounts and for a counter-discourse to emerge. This section looks at a number of ways in which public memory is being reshaped.

How does one reclaim the memory of a place and time, of a politics and youth movement, of a person who was instrumental in bringing a community together to resist injustice? The opening paper 'Remembering Olive Morris' recounts Liz Obi's journey to ensure the legacy of her friend and fellow community activist would not be forgotten. Olive Morris died in 1979 at the age of 26. Based in Brixton, South London, an area of the inner city known for its racial tensions and social problems, Olive Morris was active in campaigns – against police harassment, deaths in police custody, injustice in the courts, the suss law, inadequate housing, homelessness, insufficient state education – and a determined advocate for her community, founding the Brixton Black Women's Group and the Organisation of Women of African and Asian Descent (OWAAD). The essay chronicles a personal endeavour to produce a cultural archive and collective memory – one that found new momentum through collaboration with artist Ana Laura Lopez and the creation of the Remembering Olive Collective (ROC). Through this combined effort, a new generation is being made aware Olive Morris's legacy to community, city and nation. Liz Obi's paper expands on her input during a discussion at the festival[2], and details why she was driven to ensure this previously undocumented history of South London continues to be told.

A different approach to the exploration of (formerly) unrecorded stories is taken by artist Cathy Ward, who, for over a dozen years, has photographed mobile food wagons, primarily across Britain but also in North America, Europe and Mexico. Her project, Wagontrain, is an antidote to the seemingly unstoppable flattening out of cities by multinational companies (Ikea, Starbucks, Walmart etc). Scattered through the urban landscape – down alleys, beside unsuspecting roads, next to shopping malls and under train arches – sit portable food vans, selling fast food to passers-by. These are independent, small businesses run by entrepreneurial men and women. The fare on offer is quick to make and cheap to purchase, and, as Iain Aitch explains, it is not the terrain for soya-decaf-latte aficionados. In her paper Cathy Ward elaborates on her unique and extensive archive, which documents an aspect of national food habits that would otherwise remain misunderstood and undervalued. During the festival the archive was exhibited on Gillett Square, the main public space in Dalston Junction, just across from the Ridley Road food market.

Catherine Botibol's paper 'A City in Transition: Bucharest' raises questions about how new generations, who have not experienced the full weight of a conflictive past, are actively re-moulding the physical and collective memory of ever re-adjusting cities. Since its formation in the 15TH century, Bucharest has undergone countless periods of occupation and reconstruction. In the recent past, under the communist dictator Nicolae Ceausescu (1965-89), vast areas of the city were demolished and rebuilt to mirror ideological narratives. With the collapse of the regime, many projects remained unfinished and subsequently abandoned throughout the city. Following entry into the EU, the city has been rebuilding, transforming and expanding – driven by new political narratives. The author takes Sarah Evans' film *Bucharest: A Portrait* as a starting point for reflection. Screened at the festival[3], the film combines video stills of seemingly everyday elements of the urban environment – doorways, skateboard parks, residential buildings, hotel facades – with a poignant audio track composed of personal recollections by young Bucharesters, who share their thoughts on their architectural heritage, their perceptions of the past, and their ideas and contributions to the city's continual transformation.

Before the advent of video, digital photography and the internet, public memory was most often recorded in books. Novels, in particular, have narrated social, political and personal histories for centuries. Not tied to the confines of 'historical accuracy', novels are a generous arena, allowing for invention and speculation. The openness of the format has meant topics that are unlikely to be officially documented – personal memories, tales of everyday experiences, rumours and myths – continue to influence our understanding of place. Bram Arnold's essay argues that London is one of the most written-about cities, with pages and pages dedicated to capturing the "most enduring and endearing, alarming and terrifying things ever to be heard or fabricated by humankind. London is a book to be read: on foot, bus or the snaking underground, the past and its stories hang, clogging up its corners and dripping from its underpasses. The city is ever alive." The paper details how the popularity of the novel in England paralleled the invention of the park bench and the opening of the first municipal park in 1840. All three were by-products of industrialisation and the concept of 'leisure time'. As the vast majority of the public was unable to read, for most, novels were first experienced orally. How can this little known history of London's literary past and its relationship to the public realm invigorate the present-day city? During the festival, the performance The Park Bench Reader: A London History[4] brought these ideas together. Orchestrated by Bram Arnold, his colleagues at the Mobile Institute and a number of volunteers, public readings at the main square in Dalston Junction and a local jazz club inspired expanded interpretations of local space.

David San Millán also turns his attention to London in his photographic series Passerby, documenting fleeting encounters with people in the city over more than seven years. Though all the images are taken in the public realm, they do not show, as Zuzana Flaskova points out, "the usual thick and dense fabric of a hurried metropolis"; they do not profess to 'represent' the city nor its inhabitants. Instead, by altering the focus towards a localised experience, the photographs reveal an individual mapping of place – 'here is my journey, my observations, my narrative'. During the festival, Passerby was exhibited in Café Oto and in office windows overlooking a busy street.[5]

In recent years, accelerated by increasing access to new technologies, more individuals, collectives and organisations are articulating their own histories. This proliferation of records and archives actively counters the seemingly dominant drive to cohere space and history. For contributors to the festival, producing a public or shared memory is not a unifying impulse – instead it seeks to ensure undervalued or misread stories are understood, and to unearth the complexities that inform space.

1. Manchester International Festival, www.mif.co.uk/about-us-background-and-faq/ (accessed 24/08/09).
2. Liz Obi and Ana Laura Lopez hosted a panel discussion about founding of the Olive Morris Collective, Café Oto, 25 October 2009.
3. Screened at Space 1 on 25 and 26 October 2009.
4. Public reading took place on Gillett Square on 25 October 2009. Performance was held at the Vortex on 26 October 2009.
5. Exhibited in the windows of Metropolitan Workshop, Clerkenwell 23-26 October 2008.

Remembering Olive Morris

LIZ OBI

In July 2000 I organised an exhibition at Brixton Library entitled Remembering Olive. It was a tribute to my old friend and community activist Olive Morris. The exhibition consisted of a small collection of press clippings, photographs and posters that I had kept over the years, displayed on a background of African cloth. The idea was to use the exhibition and my relatively insignificant memorabilia as a starting point for developing a collective memory and cultural archive, which other people who had known Olive could contribute to. I felt that those of us who had known Olive needed to make sure that we passed the memories on.

I was conscious that 21 years had passed since Olive's untimely death – time in which a new generation had been born and grown, and I wondered how much of Olive's legacy had been passed on. My enquiries suggested that apart from Olive's name on the Housing and Council Tax Benefit Office, there was little or nothing known about her. The new inhabitants, who arrived in Brixton since its 'gentrification' and who received their council tax bills from Olive Morris House, had no means of accessing information about who Olive was and what she stood for. There was a plaque and photograph inside the entrance to the building, but very little else. Enquiries I made to Lambeth Archives and the Black Cultural Archives produced nothing. *The Heart Of The Race*, a book about the history of black women's lives in Britain by Stella Dadzie, Beverley Bryan and Suzanne Scaffe,[1] was the one place where Olive's contribution was documented. But this was long since out of print.

Olive died of Hodgkin's lymphoma on 12 July 1979. She was 26 years old and a highly regarded black community activist, who had made an indelible mark on the hearts and minds of the people who had known her. Olive came to Britain from Jamaica, at the age of eight, to live with her parents who had migrated some years earlier. She went to school in South London and was subjected to the inequalities and institutionalised racism that existed both in the British school system and in the society at large. She left school aged 16 without any formal qualifications, but, through her own determination and self-belief, she achieved her O and A level exams while working full time. In 1975 she was offered a place on a degree course at Manchester University.

From the age of 16, Olive had been involved in grassroots political activity. She was a member of the Black Panther Movement's youth collective based at 38 Shakespeare Road. She was active in the campaigns and issues facing black people in 1970s Britain, e.g. police harassment, deaths in police custody, the campaign against the suss law, bad housing conditions and homelessness, issues of injustice in the courts and the prison system, and issues around education and the practice of assessing black school children as educationally sub-normal. Olive was at the forefront of the black women's movement. She was a founding member of the Brixton Black Women's Group in 1974 and later established the Organisation of Women of African and Asian Descent (OWAAD). Her focus was not only on local campaigns in the community of Brixton, but also on national and international issues of the day. Olive supported workers on picket lines, marched against the immigration bill, demonstrated outside courts, defended herself inside court, rallied for the freedom of Angela Davis and the end to the Vietnam War, supported the liberation struggles of Mozambique, Guinea Bissau, South Africa and Zimbabwe and the workers movements in the Caribbean. In Manchester, she became active in the international students' groups and with women's groups in the black communities of Moss Side.

At a memorial service held a few weeks after her death, hundreds of people paid tribute to her. In 1985, to commemorate Anti-Racist Year, Lambeth Council renamed the housing benefit offices at 18 Brixton Hill, Olive Morris House, to acknowledge the contribution she made to the lives of disadvantaged people living in Lambeth. It was a fitting tribute, which by the 1990s had grown into a sad irony due to the inefficient administration of housing and council tax benefits which took place under Capita – the company employed to run the scheme. Those of us who remembered Olive would often remark that she must be turning in her grave to know what was being done to the most disadvantaged members of the community who would receive summons to court for bills they were not eligible to pay, or who would be evicted for non-payment of rent because it took Capita over three months to process claims etc. We knew that had Olive been alive she would

Portrait of Liz Obi, 2009, REHAN JAMIL

have organised and demonstrated against Capita; and we all knew she would have brought about some effective changes.

The year 2000 found a very different Brixton to the one that Olive had known – a much more prosperous place where black people from the Caribbean were no longer in the majority. In the 1970s Brixton had been known as 'Little Jamaica'. As a community we had become dispersed over the years following council re-housing schemes which saw people reallocated to Thornton Heath and Croydon – on the outskirts of London – thereby releasing the inner-city housing for sale.

We seemed to have lost a lot of the things we had fought for back in the 1970s: the Brixton Community law centre had closed, black studies as part of the school curriculum was unheard of, the suss law had been replaced by stop and search, ESN statements on black children in schools had been replaced by long-term school exclusions. Things had supposedly become better and yet it seemed that so much had stayed the same. Surely then, Olive's legacy had a relevance in 21st-century Brixton.

As part of the exhibition, a memorial gathering was held on the evening of 13 July 2000. It was attended by a dozen or so people, including members of Olive's family and past comrades and colleagues. My own children attended and listened as people shared their memories of Olive, and I know Olive's family were touched that her memory was being kept alive.

I recounted the story of when, in the summer of 1972, Olive and I had hitchhiked to Morocco, where we got stranded on our way to see Eldridge Cleaver, the US Black Panther Party's Minister for Information, living in exile in Algiers. We ended up being supported by the British Consulate in Tangiers – having become destitute without any money. Our parents had to send us money to get us back home!

Following the exhibition, my son, then aged 16, remarked that he hadn't realised what an interesting life I had led! He had listened to the memories of those gathered, myself included, and I guess my son appreciated for the first time that I had been a young woman once upon a time.

In remembering Olive, I realised we had all remembered ourselves and the young people of our generation. Because Olive had been part of a youth movement – she had not been alone in the struggle for equal rights and justice – many others had been part of that struggle which took place in Brixton in the 1970s. It was recent history and yet somehow it had got lost in the relaying of memory between the Windrush arrivals and the Riots. Olive, because of her unique energy and commitment, and maybe because she died so young, remains a symbol of that generation of youth and that era of black history in this country – the resistance of young people to the racism of the state and the general society. That is why her memory is important – she fits into the missing piece in our documented history, and that history should be told and retold.

After the exhibition I made further attempts to discover archival material and to record people's memories of Olive, but my progress was slow. Life kept me busy and although I re-established contacts with individuals who had known Olive and who were interested in sharing their memories, I failed to follow through on a lot of the contacts made. Seven years passed – don't ask me on what – then in 2007 I received an email from Lambeth Libraries putting me in touch with an artist named Ana Laura Lopez, who was interested in finding out about Olive Morris.

I was quite sceptical about Ana Laura initially – my reaction was why was this white woman interested in our history? What did she plan to get out of it? But meeting her, and getting an understanding of her work as an artist – much of it seemed to me to be like community activism – I was really impressed with her – her energy, her spirit – and I agreed to give her access to my archive and to work with her on the creation of a website dedicated to Olive's memory. Here was Ana Laura, years younger than me, with her artistic skills providing the opportunity to upgrade my efforts into the 21ST century! Olive had truly arrived in the new millennium – by 2007 she had her own website – she's doing better than me.

For my part, I have achieved what I set out to do – well almost. In October 2008, Ana Laura, myself and others formed the Remembering Olive Collective (ROC) to complete the research into Olive's life and to ensure her memory is not erased from history.

BIOGRAPHY

Liz Obi lives in Brixton and is a community activist.

1. Beverley Bryan, Stella Dadzie and Suzanne Scafe, *The Heart Of The Race* (London: Virago Press, 1985).

Wagons

Artist Note

CATHY WARD

Wagontrain was born in the last century, when London was a different city to what we experience now. One felt the change starting especially in boot-fairing – humanity's barometer of change. I'd have a weekend trawling the caste-away home-contents of a nation ridding itself of its pre-millennium past, the unwanted dumped into local areas of urban desolation and decay. I was consumed with an urgency to rescue aged, overlooked mementoes that I feared would be lost forever. I was witnessing the end of an era. This was a time before daytime TV producers created a nation of dealers and bargain hunters, and way before the East End would change forever with the bulldozers for the Olympics.

It was on a grey, rain soaked, winter's morning in 1997, in one of the most mistreated areas in East London, the Greyhound Stadium in Hackney – where the newly built stadium's windows had been pulverised by locals – that it started. Booters and stolen-goods merchants littered the terrain of greasy sludge and petrol with their piles of unwant. The place heaved with poor immigrants and the great swathe of humanity that the borough of Hackney held. Amongst this desperate conglomeration, I witnessed some of the most unappealing-looking food being sold out of the backs of unsanitary-looking wagons. Green-tinged, emaciated, battery-hen carcasses were selling fast at '3 for a £1', and the nearby belching burger-stall's odour was retching and acrid. This was the time of the CJD/BSE crisis, and the nation was talking about our questionable meat consumption. This particular day made me realise that I frequented places with an overlooked flow of humanity; where this alternative 'shopping mall' was makeshift, temporary and open air, filled with cheap and plentiful second-hand goods and below par food. I realised that the mobile food wagons were integral to these areas but had never really been documented from the humanist point of view, which was fascinating and important. Wagontrain began, and developed over the span of a dozen years.

Documenting mobile food wagons has followed me, as I go about my daily life. In travels across Britain, Europe, Mexico, Canada and the USA, I come across them in unexpected areas of our urban and transitory lives. They have become part of our consumerist social landscape, springing up in every corner, marking the shifting tides of popularity, moving where people are congregating – the operator being self-employed, a master in their own kitchen. Many are predominantly austere and, as they stand in their elemental settings of tarmac, sod or sea, they take on characteristics as diverse as their owners: some with interiors echoing the occupant's own home, with objects and slogans part of the dining experience – a memory you take away with your styrene-cased lunch. Though a few are eccentric, many function on practicality alone and are clinically hygienic, with only the basics of fast-food listings to grab your interest. They have weathered the changing tastes and the fears of successive disease epidemics with tenacity.

BIOGRAPHY

Cathy Ward is an artist with an interest in anthropology, popular culture and folk traditions. She has photographed much that is overlooked, disappearing, and transitory including fairgrounds, medical collections and graveyards. She has exhibited in the UK and internationally since graduating from the Royal College of Art in 1988.

All images are from the series Wagontrain,
1997–present, CATHY WARD

Wagontrain

IAIN AITCH

In these times when every town-centre looks the same and the countryside is becoming crammed with identikit supermarkitecture, there is very little room for individuality in the world of selling. Yet, look in the gaps between the big box retailers and motorways and you *will* find it. The roadside food vans that dot Britain's A-roads and truckers' shortcuts may all work from the same limited menu (bacon butty, sausage butty, tea or coffee) but they more than make up for it in the uniqueness of their design, presentation and the welcome that awaits you when you pull up in that lay-by. The toilet is that huddle of trees over there. Now please wash your hands, or at least wipe them on the back of your jeans.

Sit in the mobile greasy spoon's white plastic garden chairs a while and you may catch a glimpse of Cathy Ward as she passes through on her mission to catalogue food vans and their entrepreneurial proprietors. Traversing the byways, back ways and side routes of Britain as she travels to exhibitions or takes journeys to trawl obscure car-boot sales, Ward captures the spirit of individuality, practicality and fast turnaround that keeps these vans in custom.

But Ward does not stop with roadside eateries, widening her photographic lens to include any food outlet with four (or more) wheels, which means taking in pastel-coloured ice-cream vans, seaside seafood-stalls and even those of the dodgy hot-dog sellers that emerge as if by magic under the cover of night. There are the unsavoury-looking meat vans, the tourist traps selling overpriced Cokes and even those with architectural aspirations to behold, be they mock Tudor or modernist fruit-based abodes.

Frequenter of the lock-up, the cash-and-carry and the local branch of William Hill, the average food-van operator is not the sort to let the grass grow beneath his (or her) wheels. If he is not at his usual pitch just outside the town-centre or his Friday-night spot close to where the pubs turn out, then he can be found by the football ground, air show, festival or funfair. These are hard-working operations, often run by one-man bands who are up way before you and get to bed long after you are sweetly dreaming. No one ever sees them set up and no one ever sees them leaving. Some have spotless surfaces and hygiene certificates prominently displayed. Some have no such certification and do not seek it. They all detest traffic wardens. Frowned upon by the food police, the food wagon is rarely an outlet that goes out on a limb for health. The baked potato is almost exotic in its repertoire. Have it with cheese or beans. Or cheese *and* beans, if you are feeling daring. Wholemeal bread does not receive a welcome here. The condiments are described by colour rather than by flavour. 'Red or brown?'

You can almost cut the collection down the middle into the functional and the decorative. So many wagons are simply white boxes with a small price list, typed up and shoved into a plastic see-through envelope that neither rain nor cooking grease can penetrate. Then there are the bizarrely decorated, the professionally sign-painted and the pieces of pure folk art: all painted-on fried eggs, smiley-faced sausages and the proprietor's name up there in house paint rather than lights. Those solid, working-class names with their speciality as a suffix. Jim's Burgers. Bill's Butties. Union Flags, St George's or St Andrew's crosses fly from their roof. If you are really lucky you may see a badly drawn Mickey Mouse or Donald Duck. The burghers of burgers care not for intellectual property rights. This is not the corporate world.

This is not the place to ask for a grande skinny latte. This is not really the place to ask for coffee at all, if we are to be brutally honest. Tea is the thing: strong, hot and sweet. If your mug is chipped you think yourself lucky to have a real mug. You don't ask for a new one.

What is vital in Cathy Ward's Wagontrain is the cataloguing of a food landscape where things change rapidly. The wagons generally have a shorter lifespan than some of the additive-laden burgers on sale and no one else is creating as extensive an archive as she in the UK. Sure, the collection contains the odd wagon from the US or Europe, but it is the British wagons that shout loudest and really sing about a nation's culinary tastes. In an era when even Little Chef is attempting to gentrify, it is heart-warming to see these pioneers of the road doing their thing in their own way. May the Wagontrain keep on rolling.

BIOGRAPHY

Iain Aitch is the author of *We're British, Innit* and *A Fête Worse Than Death*. He writes on the arts for the *Guardian*, the *Times* and the *Daily Telegraph*.

A City
in Transition:
Bucharest

CATHERINE BOTIBOL

Sarah Evans' film, *Bucharest: A Portrait*, presents a snapshot of the city through a series of static video-captured images. Shot over two weeks in October 2006, Evans set out to capture a city that she could see was in a state of rapid transition. The narrated soundtrack comprises stories, thoughts and memories from multiple Bucharesters, interwoven to provide a collective viewpoint of present-day Bucharest. Evans recorded the interviews a year later, when she travelled back to the city with the intention of meeting residents to talk about their relationship with the city. A chance meeting with a young woman called Cinty, who spoke about the city's communist past and recounted stories from her grandmother, aroused Evans' interest in transferred memories and the city's recent history. Consequently, she began asking young Bucharesters about their second- and third-hand stories of the past, exploring their relationship with the city and their notions of its history, geography and architecture. The following collection of stills from *Bucharest: A Portrait*, combined with snippets of history, comment on elements of present-day Bucharest, and excerpts from the film's transcript, aims to explore in parallel what Evans' film presents.

The city of Bucharest has, since becoming established during the 15TH century, been forced to re-shape and rebuild itself time and time again. Wars routinely erupted between the Ottoman Empire, Austria and Russia during the 18TH and 19TH centuries, and Bucharest, being geographically situated in the middle of these conflicts, was periodically seized and destroyed. German troops occupied the city for two years during World War I, and again for four years during World War II, when it was significantly damaged by Allied bombing. Additionally, Bucharest has endured a number of serious earthquakes. In 1977, earth tremors resulted in 1,500 fatalities and an estimated $2 billion worth of damage. Large areas of the city were bulldozed and rebuilt by the communist dictator, Nicolae Ceausescu, who was in power from 1965 until the revolution of 1989. When his government was overthrown, they left a multitude of unfinished communist structures in the city. These ravages of history and geography have created a city that is a montage of architectures, narratives and memories.

Film still (SARAH EVANS, *Bucharest: A Portrait*, 2007) Time code 05:55 Apartment block, just off Una Mai

Lipscani was the trading heart of Bucharest in the 17TH and 18TH centuries. It is named after Leipzig in Germany, from where most of the goods were imported. Being a merchant in Lipscani was, at that time, something to be proud of. Much of this area has survived – it was scheduled by Ceausescu to be demolished, but was saved by the revolution of 1989. The mixture of architectural styles in the area reflects the diversity of the old trading community, where Jews, Greeks, Bulgarians, Austrians, Armenians and Serbs all jostled for business. Although it is still to fully recover from the Ceausescu years and left derelict, it is now the heart of what remains of the 'old Bucharest'.

Film still (SARAH EVANS, *Bucharest: A Portrait*, 2007) Time code 05:17 - Street in Lipscani

At one point in the last decade there are believed to have been as many as 300,000[1] stray dogs roaming in packs on waste ground and gathering outside public buildings and blocks of flats, looking for food. The dogs are a constant reminder of Bucharest's past, as their 'homelessness' is a result of the Ceausescu government's destruction of large residential parts of the city. Dog owners abandoned their pets when they were re-housed in tiny flats after their homes were bulldozed. The animals ran wild and multiplied. After many controversial culling and neutering programmes enforced by the city's administration, the numbers have been reduced, but the dogs still breed faster than the city can keep up with.

Evans' film does not visually represent the 'old Bucharest' but you hear of it second and third hand, through the narrators. One of them recalls a comment from a letter the architect Le Corbusier wrote in 1910 describing Bucharest as a glamorous city where people go to party. Rosie G. Waldeck's 1942 book, *Athene Palace*, describes Bucharest of the 40s as "Little Paris". Her book was titled after the hotel located at the corner of Calea Victoriei, on what is now known as Revolution Square, and records her stay from June 1940 to January 1941 as a correspondent for an American news publication. During the early part of World War II, the hotel housed many correspondents and provided the perfect venue for a short era of hard drinking and bohemian decadence before German occupation.

In 1948, the hotel was taken over by the Ceausescu government and the building was bugged from corner to corner. All the hotel phones were tapped; even the ashtrays were said to be equipped with microphones. The busboys were watching; the waiters were listening. In the lobby, the bell-boys, the concierge and the reception-ists were all on the government pay-roll; and outside, the taxi rank was run

Film still (SARAH EVANS,*Bucharest:A Por-trait*, 2007) Time code 02:44 – The People's Palace

by the Securitate, Romania's secret police under the communist regime. The hotel's general director was an undercover colonel in the Securitate's counter-espionage directorate; the hotel's deputy director was a colonel in the DIE, the Romanian CIA. The doormen did surveillance; the housekeeping staff photographed all documents in the guests' rooms. The hotel today provides a microcosm of the changed city. It is now a Hilton hotel with conference rooms, a business centre, a beauty salon and numerous restaurants, but, within its walls, the memory of the past remains.

Cinty, born in Bucharest in 1981, recounts a memory from her childhood (film transcript):

Eram mereu conştientă, chiar şi când eram foarte mică,
că nu am voie să discut cu alte per-soane sau la şcoală despre lucrurile pe care le aud acasă,
şi acest lucru era ceva general în soci-etatea română.

I was always aware, even when I was very small,
that I'm not supposed to talk, about things I hear at home, with other people, or at school,
and that was something general within Romanian society.

Oamenilor le era frică să vorbească cu ceilalţi pentru că nu ştiai niciodată cine poate fi un agent secret.

People were afraid to talk to the others because you never knew who could be a secret agent.

Evans' film portrays the most recent re-shapings of Bucharest: the re-found freedom of the city and its people since the downfall of Ceausescu's totalitarian regime in 1989, and the entry of Romania into the EU in 2007. A generation of Bucharesters, who did not experience the city under communism, are now reaching adulthood.

Raluca, born in 1977, talks directly about this new generation (film transcript):

Ei nu îşi aduc aminte de comunism şi nu simt acea întunecare pe care o simt eu,

pentru că acei ani m-au marcat cumva, dar ei nu ai nimic de genul acesta şi sunt atât de liberi, ştii?

They don't remember the communism and they don't have any dark things going on somewhere that I feel I have, you know,

because those years left something on me, but they have nothing of that and they are so free, you know?

Film still (SARAH EVANS, *Bucharest: A Portrait*, 2007) Time code 09:58 Skate Ramp at Herastrau Park, next to Lake Herastrau

Herastrau Park opened in 1936 around Lake Herastrau. It is the largest park in Bucharest and has very diverse vegetation, monuments and statues, a summer theatre, exhibitions, restaurants and terraces.

In direct symbiosis with the city's economic and political change, the contemporary art scene in Bucharest has also been developing over the past years. In 2004, the impressive Muzeul National De Arta Contemporana (MNAC) opened and has run an impressive series of international exhibitions since then. The museum is located on four palatial floors of Bucharest's most notorious building, the Palace of Parliament, as it was renamed after the fall of communism. Still commonly referred to by Bucharesters as 'the People's Palace', it was built by Ceausescu to be the largest, most lavish palace in the world, a place to hold all the functions of his socialist state, as well as serve as a residence for himself and his wife. In a recent article on the art scene in Bucharest in *Frieze* online, Richard Unwin states: "As a telling indication of the reactionary response to MNAC's arrival, rather than visit the museum openly, TV news cameras panned into its offices from a window in the adjacent government wing. In many ways, the physical instantiation of Ceausescu's power is a more than problematic structure for a contemporary institution to call home. Viewed against the anarchic backdrop of Bucharest's architectural history, however, MNAC's provocative location is simply another striking juxtaposition in a city of improbable parts."[2]

Evans' film reflects on this search for a balance between the old and the new. A new paradox has been created: between those that remember and those that don't. The next Bucharest Biennale in 2010 is being curated by a member of this new generation, Felix Vogel, who was born in 1987 – two years before the end of the communist period – and is too young to remember first-hand living under communism. In choosing such a young curator, the optimism of this new generation of Bucharesters is being recognised. In an interview published on the biennale's website, with reference to what the interviewer Markus Miessen calls "the weight of history"[3], Vogel says: "Even young artists of my age who did not have any personal relation to this are occupied with it and working with it in a very productive and yet different way than their older colleagues did. It seems that there is a shadow of '89 that still lasts; even if '89 itself vanished, it might be described as a spectre. I would like to try to translate these issues – not to mention morerecent issues like all those massive changes in the aftermath of 9/11 – into an optimistic and productive setting."[4]

In the film, Cinty talks about the powerful impact of the changes of the past year:

Îmi aduc aminte acum trei, patru ani cum nu existau decât unul sau două locuri în care puteai ieși să asculți muzică sau să dansezi și să bei ceva.
Și era exact aceeași situație și cu evenimentele culturale,
dar acum înflorește.
Este exact ca o floare.
Este adevărat că de abia a început, dar simt că este puternic.

I remember some three, four years ago, there were one, two places you could go out to listen to nice music, or dance and have a drink.
And the same was with cultural events and happenings and now it's flowering.
It's exactly like a flower.
It just started, it's true, but I really can feel that it's powerful.

The film *Bucharest: A Portrait* portrays a city that is being re-configured. It acts as a document of a time of transition in a city where it seems the young have the power to change things. The film raises the question of what will happen to the city in the forthcoming years. Will the memory of communism always remain as a greyness in the hearts of those who experienced it? How will the new generation embrace the cultural and capitalist excesses of the western world? This collection of images and texts, along with Evans' film, is not meant to present answers, but to raise questions and provoke thought about how the collective memory of the city will re-mould itself as this new generation of adults find their voice.

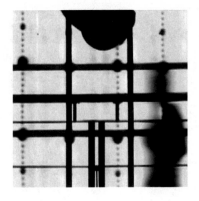

Film still (SARAH EVANS, *Bucharest: A Portrait*, 2007) Time code 10:52 Studio Martin

Studio Martin is located in a building that was constructed in the inter-war period. In 1990, it became a cinema – Volga – and 15 years ago it was turned into the first house music club in Romania. It was closed between 2004 and 2005, and since it reopened, with new management, all the best DJs in the world have played there at least once.

BIOGRAPHIES

Catherine Botibol is an artist and writer, living in London. She is the Creative Development Director at Pd3, where she develops and produces innovative collaborations between commercial brands and artists.

Sarah Evans is a filmmaker, video artist and writer. She teaches video and photography at London Metropolitan University.

1. BBC online, 2 March 2001, *news.bbc.co.uk/2/hi/europe/1196712.stm* (accessed 27/02/09).
2. R. Unwin, 'Bucharest', *Frieze* online, 12 January 2009, www.frieze.com/comment/article/bucharest/ (accessed 25/02/09).
3. 'Producing Possibilities, Markus Miessen in conversation with Felix Vogel (July 2008)', excerpt from: Markus Miessen (ed.), *East Coast Europe* (Berlin and New York: Sternberg Press, 2008) bucharestbiennale.org/concept.html (accessed 25/02/09).
4. *ibid.*

The Park Bench Reader

Urbanism, Literature
and the Reclamation of Public Space

BRAM THOMAS ARNOLD

The beginnings of this project lay in a few obsessions of mine and their collision during some research I was undertaking into reading. The park bench is a strange thing, a hangover from a more sociable society, from the excitement of leisure time that was created by the invention of industrialised work in Victorian England. The novel began to emerge a rough century earlier than this, with Defoe's *Robinson Crusoe* in 1719, but only really began to take off in the 1800s and saw its real breakthrough in the 1840s when a whole new generation of writers published an array of classics – from Thackeray's *Vanity Fair* to Dickens' *Bleak House.* [1]

In 1840, the year of Thomas Hardy's birth, Joseph Strutt opened England's first municipal park to the public on Wednesday 16 September. And with it came the park bench. On Sunday 23 March 2006, I enlisted the help of six volunteers to commemorate this collision by reading out loud from six of Hardy's works on six park benches that were situated near to each other in the grounds of Dartington Hall, South Devon. The piece interacted with the environment, with the students of the college and with members of the public strolling past first one bench, then another and another, each alive with a different Thomas Hardy tale.

In the beginning, novels were an elusive exclusive possession, as indeed was the capacity to read, and so this lead to a culture where 'reading' meant to 'read aloud' from a paper or a book to loved ones or friends, or to all the illiterate chaps down the pub. Indeed even in ancient Greece reading was considered something that was only to be done out loud, for the Greeks were worried about the written word and the way it may have encouraged laziness in understanding – permitting a reader to say they had *read* a text without ever having to prove they had *understood* it.[2] And so novels, in their initial instance, were read aloud and serialised into pamphlets or published weekly as though they were an episode of *Eastenders*.[3] They were also and inevitably, for the wealthy, an opportunity to display one's wealth through the acquisition and possession of rare things, an activity which the Victorians found most absorbing.

But I only found all this out later. At the time I was reading an article by Blake Morrison about bibliotherapy,[4] a new line of thought experimenting with reading aloud as a form of theraputic occupation. "The usual pattern is for a complete book to be read aloud, cover to cover, at weekly sessions, which for a group spending an hour a week on a Dickens novel can mean six months devoted to a single work."[5] And so I took this idea of healing through reading aloud and smashed it into society: took it outside, played around with it, and even if no one listened that week, even if no one found the bench, it felt like an achievement of sorts. Reinvigorating urban space with public interaction.

It is, at heart, a simple formula and as such could form the ground for a type of work that could be called site-generic, as opposed to the site-specific artwork. It requires, as a thing, *a* park bench – not *this* particular park bench. It requires a *novel* – not *this* particular novel. It requires a reader and an advertisement of the event for which I developed a certain style, another very simple construction that sought to echo Victoriana posters announcing events. And that was all really. It was a performance that went on as long as the situation required, and was about the small collection of people who had sought out the experience.

Fiona Bradley wrote: "artists working today make increasingly inventive use of language, their discoveries often rooted in the researches of the past",[6] and this was little more than that. A re-contextualisation of a series of developments, jumbled up together and played out again and again. In this may be the reason for the project's popularity. The project began on a bench in the pouring rain on 4 February 2008, a reading attended only by my housemate that lasted for as long as it took the pages to become too damp to turn; by that September, The Park Bench Reader had gone on to be featured in both Live Art Falmouth and Conflux, a festival of psycho-geography in New York. Each time the project was looked at from a slightly different angle or viewed through a different pane, but at its heart it was always the same: a person on a park bench, reading out loud a classic work of literature to friends and strangers alike.

In New York, a Dutch artist read *Animal Farm* to an old lady who, after sitting there for half an hour, proclaimed "that was delightful, I haven't read that book for years" and promised to go off and buy herself another copy and step back in time.[7] We have all been read to in the past, and we all have warm memories of these moments and can appreciate the warmth the situation suggests. Another woman sat in Washington Square next to a volunteer who read from the pages of a Charles Dickens novel, and after the performance wound down, she turned to the reader to explain that she had not only been listening and enjoying the surreality of the experience, but had been writing it up on a postcard as she listened. It was her first day in New York and the postcard was bound for Finland that evening.

London could probably stake a big claim as being the most written about city in the western world – a palimpsest of memoirs and tales, histories and fictions, written and rewritten over the same square miles, stretching out in all directions to the noose of the M25. The city has hung itself. But between all these pages have been captured some of the most enduring and endearing, alarming and terrifying things ever to be heard or fabricated by humankind. London is a book to be read: on foot, bus or the snaking underground, the past and its stories hang, clogging up its corners and dripping from its underpasses. The city is ever alive.

It was with this in mind that the Mobile Institute[8] approached TINAG with a proposition, a proposal if you will. This was The Park Bench Reader: A London History. Take a number of volunteers and a public square in Dalston, that goodly square mile or so that regularly receives a meander from Iain Sinclair or Stewart Home, not to mention being the proud owner of a number of the *Hackney Gazette*'s more grizzly headlines. Invite these volunteers to choose a work on London, be it fiction or fact, dense theory or elaborate fantasy, and bring it to a public reading, advertised on the fly-postered walls of the area like it were the next best club-night. And for an ill-defined period of time, let these readers, these orators, dispel their own version of London onto its own streets, reading its own historical fiction back to it.

Besides this, the festival and the case demanded something more than this fleeting glance, something that was concrete and performative, something that could hang through time more heavily than our voices, whittled away by the wind of an October day as they were. To this regard, take an extract from each participating book, and weave them together, interceded by the collaborative efforts of the Mobile Institute to form a bulk of text that weaves from classic literature to social theory to eloquent architectural diorama, but at the same time exists as its own piece of text, its own thing, scrawling again on the sheets of the city. In order to prove, as Walt Whitman suggests:

> *That you are here – that life exists and identity; That the powerful*
> *play goes on, and you will contribute a verse.*[9]

This performance, this whole idea, is about reclaiming something we have lost, reclaiming space, reclaiming culture, reclaiming our own presence, reclaiming collaboration, reclaiming our ability to dream, and reclaiming society from the jaws of Thatcher's demise. "There is no such thing as society,"[10] she still echoes at us, but there is. And the Mobile Institute exists to remind one of that.

BIOGRAPHY

Bram Thomas Arnold is an artist, writer and pedestrian. He is one of the co-founders of the Mobile Institute. Currently based in London, he lives and works between places. (www.bramthomasarnold.com)

1. For more on this see the introduction to Charles Dickens' *Dombey & Son* (London: Penguin, 1968).
2. For more on this and some fascinating insights into the development of both reading and language please see *The Adventure of English* by Melvyn Bragg (London: Sceptre Books, 2004) and *Proust and the Squid* by Maryanne Wolf (Thriplow: Icon Books, 2006).
3. *Eastenders* is a long running British soap opera that is now screened several times a week with an omnibus on Sunday afternoons so people can catch up on what's been going on. The programme is supposedly set in the present in a neighbourhood in East London, hence the name.
4. See the article 'The Reading Cure' by Blake Morrison published in the *Guardian*, Saturday 5 January 2008. Or go to www.guardian.co.uk/books/2008/jan/05/fiction.scienceandnature to read the article online.
5. Quoted from the above article.
6. Fiona Bradley, Isobel Johnstone and Martin Thomas, *Words: from the Arts Council Collection* (London: Hayward Gallery Publishing, 2002) p.9.
7. Here I would like to thank Dutch artist Ties Ten Bosch for his recalling of this story after a performance in Washington Square Park in Greenwich Village, NY, September 2008.
8. The Mobile Institute is an interdisciplinary arts organisation centred around the concerns of place, site specifics and the arts as social engagement. It was co-founded in 2008 by Bram Thomas Arnold, Eleanor Wynne Davis and Penny Skerret.
9. These lines form the 'Answer' part of the two-part poem by Walt Whitman entitled 'O me, O Life!' This poem can also be recalled from the Peter Weir film *Dead Poets' Society*. See www.poets.org/viewmedia. php/prmMID/20247 for a full transcript of this poem.
10. Jonathan Sacks, *The Politics of Hope* (London: Vintage, 2000) p.50.

Fleeting Urban Encounters

The Photographs of David San Millán

ZUZANA FLASKOVA

Photographer David San Millán lives and works in London, a city that often lays claim to being one of the most diverse and vibrant in the world.

The city, a growing organic entity, constantly alters the nature of habitation along with the nature of its inhabitants, challenging their capacity to adapt to an ever-changing milieu with a constant flow of stimuli. Despite, or rather due to, the vast numbers of people living in London, one of its notorious urban paradoxes lies in the city as an embodiment of distant and impersonal relationships. Alienation, or co-habitation by mutual indifference, is a very contemporary urban experience.

David San Millán's black and white street photography series Passerby captures something beyond the city dwellers' everyday experience. Despite inhabiting the same city, I have in front of me images of a space I somehow haven't noticed before. Taken over the course of seven years, the images are far from the usual thick and dense fabric of a hurried metropolis with its competing economies. A contemporary flaneur, David catches the ephemeral fleeting moments within the frantic daily experiences. Nothing extraordinary, yet these images are intriguing with their arresting beauty and unusually quiet pace. Rather than exposing the dynamic complexities of urban existence or its physical environment, they present externalised narratives of the human condition. Personifications of the still moments of a city in a constant state of flux, they capture the particular flair unique to the individual subject but universal to the urban dweller, the anonymous metropolitan mind. David's deeply emphatic personal view of the world passing by gives his images a great emotional resonance and creates a fascinating level of intimacy despite the unexplored potential of the encounter.

BIOGRAPHIES

Zuzana Flaskova is a Slovakian freelance writer and translator currently studying for an MA in Contemporary Art Theory at Goldsmiths College, London.

David San Millán Del Río is a Spanish former press photographer currently living in London working on personal projects.

Public Memory

All images from the series Passerby, DAVID SAN MILLÁN DEL RÍO

CREATIVE DESTRUCTION

Introduction

DEEPA NAIK & TRENTON OLDFIELD

'Creative Destruction', the term coined by economist Joseph Schumpeter in 1942[1], has been chosen as the title for this section for two main reasons. Firstly, it is frequently offered in an off-the-cuff way by academia and built-environment professionals to explain the trend to never look back, never protect and never lament as the future is always full of possibilities. For most cities this is experienced as continual demolition and construction (offices, homes, factories, shops etc).[2] The argument suggests that failure occurs without re-invention. The allegory offered most often is that of the human body, which is continually destroying and renewing itself from within.

Secondly, Schumpeter's driving thesis argues that failure will occur unless decision-making processes are opened up, controls relaxed, new ideas identified and motivations re-assessed. This was meant as a guide for companies experiencing decline due to new technologies. What is interesting about this business analogy is the fracture between the concept and the lived experience of urban dwellers. In reality, cities are not department stores or companies 'in decline' but places and spaces where ten of millions of people are trying each day to establish a home and maintain a life. In cities, creative destruction matters, as it affects the daily lives of all but the most mobile inhabitants.

Creative destruction is a highly seductive notion, trumpeting the endless potential of human creativity, ingenuity and renewal. However, it is based on the belief that there are never-ending resources (including people) to be mined. At best, this approach might contribute to the replacement of the status quo (perhaps even the establishment?) from within. At worst, it elevates lazy neo-liberal notions of business-led urban renewal, along with the agenda to remove any impediments that are perceived to inhibit it, including sustainability agendas, conservation, community participation and planning. The most active advocate for this approach, perhaps more so than pragmatic developers, is a potent group of architects and intellectuals embarrassed and frustrated that their unique creativity and vision is being tempered and limited (worst of all by governments or communities). Though little discussed, 'waste' (people, livelihoods, communities, materials, histories, sites) is understood as an inevitable outcome of the process. Charities, not-for-profit organisations and sometimes government departments are occasionally funded to 'clean up' afterwards (i.e. through public art commissions, church or community activities). Whatever is considered to be 'progress' must triumph and the 'wastage' can be addressed, if need be, by some of the resulting profits.

Schumpeter's ideas for businesses facing decline, though applied quite different-ly, have unknowingly paralleled the ideas propelling the establishment of the This Is Not A Gateway Festival. In particular, the argument for openness, rigour and continuous 'reality checks' has resonated.

In the years leading up to the inaugural festival and even after the collapse of Lehman Brothers, most built-environment discussions and certain-ly most architecture festivals steadfastly chose against acknowledging an 'elephant in the room'. Few architects, planners or academics wanted to ques-tion the aggressive pursuit of ever-widening margins of profit, their role in lubricating the process, or the consequences of these values and poli-cies on those who were trying to make the city their home. The many working on the ground who did ask questions, be they in Italy, Spain, Is-tanbul or Moscow, were offered up as 'out of date', 'anti-progress' and even 'anti-intellectual'. The trickle-down theory, though long disproved, was back in vogue. And yet, the questions continued at the salons and festival: How much profit is enough? How significantly have the built-environment professions been implicated in the global financial crisis? What roles did they play? What was it that prevented most built-environment institutions or architectural founda-tions from addressing any of these questions? How were so many in denial of the fault lines?

Schumpeter's theory was addressed in a workshop The Architecture of Financial Crisis[3] organised by Louis Moreno. Speakers, including a range of established aca-demics and emerging researchers, questioned the effects of globalised capital on ur-ban geography, culture and representation, with a particular focus on the last period of economic growth in the UK. Sessions addressed "the impact of global markets on geography and culture, the effect of the UK's economic boom on urban lifestyles and work patterns, and the way financial capital is institutionally and culturally ar-ticulated in architecture and media." Moreno's paper offers a detailed account of the presentations and adds further reflections and research. As the workshop was held in 'the eye' of the financial storm, reading the text one feels both the sense of anxiety and sense of possibility evident at that time.

Anxiety is a pervasive factor in the essay 'Water, Politics and Cinematic Space in Contemporary Mumbai', which takes a documentary film, *Liquid City*[4], as its starting point. With 60% of Mumbai's reported 18 million residents living in slums, access to water is a daily pre-occupation for all but a small elite. The film's director, Matthew Gandy, elaborates on the effects of accelerated economic growth on urban infrastructure and reflects on the collaborative filmmaking process involving researchers, technicians, academics, not-for-profit organisations and editors in London and Mumbai. Drawing on diverse perspectives from a range of practitioners – activists, theorists, engineers and residents – Gandy maps the complex power relations linked to the mega–city's water supply. He highlights the devastating consequences for poor residents and neighbourhoods when water – essential for life – is made a site for entrepreneurship.

Have the generative aspects of creative destruction been hijacked by neo-liberal values? How has the language of independence and choice affected essentials such as health? In 'Paradoxical Frogs', Phil Gusack expands on his presentation at the Medical City salon[5] exploring the complex interactions of public health care and the urban environment. The essay charts the evolution of hospitals in Britain, mapping the three main waves of their production: in the 19TH century, post World War II (which saw the establishment of the National Health Service), and under the Blair government (with public/private initiatives). The urgency surrounding the first public health initiatives is made apparent in the alarming statistics: up to 50% of deaths in UK cities in the 19TH century were attributable to infectious diseases; the average lifespan (in Whitechapel, East London) of the upper classes was 45, while labourers were lucky to live past the age of 22. Gusack urges urbanists to propose new ways of understanding the connections between the built environment and health. His analogy – Trinidad and Tobago's paradoxical frogs that reduce rather than increase in size as they grow from tadpoles into frogs – is offered as a challenge urbanists to not allow their aspirations and values to be reduced by mediocre policies.

Sukhdev Sandhu's paper 'Precarities and Dissensualities: Arts, Policy and Space on the Eve of an Election' elaborates on questions raised at the Cultural City salon[6] in which academics, cultural practitioners and a policy researcher for the Conservative Party considered the ways cultural policy has been translated into the built environment and, perhaps more urgently, what a post-New-Labour cultural landscape might look and feel like. Sandhu examines the entangled relationship that artists, cultural theorists and corporate creatives have with the political economy and their recent rapid elevation as key agents for urban transformation. Positioned as the new entrepreneurs, 'creatives' have been replacing Britain's now largely redundant manufacturing and maritime industries. New Labour policies culminated in the building of new cultural quarters and arts centres (often as a result of campaigns initiated by local communities), many of which have subsequently failed to find relevance as the dynamics and needs of the surrounding neighbourhood change. How might Conservative cultural policies differ and what are the potential impacts on urban space? Unravelling the theory underpinning past and present Conservative policies, which have advanced notions of individualism and art operating in a transcendental sphere 'beyond the market economy', the author argues these ideas are simplified, misguided and do not address the extent to which the arts are enfolded within the economic, social and spatial make-up of cities. This moment of uncertainty – between the economic crash and the election – is also one of potentiality: "How can arts organisations that often develop crookedly and unevenly over the course of many years, dealing in the process with an ever-changing roll-call of bureaucrats and cultural gatekeepers, cleave to their original goals and respond to the transformed landscapes they encounter when they finally get up and running?"

The final two essays arose from the salon How Vermin are Shaping our Future Cities.[7] The discussion brought together a pest controller, urban archaeologist and architectural theorist to examine the entrenched relationship between vermin and the built environment. In his paper 'The Cleansing of Slumland and the Return of the Bed Bug', Ben Campkin provides "a historical perspective from which to consider concerns with urban pests in the early 21ST-century metropolis". He details how the threat of pest infestation was used to propagate housing reform schemes and development policies in 1920s Somers Town. In the name of progress, the resulting slum clearance and flat building produced radical urban transformation. The paper explains that the construction materials used, density of buildings and lack of infrastructure created ideal habitats for vermin – allowing for continual infestations. What is particularly interesting is how notions of dirt and decay have perpetuated constructions and representations of class difference. The drive to sanitise the slums led to the establishment of organisations such as the St Pancras Improvement Society that described the slums as "devil's architecture". Their demolition and renewal allowed a triumphant re-imagining of entire neighbourhoods, along with the establishment of a well-respected profession of pest-controllers. However, despite best attempts to sanitise cities, there appears to be a resurgence in vermin infestations. Campkin argues that one of the reasons is yet another phase of 'creative destruction', this time driven by the privatisation of infrastructure and environmental health, and the reneging of state responsibility for housing and the public realm.

'Vermin: The Future Development of Cities...and Other Stories' by Alan Thompson draws out the key ideas raised during the salon discussion. Referencing literature, history, policy, art, urban myths and legends, he charts the way cities have been shaped by the drive to keep vermin out. Paradoxically, 'improvements' and attempts to isolate or constrain pests have created even better environments for them to thrive (pipes, spaces between walls, alcoves and waste disposal areas) and multiple factors combine to facilitate their proliferation (from waste management and treatment schemes to the movement of people across the globe). Our attitudes towards these causes and the actions we take, collectively and individually, will determine how we are affected by vermin in the future. Importantly, the author argues "it is our collective 'inaction' that might well precipitate greater changes ... our commitment to the responsible management of waste and the ongoing provision of an effective public health system, are central to our future stable relations with our vermin populations."

How are the notions of creative destruction taught to city builders? Is the theory explicit in urban policy? Do outputs resulting from creative destruction signal something better, something enhanced? Do they have a net benefit for society? How are the subsequent social disruptions, the waste and detritus (including people and place) considered by urbanists? How do cities manage the openness of democracy and innovation alongside capitalism's drive to monopolise? How can the processes of creative destruction come to address issues of climate change and poverty rather than perpetuate to these conditions? These questions continually surfaced in the salons and the festival as participants queried whether they contribute to, or were the 'cleaners' of, the waste created from the processes of creative destruction. Are 'social cohesion' and 'sustainable communities' policies an attempt to redress and mitigate the consequences of the crisis implicit in the built environment?

Social cohesion works on the basis that there is 'a glue', a commonality that binds us together and helps to reduce social exclusion. The British Government's *State of the English Cities report*[8] used five factors to assess levels of social cohesion: material conditions, passive relationships, active relationships, inclusion and equality. The architects of these terms, it can only be guessed, did not consult the numerous libertarians and constructivists practicing, theorising and teaching across the built-environment disciplines. For property foundations, splitter groups from the Revolutionary Communist Party (ManTowNHuman, Institute of Ideas) and a number of centres of learning, the idea that governments are involved in forging community ties or creating policies to limit the impacts of creative destruction is bureaucratic and anti-intellectual.

The tensions resulting from these divergent ideas rubbing up against each other were evident throughout the salons and festival. The ideas at stake, including notions of progress, libertarianism, social cohesion and social justice, have, of course, been part of a longstanding struggle played out in many fields. It seems, however, that not since the adventures of 'architectural modernism' have the built environment and the urban disciplines been at the centre of this struggle. Cities, as the magnet for mass migration, and the extraordinary rate of demolition and new development, have thrust 'city-builders' to the forefront in debates at the junction of climate change, financial-market collapse, unsustainable resource use and lack of social cohesion. Alongside these concerns is a resurgent discourse ostensibly led by a school of thought within architecture arguing for the removal of restraints, policies and social obligations perceived to be hindering human focused solutions, expression and the generation of profit. It became apparent to us at the festival, salons and through reading the papers within this book that this debate is experiencing a new turn – propelled by the weight of the issues and the diversity of agents injecting ideas, knowledge and new agitation.

1. Joseph A. Schumpeter, *Capitalism, Socialism and Democracy* (New York: Harper & Row, 1942) pp. 381.
2. We argue this has resulted in a strategy of 'erase, stretch and relinquish', which is expanded in the section 'Legalities of Space' (p.07)
3. Held at the University College London (UCL) on 24 October 2008.
4. Screened at Space 1 on 25 and 26 October 2008.
5. Held in London at public works on 14 July 2008.
6. Held in London at St. Anne's Community Hall on 24 June 2009.
7. Held in London at public works on 26 November 2007.
8. *State of the English Cities* (London: Department for Communities and Local Government, United Kingdom Government, 2006).
9. Such as environmental regulations, community consultation and planning codes.

The Architecture Of Financial Crisis

LOUIS MORENO

Once currencies could float, the world changed.

The Economist, 18 October 2008

The urban flaw

On 23 October 2008, under interrogation by the Senate Oversight and Government Reform Committee, former Federal Reserve chairman Alan Greenspan admitted he had found "a flaw" in his "ideology". Perplexed by the remark, committee chair Senator Waxman asked for clarification: "You found a flaw in the reality?" Greenspan elaborated:

> *I found a flaw in the model that I perceived is the critical functioning structure that defines how the world works, so to speak.*[1]

It was barely a month since Lehman Brothers collapsed, eight months following Northern Rock's nationalisation, over a year since the scale of US home loan default shook the markets, and nearly four decades[2] since the formation of an intellectual framework which no longer explained Greenspan's world. To an economic outsider the bald simplicity and uninflected contrition of his confession is startling. However, a striking definition, provided by Martin Wolf in the *Financial Times* on 1 October 2008, helps frame the confession's significance: "Finance is the web of intermediation binding economic agents to one another across space and time." Wolf, like Greenspan, understood that the free market compass was broken – the terrain of trade was now hostile. But what about that other socially critical web of temporal and spatial intermediation, the built environment; had flaws in structured finance affected the functioning and production of architecture and cities?

The day after Greenspan's hearing a workshop was held at the Bartlett School of Architecture to explore the way place and space are affected by financial expansion and collapse. Contributions were invited from a group of leading experts and emerging researchers covering a spectrum of urban inquiry whose interests connect urban and economic problems. To comfortably accommodate interests as diverse as geography, history, economics, architecture, business, planning, film studies and anthropology, the day was divided into sessions addressing three interrelated problems: the impact of global markets on geography and culture, the effect of the UK's economic boom on urban lifestyles and work patterns, and the way financial capital is institutionally and culturally articulated in architecture and media.

Dusting down the economic and sociological theories of Kondratieff and Schumpeter, Peter Hall's keynote talk reflected on research published in his 1998 book *Cities and Civilization*,[3] suggesting patterns in the way urban structure and culture is influenced by the technological transformations of industrial and financial capital. Dariusz Wójcik, an economic geographer at the University of Cambridge set out his recent research into the geographical concentration of global financial activity. Andrew Harris, lecturer at UCL's Urban Laboratory, linked the rise of London as a global city to the dual trajectories of finance and art markets. Max Nathan, a researcher at LSE, reflected on city-centre-led regeneration and the prospects for northern towns today. Davida Hamilton, director at space planning practice DEGW, explained the economic tendencies changing work styles and space usage. Maria Kaika, professor of geography at University of Manchester, gave a critical account of the changing architectural image of the City of London. Lawrence Webb, a researcher in the film studies department at King's College London, examined how the economic crisis of the 1970s affected cinematic representations of cities.

The purpose of this essay is to offer a report on their presentations. In doing so I try to build on the array of evidence and arguments to try and sketch out a way of thinking about the relationship between cities and capital today. I argue that the financial crisis necessitates a cultural and economic approach to analyse the production of urban experience today; which, as David Harvey said, can "unravel the meanings" of political economic life.[4]

Business cycles, technological innovation and cultural logic

In *Cities and Civilization* (1998), Peter Hall produced a multi-layered account of the interconnections between technological innovation and cultural production to explain the mysterious, complex and contradictory sense of order in everyday life.[5] At the centre of his account lay a palpable industrial heartbeat first detected by Nikolai Kondratieff and then later amplified by Joseph Schumpeter. To open up the debate about the way economic swings affect urban structure and culture, Peter Hall was invited to present this 'composite theory' of economics, geography and history.

Hall argued that Schumpeter's greatest achievement was to have adapted Kondratieff's long wave theory, established in the 1920s, into a dynamic economic history of industrial capitalism. In the two-volume work *Business Cycles*, published in 1939, Schumpeter linked boom and bust with technological revolution. Punctuating waves of financial euphoria and depression, entrepreneurs, in places far from the centres of political and economic life, develop new innovations in industrial technology and social organisation. From the late 18TH to the late 20TH centuries, new modes of production in places like Glasgow, Manchester, Berlin and Detroit centred on the installation of a low-cost social and technological input that increased production and reduced the cost of transportation and communication. The value created generated fantastic wealth for entrepreneurs and investors, whose success lay in their ability to harness the new idea to revolutionise production techniques. Hall laid out the sequence Schumpeter established and other economists later developed:

> *The first wave was in the late 18TH century especially in England with developments in the cotton industry and the iron and steel industry. The second associated with rail and ship building and the Bessemer process in iron and steel that greatly cheapened steel production. The third from the 1890s associated with the new motor car industry and with chemicals, especially pharmaceutical industries, this is when a lot basic drugs like aspirin came on the market for instance, and also the beginnings of the electrical industry. And the fourth was essentially associated with electronics but also with air travel; this was the wave that began*

215

with the mass production of television in the 1950s and went on to the development of the personal computer in the 1970s.[6]

According to this theory new technology and infrastructure influence change in social institutions, gradually altering the structure and character of places, inventing new routines of everyday life. The success of an innovation is measured then not only by its technological novelty but the entrepreneur's ability to exploit the potential of new ideas in the production process. Thus, "Henry Ford didn't invent the motor car, this was invented in Germany in the 1880s, but he did invent the mass production of the car for everyone in Detroit in 1907 with the Model T." Hall said this theory helps explain the last wave of development in the post-war period, where, in the area south of San Francisco now called Silicon Valley, a chain of critical innovations took place. From transistors to search engines, successive waves of technological discoveries took place in an area which up until the 1930s had served as agricultural land.

This process of continuous innovation Hall said had extraordinary parallels with "what happened in Lancashire in the first industrial revolution in the late 18TH and early 19TH industry centuries." But while the pattern of economic development of industrial Lancashire and Silicon Valley may follow similar geographical processes of development, the competitive pressures of fresh technical and social innovation can degrade the social and economic resources of places historically dependent on the activity of less adaptable industrial structures (for example, Detroit on car manufacturing). The emergence of a technological revolution signals increasing competition for resources which can dislocate the economy of places unable to weather, what Schumpeter famously described as, the "gales of creative destruction" whipped up by technological revolution. The fixed nature of physical capital can lock places into paths of decline through the devalorisation of physical assets and institutionalisation of poor job prospects. Over time, places are depopulated, leaving sinks of deprivation with dependent populations trapped and stigmatised by their decayed landscape and decomposing skill sets. However, the development of new industries and new firms seeking sites for production can, through geographical concentration and new modes of transportation and communication, transform the potential of abandoned places: "as a result, urban space is revalorized: rural areas, previously almost valueless, suddenly become valuable, central areas with certain properties have suddenly new potential".[7] But often, this process of urban renewal generates new sets of winners and losers.

Lawrence Webb developed this point, arguing that the new forms of urban representation emerging in 1970s US cinema were a product of socio-economic

Creative Destruction

contradictions inherent in real estate, industrial production and urban experience. Building on Michael Storper's analysis of the restructuring of Hollywood in the late 1960s and early 70s, Webb argued that the interregnum in cinematic production opened for a brief moment a window of experimentation in mainstream film. The financial crisis, which precipitated the reconfiguration of film production, paralleled the urban crisis of industrial heartland cities such as Detroit and Baltimore. This, according to Webb, provided filmmakers with "an urgent subject for enquiry and an intriguing set of forms and surfaces to work with".[8]

Webb applied the literary theories of Franco Moretti and Fredric Jameson to suggest that the New Hollywood processes of location shooting and de-dramatised narratives were attempts to represent the actually existing state of stagflation in that period. Using a pair of movies whose locations bookend a period of urban renewal in Atlantic City, Webb argued that *The King of Marvin Gardens* (1972) and *Atlantic City* (1980), in story line, aesthetic and production form respectively "plot out" the transition between two phases or periods of financial capitalism: "monopoly capitalism" and "casino capitalism". The role of finance in the economic 'plot' underpinning urban culture comes into view. The development and cultural conditions of cities expand to the limits set by the "design, product and profit space"[9] of an innovation and the new circuits of speculation set in motion by a new regime of finance capital.

The geographical concentration of financial capital

In *The Global City*,[10] the urban sociologist Saskia Sassen produced a benchmark account of the urban command and control of capital flows through a handful of core centres of financial production. For the workshop, Dariusz Wójcik took a fresh look at the notion of global cities with a geographical account of the financial sector's recent decoupling from the 'real' economy. Wójcik argued that there was a need to explain both the intense concentration of financial services in London and New York, and how one of the basic financial innovations of the deregulation era - securitisation - has become a structural fault line, along which local suburban real-estate markets have shaken the global economy to its core.

The process of deregulation in Wall Street, in the mid 70s, and Big Bang[11] in the City in 1986, meant these investment centres were freed up to exploit new markets. In this time of transition, a novel set of relationships developed between Wall Street and the City of London around new classes of investment products and processes (collectively known as structured finance). The concentration in the City and Wall Street of services and expertise in dealing in transparent assets, which needed little place-specific activity like foreign currency, Wójcik argued, explains the pronounced rise in the US and UK global share of interest rate derivatives between 1995 and 2005 – a period he called the 'heyday' for international capitalism. The vast proportion of domestic debt owned in the US was also a critical factor in the growth of this field: "the value of US domestic debt securities is 50% larger than the amount of all debt securities in international circulation in the whole world."[12] By being the world's single largest, most liquid financial market, the US became a laboratory to experiment in securitisation – complex processes to monetise debt.

One of the most significant innovations in this period was in asset backed securities; including the infamous mortgage backed securities upon which so many of the UK's large banks and building societies came unstuck. The tremendous growth and scale of these markets, intensified by the growth of hedge funds (effectively unregulated banks), the climate of permissive regulation and bonus incentives, increased the extent of financial innovation and risk taking. Another notorious invention over this period has been that of credit default swaps – the trading securities that brought down the insurance firm AIG. These were created in Wall Street, produced by financial mathematicians known as quantitative analysts, and exported worldwide by the City of London, with the tremendous sums farmed out through a global archipelago of offshore tax havens (in the Cayman Islands, the Seychelles, etc.)

Investors from all around the world called on London and Wall Street for products like interest rate swaps, because these cities were key marketplaces with concentrated knowledge and expertise in macroeconomic information, such as international interest rates. But what was overlooked in the race to get these exotic assets was information on the firmness of the local real-estate markets these securities rested on. The break in the geography of information, the link between real estate in places like suburban Detroit and financial activity in the City, was, in Wójcik's view, one of the critical failures causing capital markets to topple over.

The investment institutions that have congregated in these financial capitals form, in Wójcik's terms, the "connective tissue" binding the contemporary international money system together. But despite the tissue damage, Wójcik concluded that due to the concentration of institutions it is unlikely that Wall Street and London will be seriously challenged for some time. From the point of view of history, Wójcik said, "the significance of connectivity and mobile international bankers is, if anything, more true today than ever before". The recent wave of financial innovation has therefore consolidated the City of London's reputation, established in the early 19TH century, as the world's leading financial centre. By extension, financial and business services have maintained the significance of the UK in the global economy despite an increasing diminution of production activity, which, Wojick said, is consistent with the lessons of economic history.

The decline of London's manufacturing and maritime functions has been to the City's advantage. The disinvestment of London's docklands opened up arable real estate for commercial banking activities. During this time of growth the City experienced its own form of urban renewal, with new tall buildings like Richard Rogers' Lloyd's Building, and more recently, Norman Foster's 30 St Mary Axe ('the Gherkin'), accommodating the global reinsurance firm, Swiss Re. The redevelopment of the City has been physically marked by a new set of financial clusters: a base of hedge funds in Mayfair, a concentration of international firms in Canary Wharf and, of course, the political core, the City of London. Furthermore, a new cultural and creative economy has taken root in the late Victorian-era workshops and studios on the fringes of the City. The presentations from Maria Kaika and Andrew Harris reflected on how this financial transformation has culturally and spatially taken shape.

Cultural instruments of financial manipulation

Maria Kaika complemented Wójcik's account with a combined institutional and architectural critique of the City's recent evolution. Like many of the other presentations, her story began in the 1970s, with the Corporation of London described as a powerful but introspective city-state ("London's Vatican" as Kaika put it). Recalcitrant in the face of the changing character of financial capitalism, the Corporation's planners proudly repelled American towers from besmirching the City's historic character. This resistance to corporate modernism was, Kaika argued, symptomatic of a club-like code blocking the promulgation of new technologies and overseas companies. But the cumulative effect of liberalisation - the entry of foreign firms awash with capital into the market, the complexity of new products and new communications technology – forced a crisis. The Thatcher government's restructuring of the London Stock Exchange in 1986 meant a structural and cultural break with the City's past, forcing it open to international competition.

In the years that followed the Big Bang, the Stock Exchange of London turned from the preeminent stock exchange in Europe to being surpassed by its

European competitors, even the originally very successful LIFFE (London
International Financial Futures and Options Exchange) experienced
a deep plunge after the Corporation failed to move quickly to an electronic system.[13]

The shock of losing the European Central Bank to Frankfurt in the early 90s provoked an institutional moment of clarity. The Corporation finally began to transform; it accepted the need to adapt its urban layout and architecture to become a more viable location for international finance. This required new planning approaches to make room for change, but also a type of building and skyline attractive to global capital; a brief eventually fulfilled by the voluptuous form of Foster's icon at 30 St. Mary Axe.

London's skyline has, for the most part, bypassed 20TH-century corporate modernism, and adopted the haute-architecture of the 21ST-century cosmopolis. For Kaika the obeisance to finance and neglect of the public raises a question of ethics for architectural practice. Animated by the objectives of pecuniary power, guided by the strategic logic of development, the leading edge of architecture has, knowingly or otherwise, rejected the public sphere and become, for Kaika, "autistic" – repetitively casting meaninglessly distinctive urban forms. The related phenomena of the star-architect and iconic architecture are, in Kaika's critique, the fruition of a tendency which the architectural critic Manfredo Tafuri observed in the 70s: a capitalised avant garde whose freedom of expression correlates with the motivation of finance and real-estate actors.

In fact, despite the Corporation's resistance to change, the use of architecture to culturally mediate a new economic order was nothing new for the City. In *The Constitution of Society*, Anthony Giddens argued that the bankers of the 19TH century assumed the neo-classical tastes of Burlington-era aristocracy because of wealth accrued financing the industrial revolution.[14] Their entry into the English social elite was an exchange for bailing out gentry threatened by an earlier long wave effect–the collapse of agrarian production. Culture has long played an instrumental role in economic transformation. Andrew Harris brought this story up to date by comparing the trajectory of British artist Damien Hirst's career with the investiture of a new power-elite of hedge fund managers, Russian oligarchs and Gulf oil magnates. Using the conjuncture of two extraordinary events – the collapse of Lehman Brothers and Hirst's Sotheby's auction – Harris gave an exploratory account of the way this era of finance mobilised the value and influence of the art world. But instead of merely defining art as a passive target of speculation,

Harris suggested contemporary art mediated and expressed the social relations of the new era of finance.

From a geographical perspective Harris also linked the simultaneous success of Hirst and finance to the growth of a creative economy on the City's fringe. Not only were Hirst's first major exhibitions funded by Canary Wharf development company, they also took place in areas of London, like Shoreditch, which would later see a revival of new economic activity. This links with Hall's observation that the economic synthesis of art and technology, fuelled by speculative capital, can revive the urban core of cities. Thus, "terrains of disinvestment"[15] like East London, or Baumwollspinnerei in Leipzig, or SOMA in San Francisco have, since the mid 90s, become sites for new 'knowledge intensive' industries. These enterprises rely on intangible, creative services such as branding, design and marketing to define the distinctiveness of high-value goods. Alongside this, core manufacturing cities such as Leeds have, over the past 15 years, adapted their economic resources to accommodate the growth of financial and business services, picking up activities outsourced from London. The substitution of new economies for traditional industries has not only changed the physical landscape, but new modes of reindustrialisation have altered the social and cultural character of places.

The new inner city has produced a new work experience blurring the boundaries of employment, culture and leisure. Again architecture has played an instrumental role in reshaping the economic life of places, designing flexible spaces and distinctive images which contour new sites of production and consumption. Davida Hamilton and Max Nathan explained the changing style of work and use of space that have emerged over the last decade.

The demand for urbanness and spatiality

Davida Hamilton's presentation discussed the lifestyle changes new technology has stimulated and the spatial impact on those cities transformed by financial services. Hamilton's observations on the future industrial demand for work-space, based on analysis for Northamptonshire County Council, provided an insight into the changing time-space structure of labour. Communications technology and the need for proximity mean that workers are being pushed and pulled in many different physical directions. A diverse palate of physical and virtual places, such as cafés, websites and hotel lobbies, have become the new production floor of the knowledge economy, populated by users equipped with wifi-enabled mobile phones, laptops, etc. Forces of technology, real estate, employment and industrial competition have led employers to 'expect' workers to be highly networked, with diverse skill sets and flexible attitudes to work. But zoning typologies of residential, industrial and office space, and management processes, are lagging the changing socio-economic character of work staged on a highly differentiated range of sites. Hamilton's analysis could be said to present the demand for space and labour for what Allen Scott described as the new "cognitive cultural economy".[16]

A feature of this new economy is, in Hamilton's view, the tremendous growth rate of microlevel organisations; firms of up to ten people, which are crucial sources of employment in city regions. Hamilton suggested that this trend of micro start-ups is likely to increase following the contraction of financial services, but worryingly, she pointed out that it is not clear how the knowledge economy can absorb the scale of job loss northern financial centres, like Leeds and Halifax, are likely to experience. The dot com bust has shown how sensitive the new inner city economies can be. Due to the dependency of the knowledge and cultural economy on volatile financial capital, the "durability of the community regeneration mission" freighted by policymakers on these new industries is, as Thomas Hutton suggests, [17] doubtful.

Max Nathan looked at the municipal dimensions of real-estate and culture-led regeneration, and in particular the way housing investment models have changed in a relatively short span of time – what Storper has called the "demand for urbanness". The lineaments of the UK's urban-housing-market failure are similar to those Wójcik identified; namely, investment problems in the geography of information. "When housing markets are investor driven, when purchasers are geographically and systematically further away from the product, as city centre markets have turned out to be, they are particularly vulnerable to information problems around the housing product."[18] This is a critical area where the planning and regulatory system failed. While many on the ground knew the demand for housing products like one-bedroom flats was weak, the force of the business model that needed investors to bulk buy off-plan meant deals were taking place far removed from final demand.

The aspirational desire for a particular product, encouraged by place marketing, iconic architecture and real-estate media, helped inflate a housing bubble, and constructed a new political and consumer sense of urban value. "The increasing commodification of urban experience via spatial concentration of consumer sectors, and the blurring of retail, leisure and tourism" was, Nathan argued, conditioned by the political economy of speculation, rather than the objective for good standard, long-term social infrastructure. The robust real-estate acumen of US city leaders was enthusiastically emulated by their UK counterparts. As Mike Storey, one time leader of Liverpool City Council, said of the advice received from his New York mentors: "You talk the city up to everyone you can, you sell it and sell it, and then you look for the big cranes on the skyline."

The commercial role of architecture in places like Liverpool and Leeds was, as in the City, to excite effective demand so a speculative economy would take off. This business model responded to a demand for city-centre lifestyle 'packages' built on the new economic foundations of inner city restructuring. The risk of this model was assuaged by structured finance and permitted by central and local government eager to raise tax revenues and offset costs of physical and social infrastructure onto the private sector. New financial instruments, like mortgage backed securities, opened new routes for growth for banks. With that, the control over capital investment and urban development processes were assumed by those who, as Keynes said, "do not manage and have no special knowledge of the circumstances, either actual or prospective, of the business in question"[19]. This produced an over-supply of built environment, like city-centre flats, the remnants of which may become the liberal market equivalent of post-war housing estates. And here we find the various threads of the story – technological innovation, financial deregulation, financial innovation, revolutions in production, changes in consumption, redevelopment of urban fabric, cultural production, the changing space and time of the working day – converge to a critical point with a frenzy of speculation on the simplest expression of architecture: the home.

What do these houses mean? [20]

In 1970, the evening prior to the dawn of deregulation, the philosopher Henri Lefebvre sensed that a new urban order was emerging. He asked if the new phenomenon of 'global cities' indicates that urbanism "doesn't today play the role of ideology";[21] an ideology which produced so many models that were, in reality, barriers to the future. Nearly 40 years later, Alan Greenspan reflected on the failure of his ideology which no longer identified a path towards anything. He described this state of being as "distressing". "Everybody has an ideology, it's how you relate to the world." Given that economic rationality has, as Greenspan said, defined the way the world worked, some account of how this era of finance crystallised out through the materiality and space of cities is still an urgent question – perhaps more so now. Could Greenspan's flaw be perceived in the critical functioning structures that define the built environment?

To answer this question we need to be careful – an overhasty treatment of Green-span's predicament may contaminate the evidence, so to speak. In teasing out the urban dimensions, let us be clear about the ideology Greenspan operated. A recent online forum on Greenspan's legacy, hosted by *The Economist*, provides a useful guide to understand what is meant by the term 'financial architecture'.

Previous financial crises did not cause us to seriously question our informational architecture like this one has. This crisis has wiped out or discredited major sources of financial-market information that are crucial for credit markets to function. The ratings agencies are an obvious example. They are supposed to solve an asymmetric information problem between borrowers and lenders by giving those doing the lending a reliable assessment of the riskiness of financial investments. They failed in that mission.[22]

In *The Architecture of Markets*, the economic sociologist Neil Fligstein called normative market trends and policies reflexive 'conceptions of control', which co-ordinate the widely distributed actions of economic actors such as firms and households. In times of financial crisis these 'collective identities' and 'social movements', which concentrate in a boom around particular sets of markets, are often destablised.[23] What the urban dimensions of this financial crisis reveal is how buildings and cities intermediate, but do not define, the conceptions of control which condition the order of everyday life today. With sub-prime, urban areas became asset farms to be exploited by new financial practices of securitisa-tion; but the astonishing gains were dependent on systematic ignorance of their social and historical realities. The liberal financial architecture, according to Greenspan's world view, was founded on the "self interest of banks and others... such they were best capable of protecting their own shareholders".[24] But to feed the self interest of lenders and shareholders the financial architecture was over-cranked to exact rent from the vulnerable. Dariusz Wójcik's conclusion clinically summarised the results:

The crisis has been triggered by a failure of mismanaged and unregulated globalisation of non-transparent financial assets. Residential real estate that otherwise belongs to the realm of local markets by its nature. By refinancing mortgages, securitising them (creating mortgage backed securities), creating in-surance contracts on these securities (the infamous CDS), selling and buying these

*securities and contracts on a global basis, financial institutions
maximised the international financial system's exposure to what is otherwise
very localised risks...effectively what they did was tie their fortunes
and the fortunes of the global economy to the change in prices of ordinary homes
in places like suburban Detroit and Kansas City, etc.*

From a cultural perspective, art and architecture have played an active role in manipulating perceptions of value. The City of London not only offered a permissive business climate but also a supplicant guild ready to craft icons like Foster's Gherkin or Hirst's *For The Love of God*; architecture and culture have both instantiated and encapsulated new routes to growth. The instrumental economic role of culture suggests a tendency where normative conceptions of welfare, structured through our experience of space and society, are increasingly conditioned by a global information network of finance, politics and media.[25] For example, in terms of housing, the surpluses of inner-city flats are evidence of structural flaws in the information architecture of markets reproduced through the designed environments of cities.

In April 2008, a Wall Street fixed income broker-dealer was quoted in *The Financial Times* saying that "[t]he most compelling evidence that we are going through a crisis is that we have already redefined the meanings of words and symbols that were part of our cultural archetypes".[26] However, even if the crash has shaken the economic culture to the core, the spectacular forms rising in the new cadre of global cities suggest an ongoing demand for spectacular architecture. But perhaps the crisis opens up new opportunities for linkages between spatial research and architectural practice to examine weakening industrial territories like Detroit or Stoke-on-Trent and to critique the political economy of urban devalorisation and the logic preventing development, movement and centrality and blocking what Lefebvre called "the right to the city". Efforts could focus on multiple, interdisciplinary responses to Lefebvre's challenge to "put things the right way round", to envision the urban recasting of physical and financial dimensions so that economic logic subordinates to habiting and labour as creative ends.[27] The notion resonates with the work of sociologist Pierre Bourdieu. Investigating the social structure of the housing economy, Bourdieu argued for an economic anthropology which explains that "the economic field is a field of struggles".[28] Indirectly, this approach has been taken up by the architecture of Teddy Cruz, suggesting that urban practice should be animated by informal housing which encapsulates economic struggle in the margins of society.[29] In the aftermath of sub-prime and the failures of regeneration, urban practice and research could build new approaches to urban production which counter the "mis-scaled urbanism" (to borrow Neil Smith's phrase[30]) and 'real-estate-politik' which have driven urban development and governance.

The workshop tried to initiate a preliminary survey of the spaces, institutions and actors that have shaped cities in the lead up to what HSBC chairman Stephen Green has called the "first crisis in the era of globalised securitization".[31] The next step is to develop research and design approaches that track the financial fallout and make visible the crisis–creating capacities of structured finance. The urban challenge involves explaining not just how "all that is solid melts into air", but to avoid, as Marx said, the assertion of economic gravity which returns credit to earth causing a person's house to collapse.[32]

BIOGRAPHY

Louis Moreno studied Architectural History at the Bartlett School of Architecture and is a PhD student at the UCL Urban Laboratory exploring the relationship of business cycles and the production of the built environment.

Dalston Junction, London, 2009, MAX NATHAN

Creative Destruction

1. washingtontimes.com/weblogs/potus-notes/2008/Oct/24/he-found-flaw/ (accessed: 15/07/09)
2. In an article called 'A Short History of Modern Finance', *The Economist* (18 October 2008) attributed the origin of financial deregulation to Richard Nixon's decision to suspend the dollar's convertibility to gold in 1971.
3. P. Hall, *Cities and Civilization: Culture, Innovation and Urban Order* (London: Phoenix, 1999).
4. D. Harvey, *The Urban Experience* (Baltimore: Johns Hopkins University Press, 1989) p. 255.
5. *ibid*. Hall (1999) pp. 614-618.
6. P. Hall, 'Come Back Schumpeter, Come Back Kondratieff All is Forgiven', The Architecture and Urban Culture of Financial Crisis, Bartlett School of Architecture, 24 October 2008 (unpublished workshop transcript).
7. *ibid*. Hall (1999) p. 616.
8. L.Webb, Learning from 'Las Vegas East': economic crisis and cinematic space in The King of Marvin Gardens and Atlantic City (unpublished workshop transcript).
9. C. Perez, *Technological Revolutions and Finance Capital: the dynamics of bubbles and golden ages* (Gloucester: Edward Elgar Publishing, 2003).
10. S. Sassen, *The Global City: New York, London, Tokyo* (Princeton: Princeton University Press, 2001).
11. The modernisation and globalisation of the City's securities markets.
12. D. Wójcik, Geographical Concentration in Finance (unpublished workshop transcript).
13. M.Kaika, Autistic Architecture: re-imagi(ni)ng London and reinventing the Square Mile (unpublished workshop transcript).
14. A. Giddens, *The Constitution of Society: outline of the theory of structuration* (Berkeley: University of California Press, 1986) p. 321.
15. T. Hutton, 'The Inner City as Site of Cultural Production *sui generis*: A Review Essay', *Geography Compass* 3(2), 2009, pp. 600-629(611).
16. *ibid*. Hutton (2009) p. 625.
17. *ibid*.
18. M.Nathan, Counting Cranes: economic geography and the rise and fall of city centre living in the UK (unpublished workshop transcript)
19. *ibid*. Perez (2003) p. 124.
20. Nietzsche's question quoted by Lefebvre in *The Urban Revolution*.
21. H. Lefebvre, *The Urban Revolution* (Minneapolis: University of Minnesota Press, 2003 (1970)) p. 162.
22. www.economist.com/blogs/freeexchange/greenspan_roundtable/ (accessed: 15/07/09)
23. N. Fligstein, *The Architecture of Markets: An economic sociology of twenty-first century capitalist societies* (Princeton: Princeton University Press, 2002) p. 77.
24. Alan Greenspan, quoted by Paul Mason, http://paulmason.typepad.com/MASON%20CRUNCH%20KPMG%20PREZ.ppt (accessed 17/07/09)
25. On the political economic influence of communication networks see Manuel Castell's latest book *Communication Power* (Oxford: Oxford University Press, 2009)
26. *Financial Times*, 11 March 2008.
27. *ibid*. Lefebvre (1970) p. 85.
28. P. Bourdieu, *The Social Structures of the Economy* (Cambridge, UK: Polity Press, 2005).
29. www.thenation.com/doc/20090216/cruz?rel=hp_currently
30. N. Smith, 'New Globalism, New Urbanism: Gentrification as Global Urban Strategy', *Antipode* 34(3), 2002, pp. 427-450.
31. www.hsbc.com/1/2/newsroom/news/news-archive-2009/hsbc-holdings-plc-2008-final-results-highlights (accessed: 15/07/09)
32. K. Marx, *Capital*, Volume One (London: Penguin Books, 1976) p. 168.

Water, Politics and Cinematic Space

in Contemporary Mumbai

MATTHEW GANDY

Contemporary Mumbai is a paradoxical urban space characterised by choking fumes, forests of billboards and worsening levels of road congestion that are merely the outward signs of a city torn between attempts to build a more inclusive and functional public realm and counter impulses towards ever greater degrees of social iniquity and religious tension. Since the devastating anti-Muslim riots and retaliatory bomb blasts of the early 1990s, the city of Mumbai has faced heightened concerns over its security rooted in the political manipulation of community tensions by right-wing fundamentalist groups and acts of revenge linked to international criminal networks. This sense of anxiety has been raised more recently through the bomb blasts on commuter trains in July 2006 and the co-ordinated attacks on high-profile targets in December 2008.

The Indian city of Bombay – renamed Mumbai in 1995 – is undergoing an accelerated modernity whereby political and economic elites are seeking to transform the city into a hyper-modern Indian counterpart to cities such as Shanghai. This involves extensive slum clearances, airport upgrading and the building of new highways that often pass directly through or over poorer neighbourhoods. A massive construction boom is taking place for luxury apartments, shopping malls and other facilities aimed at the needs of transnational elites and powerful real-estate interests. In addition to sectarian and religious tensions, a key dilemma facing the city is the degree to which the urban environmental agenda has been effectively captured by the middle classes so that the public health crisis facing the poor has been marginalised. The city's middle classes, who have long been the greatest beneficiaries of municipal services, are increasingly militant in their desire to remove the poor from wealthy neighbourhoods.

If we consider poverty and social inequality over the last 30 years, it is striking that the proportion of slum dwellers has increased in both relative and absolute terms so that over 60% of the city's population now live in slums. The inequalities and injustices that mark everyday life in contemporary Mumbai are exemplified by problems of access to water. The city's municipal water supply system is reliant on a vast transfer of water from the jungles, lakes and mountains of the state of Maharashtra but this does not currently meet the city's needs: many businesses and local communities rely on thousands of wells and boreholes scattered across the metropolitan region, along with hundreds of private tankers and innumerable illegal connections. In the case of water and sanitation, Mumbai has never been able to provide the most basic services to all of its population, high infant-mortality rates persist throughout poorer parts of the city and the rudimentary sewer system is regularly overwhelmed by heavy rains. In the record monsoon of 2005, for example, over 400 people lost their lives in the city as makeshift dwellings were washed away, buried in landslips or simply inundated with rising flood waters that could not disperse through blocked or absent drains.[1]

In order to investigate some of these questions I completed a documentary film in 2007 called *Liquid City* on the theme of water and urban infrastructure in Mumbai.[2] Having written about cinema – principally on the representation of landscape in European film – it was a major challenge to actually make a film for the first time. After my first visit to Mumbai in 2002, I began to reflect on the centrality of cinematic culture to the city and also wondered whether my research could be developed through the making of a documentary. I had already made some experimental footage of the city from moving trains, and also taken many photographs that began to suggest some kind of visual narrative structure for the city that might be arranged around the themes of water, infrastructure and urban landscape.[3]

During the planning stage of the project, I watched with interest many examples of documentary films made in India. These ranged from European impressions such as Louis Malle's *L'Inde Fantôme* (1968), Pier Paolo Pasolini's *Notes for a film on India* (1968) and Roberto Rosselini's *India: Matri Bhumi* (1959) to more recent work by Indian filmmakers such as Anand Patwardhan's powerful account of a slum under siege in *Bombay our city* (1985), Dev Benegal's depiction of water politics in *Split Wide Open* (2000) and Paromita Vohra's pithy exploration of

gender and sanitation issues in *QTP* (2006). A distinctive feature of Mumbai is its role as a stage for an exuberant cinematic culture reflected not only through the economic significance of Bollywood, but also by the enduring relationship between cinema and popular culture. The city's visual culture has generated a diversity of representational forms that range from musical dramas aimed at mass audiences to a plethora of more experimental forms linked with the use of digital technologies for documentary filmmaking and a range of new developments within the visual arts.

In building a picture of water politics in the city, I decided to focus on four main groups of interviewees: academics, engineers, activists and ordinary voices from the locations where we were shooting. In practice, however, it became immediately apparent that these categories were not so clear cut: street-level encounters, for example, often yielded insights far more significant than many published sources, whilst engineers often confounded theoretical conceptions of the state and its relationship with civil society. A documentary film, like any piece of academic writing, normally has an intended audience. In this case, I felt that there were three key groups of people I wanted to reach: firstly, an interested general public, and especially the people of Mumbai; secondly, an academic audience, some of whom might choose to use the film for pedagogic purposes; and thirdly, a cinematic audience who had some interest in documentary filmmaking.

The film opens with a sequence of paintings by Sudhir Patwardhan – a local artist who has focused his work on the rapidly changing landscapes of the urban fringe. I took the idea for this opening scene from the depiction of New York City in John Cassavetes's *Gloria* (1980), where paintings set to music provide a dramatic segue to aerial views of the city itself. Though my panoramic views of Mumbai had to make do with the tops of residential towers, I nonetheless sought to juxtapose ways of seeing or conceiving the city as a larger entity interspersed with everyday experiences. The first part of the film is focused on the use and meaning of water in the city where we encounter the power of water as a focus of anxiety for all but the wealthiest strata. In a telling observation, one of the interviewees, the anthropologist Arjun Appadurai, contrasts the "vertical city" of modernity, characterised by its hidden underground networks, with the "horizontal" or "infrastructure free" city of informal settlements, where everything is "fully available to the gaze". The film explores a series of specific encounters with water: slum dwellers explain their precarious access to municipal stand pipes and other sources; a local politician reveals the involvement of gangsters and organised crime on the urban fringe;

*fig.*02

*fig.*03

and environmental activists describe the intricate set of structural and social barriers affecting access to water. In the second part of the film, the emphasis shifts to
some of the wider dilemmas facing the city: the ability of engineers to meet future
needs in what the UN predicts will be the largest city in the world; the intensify-
ing threat of flooding; and pressures to adapt urban planning and infrastructure
provision to new political constellations associated with the global economy. The
premise of a water crisis, as the educationist Nirupa Bhangar explains, is true but
it also provides a convenient pretext for the mooted privatisation of the city's water supply system or other forced 'modernisations' that may serve to worsen an
already serious situation.

From the outset I wanted to ensure that the film was a genuine collaboration
between London and Mumbai. An indispensable element in the production process
was our connection with the Mumbai–based organisation PUKAR – Partners for
Urban Knowledge and Action Research – a grassroots research collective that operates independently from the formal university sector though it benefits from an
international network of scholars, activists and artists.[4] A critical feature of the
post-production phase was my decision to bring the key members of our Mumbai
team to London and ensure that the international collaboration extended to the
final stages of the project. I wanted to avoid a scenario where material is simply
extracted from its local context and then handled by a post-production team unfamiliar with the wider rationale of the project.

In December 2007, almost exactly one year after we completed the shooting,
the film was given a public premiere at the Max Mueller Bhavan in downtown
Mumbai, followed by an uptown screening at the Rachana Sansad Academy of
Architecture a couple of days later. These mostly local audiences, including some
of our interviewees, provided an opportunity for me to see whether the film had
achieved its aims. The screenings were followed by question and answer sessions
that focused very intensely on both the content and purpose of the film. An important criticism raised by one of the interviewees after seeing the film was that I
did not state clearly what the city should do in order to tackle its water and sanitation crisis. My response, which I still believe, is that it is not appropriate for a
London-based academic or filmmaker to present a set of prescriptions for a city in
which there is no shortage of ideas or expertise. There is in any case a plethora of
'developmentalist' commentaries on the future of Mumbai that actually offer very
little insight into the life in the city or simply replicate stereotypical conceptions
of cities in the global South. On one occasion, for example, we stopped by the

heavily polluted Mahim Creek and noticed a huddled group of figures in the distance sitting under tarpaulin sheeting between two giant water pipes. The dramatic setting seemed reminiscent of a Sebastião Salgado composition and we tentatively approached them to ask if we could have permission to film, only to discover that they were not a displaced family at all but a maintenance crew from the municipal water department who were more than happy to be interviewed.

BIOGRAPHY

Matthew Gandy is Professor of Geography at University College London and Director of the UCL Urban Laboratory.

*fig.*01: Street Scene, 2002
Nearly 80% of Mumbai households live in a single room with intense competition over space and resources. Mumbai is a complex patchwork of Hindu, Muslim, Christian, Jainist, Buddhist, Zoroastrian and other religious practices intersected by regional, class and caste-based forms of social differentiation.

*fig.*02: Banganga Tank, 2002
Modern means of storing and distributing water in the city are juxtaposed with complex patterns of water use originating in the pre-colonial era. A number of so-called 'tanks' – elaborate bodies of water surrounded by stone steps – still exist in the city but these are now mainly used for recreation or ceremonial bathing.

*fig.*03: Water Pipes, Mahim, 2002
The city is dissected by giant water pipes often passing through slum settlements with little or no access to municipal supplies. These pipes are used as pedestrian walkways by the poor.

Previous page: Cinema, 2002
A distinctive feature of Mumbai is its role as a stage for an exuberant cinematic culture reflected not only through the economic significance of Bollywood but also by the enduring relationship between cinema and popular culture.

All photos: MATTHEW GANDY

1. For further details of water politics in Mumbai, see Matthew Gandy, 'Landscapes of disaster: water, poverty and urban fragmentation in Mumbai', *Environment and Planning A* 40 (1), 2008, pp. 108-30.
2. *Liquid City*, 2007, UK/India, 30 minutes, English, Hindi and Marathi with English subtitles, directed and produced by Matthew Gandy, with assistant director: Savitri Medhatul; camera: Krystallia Kamvasinou; editors: Savitri Medhatul and Krystallia Kamvasinou; sound designer: Amala Popuri; research and production coordinator: Andrew Harris; and, assistant producer: Johan Andersson. Copies of the film may be obtained from the director or from the UCL Urban Laboratory www.ucl.ac.uk/urbanlab
3. The film was funded by the UK Arts and Humanities Research Council and is one of the first projects to be completed at the newly created UCL Urban Laboratory. A version of this essay appears in the journal *Cultural Geographies*.
4. Other Mumbai-based NGOs that played a critical role in the film were SPARC (Society for Promotion of Area Resource Centres), CRIT (Collective Research Initiatives Trust) and VAK (Vikas Adhyayan Kendra).

Paradoxical Frogs

PHIL GUSACK

I will not cease from Mental Fight,
Nor shall my sword sleep in my hand,
Till we have built Jerusalem,
In England's green & pleasant Land.

'Jerusalem', William Blake, 1804

Hurray for Dan Cruikshank! Thanks to his tireless explorations, we can marvel at lost cities such as the Aztec Tenochtitlan and Harappa in the Indus Valley. Despite a separation of 3,000 years and 12,000 miles, these are cities of rectilinear urban blocks with engineered water supply and sewage systems.

Engravings of medieval European cities[1] remind us that they were more often shaped by the geometry of defence, not public health. In Europe these priorities surfaced in 19TH-century Paris once it was clear that the threat to civil life was no longer from besieging armies, but from its own proletariat, one that had a track record in revolution. Haussmann's Parisian boulevards created great perspectives of urban grandeur but they are there, like firebreaks in forests, to stop trouble getting out of control.[2]

By 1851, Britain was displaying its manufacturing power in the Great Exhibition in Paxton's visionary Crystal Palace, clad in 293,000 prefabricated glass panels. At the time, over two million people worked on the land, but even more now worked on the coalfields, in textile mills, and in workshops and factories.

TABLE 1: Selected industry employment data 1851-1951[3]

	1851	1901	1921	1951
COAL MINING	383,000	931,000	1,240,000	675,000
METAL BASHING	536,000	1,485,000	2,125,000	2,157,000
TEXTILES	1,300,000	1,352,000	1,110,000	633,000
RAILWAYS	29,000	320,000	318,500	318,000
AGRICULTURE	2,017,000	1,485,000	1,440,000	1,219,000
TOTAL IN WORK	9,377,000	16,299,000	19,355,000	22,610,000
GB POPULATION	20,800,000	37,000,000	42,000,000	48,000,000

Between 1700 and 1800 the British population grew by four million, but from 1801 to 1851 it grew by eight million. The 1851 census found that half of the population now lived in urban areas. Urban Britain expanded around its industrial and transport hubs, its towns and cities shaped pragmatically by local topography. The growing millions in the industrial workforce crowded into factory housing and lodgings within earshot of factory hooters.

TABLE 2: People per dwelling 1801-1951[4]

	ENGLISH POPULATION (MILLIONS)	ENGLISH DWELLINGS (MILLIONS)	PEOPLE PER DWELLING
1700	4	–	–
1801	8	1.5	5.33
1851	16.75	3.2	5.23
1901	30	6.3	4.76
1951	41	11.6	3.53

It took 100 years of reform, scientific advances, one great depression and two world wars to shift the balance of political power before the ratio of occupants to dwelling was significantly reduced. Life was not just tough, it was also short.

TABLE 3: Human life expectancy data, combined male + female estimated averages[5]

NEANDERTHAL	20
BRONZE AGE	18
CLASSICAL GREECE	20-30
CLASSICAL ROME	20-30
MEDIEVAL BRITAIN	20-30
EARLY 20TH CENTURY	30-40

In 1837 the British national average was only 38 years. In 1840, in the Whitechapel district of London, it was 45 years for the upper class, 27 for tradesmen and 22 for labourers and servants. Recent analysis now attributes 50% of all deaths in cities during that period to infectious diseases. However, as nutrition improved, reforms were enacted and medical science advanced, life expectancy increased, and by 1901 it was 48 years.

Key ideas about how disease spreads can be pinpointed to 1854. In London, John Snow had traced an outbreak of cholera to a contaminated water pump in Soho, and in the Crimea, Florence Nightingale discovered that most casualties did not die from wounds but from various infectious diseases. Their research put the new science of epidemiology – the geography of disease – on the map, and Nightingale not only fixed space (between patients), ventilation, light and hygiene as the basis of future nursing practice and hospital design, but also injected a shot of medical evidence into the Victorian agenda of moral and physical rectitude.

Conditions in Victorian Britain inspired every kind of political, social and urban theory. For example, Marx and Engels published the *Communist Manifesto* in 1848, and James Silk Buckingham, an adventurer cum Member of Parliament for Sheffield, published *The Model Town Plan of Victoria* in 1849, he said, "to avoid the evils of communism".[6] The plan for Victoria was a series of precisely dimensioned concentric square rings of buildings. The elite lived around the centre and the workers round the edge because the various farms and factories that sustained them were some distance away. The text ticked all the boxes anyone could think of at the time: breezy greens, pedestrian arcades, clean water, public bathhouses and indoor toilets, and there were no blind spots or alleyways, hence no crime or brothels. In the chaotic British urban landscape at that time, the graphic impact of Buckingham's antidote to communism was new, shocking and totalitarian.

The first signs of a real change in thinking came 40 years later with the publication of *To-morrow: A Peaceful Path to Real Reform*, Sir Ebenezer Howard's Garden City manifesto.[7] Howard drew some elements from Victoria but, more importantly, he also knew what to leave out. Out went Buckingham's iron construction and flat roofs. In came "air and space, wood and water, schools and churches, shrubberies and gardens, around pretty self contained cottages in a group neither too large to deprive it of country character, nor too small to diminish the probabilities of social intercourse." The green and pleasant land at last.

In its organisation, however, it segregates anything obviously incompatible with cottage life. Unlike the so-called utopian townships (Saltaire, Port Sunlight, Bourneville), which wrap workers' housing around their factories, everyone still walked to work, as they would have in the towns they had left behind – cottage life turned them into commuters.

Without Howard himself, the equation would simply have been: Garden Cities = suburbs + green belts. But Howard moved forward. In two years he (1) founded the Garden City Association (later renamed the Town and Country Planning Association that is still going), (2) republished his book with a catchier title, *Garden Cities of Tomorrow*, (3) raised £20,000 and (4) registered the Garden City Pioneer Company Limited to start work on Letchworth. Then he (5) held a masterplan competition, which was won by Parker and Unwin in 1903, (6) purchased 1,260 acres, (7) launched the town design effort for 30,000 people, (8) held the Cheap Cottages Exhibitions in 1905 and 1907 (60,000 visitors), and (9) started construction in 1908.

All this spin worked. Letchworth attracted industry, although not industry as the Victorians knew it. It seems entirely appropriate that the first manufacturer to move to the town encircled by a (green) belt was the Spirella Corset Company. Work on its central Letchworth site began in 1912. With an Arts and Crafts skin stretched over an unyielding concrete frame, it proved that Garden Cities could impose strict stylistic discipline to deal with deviation from the original ideas.

Most visitors to Hampstead Garden Suburb today, and even many of its residents, may be unaware that its architect, Sir Raymond Unwin, had been a leading member of William Morris's Socialist League, and that it was conceived as Letchworth Mark II. Experts continue to examine the differences between them to decide which one is truer to the Garden City ideal. But it was more the fact that Unwin had both in his portfolio that led to his lead role in drawing up the government's housing design standards published in the 1917 Tudor Walters Report.

The extent of unplanned urban expansion – sprawl – is clear in Department of Communities and Local Government historical data. Over 4.2 million new homes were built between 1921 and 1951, despite the Depression, war damage and post-war material shortages. This included over 160,000 'prefabs', most of which were in use decades after their designed life of 10 years.[8]

It meant that even though one million homes had been destroyed or damaged in London during the war, by July 1948 – the official start of the Welfare State – about a third of English homes were actually no more than 25 years old! The flip side was that over 60% of the stock pre-dating the Tudor Walters Report did not have their own indoor bathrooms and toilets. Welfare State or not, post-war government would have to get to grips with growth.

Clement Attlee's 1945 landslide election victory was a mandate for fast action. The task of masterminding Britain's Town and Country Planning system, with land use classification, local planning, building control and compulsory purchase powers – all of which required considerable cunning and bravado – was given to Hugh Dalton, fresh from his wartime role as the head of the Special Operations Executive set up to sabotage the Third Reich. Ironically, the best view of Britain's industrial and suburban sprawl came from thousands of Luftwaffe aerial photographs.

In the 1945 election campaign, Aneurin Bevan told the crowds: "We have been the dreamers, we have been the sufferers, now we are the builders. We enter this campaign at this general election, not merely to get rid of the Tory majority. We want the complete political extinction of the Tory Party!"

Attlee took him at his word. He put him in charge of post-war housing and in charge of post-war health services. His record as builder – over 425,000 new homes in 1946-48 – and as sufferer – launching the National Health Service (NHS) – overshadow his failure with the extinction of the Tory Party. But it is still on every dreamer's *to do* list.

Bevan took charge of over 250,000 nurses, consultants and hospital workers. He got 480,000 beds in 2,700 hospitals of all shapes and sizes: venerable teaching hospitals, municipal infirmaries, tuberculosis sanatoria, fever hospitals and mental asylums, many teetering on the edge of bankruptcy. Not surprisingly, in 1939, a major survey by the Nuffield Provincial Hospitals Trust with Ministry of Health support – not just the first survey but still the *only* survey – found: (1) inadequate accommodation, (2) shortage and mal-distribution of consultants and specialists, and (3) lack of co-ordination.

Bevan wanted to take charge of the 19,000 general practitioners (GPs, family doctors) too. In the 1930s, around 14 million employed people were entitled to free treatment. A GP who treated 1,000 insured patients would receive £400-500 a year. Most depended on wealthier private patients and many did what they could to care for the poor who might have five shillings on their mantelpiece for the doctor. Many GPs wanted to join the NHS as salaried employees. Others did not. After lots of political infighting within the British Medical Association (BMA) and within Attlee's cabinet and in Parliament, the NHS was launched in July 1948 (one week after the Town and Country Planning system), free to all, 'from cradle to grave', with GPs participating as independent contractors as they still do.

> *While history is tellin' you*
> *The same old thing*
> *This is tomorrow callin'*
> *Y'all come on in.*

'This is Tomorrow', Bryan Ferry, 1977

Hurray for Reyner Banham! Thanks to his tireless exploration of the modern, the rest of us can look back to the struggle between the ideologies of the left within the London County Council's post-war housing architects.[9] Those closest to Moscow, embarrassed by Stalin's prohibition of the International Style, turned to Swedish design, like Ryvita and Saabs – different but not really new.

The majority of other architects who wanted to make their mark in post-war Britain were lured by three visionaries. Frank Lloyd Wright, like Gary Cooper who played him in *The Fountainhead*, was clearly only at home on the range. Wright had his own 'high noons' too. Mies van der Rohe, born again in Chicago after failing to get Hitler to drop Speer, had propelled the glass box into every architect's mind's eye but, in the context of post-war austerity, every architect in Britain knew this was only ever going to work on special occasions. Le Corbusier had political baggage too. In 1934 he had lectured in Rome at Mussolini's personal invitation. Today it is clear that churning out a back catalogue of urban fantasies works as a career strategy if the drawings are edgy and the volumes are XXL!

Young British hopefuls, who favoured paté on baguette over herring on Ryvita, took Corbusier's texts with a grain of *sel de mer*. They could cherry-pick the 1,700 pages of Corbusier's *Oeuvre Complet*, turn a blind eye to the issues of the destruction of existing communities, and get Corbusier's ingenious scissor-sectioned (cross-ventilated) deck-access (streets in the air) diagrams to work as well in Britain as the Unité d'Habitation in Marseilles. They recognised that raising blocks up a storey on *piloti* would instantly dramatise their elevations (the proteins in the double helix of architectural evolution). Better still, the promise of cheap concrete and continuous greenery meant it would make it easier to convince hesitant borough councillors and housing managers that this was the best way to build 'Tomorrow'.

The NHS arrived just in time to give 'Tomorrow' a fighting chance. With a budget of £280 million, its front line of 16,800 GPs promised better care for everyone. The fact that GPs were thinner on the ground in poorer areas (1,500 patients per GP in Harrogate but 3,500 per GP in Wakefield) was a problem that, it was assumed, would be dealt with in time. Besides which, the new antibiotics and vaccinations led to a huge drop in deaths from infectious diseases such as diphtheria and tuberculosis (over 20,000 in 1948 but under 5,000 in 1958).[10]

Dramatic results reinforced NHS authority and autonomy. It projected itself into the public eye as a centre of scientific prowess, military dedication and Church of England virtue. And while everyone in it knew they were in it to serve the public, they also knew that the public they served was, in essence, a captive market.

The early success of the NHS was good news for local authorities. It relieved them of the prime responsibility in planning and provision of health services. If drugs could prevent or cure diseases, and if GPs and hospital care was free, local authorities could take more risks in the way they tackled housing. It cleared the way for prefabricated point blocks – cheap, but anything but cheerful.

In the years 1948-68, the population grew by five million, but five million new homes were added to total housing stock. The average number of occupants in a household dropped from 3.6 to 2.8. The process of building 'Tomorrow' was controversial. The chattering classes derided it for the same reason they derided garlic, Lambrettas and immigrants. And when Willmott and Young asked them, the working class complained that the old neighbourhoods had been destroyed.[11]

On 16 May 1968, a gas leak exploded in Ronan Point,[12] a brand-new 23-storey tower block built by Taylor Woodrow Anglian in West Ham, East London. It blew out a concrete wall panel and a number of flats collapsed. Four people were killed. It would be handy to pose this as council housing's 9/11 but, astonishingly, Ronan Point was repaired, re-occupied and used for another 18 years. What it really showed was how governments could slam the door on communities and lock themselves in denial.

The four governments in these 18 years – Harold Wilson's (Labour), Edward Heath's (Tory), James Callaghan's (Labour) and Margaret Thatcher's (Tory) – showed that denial was not exclusive to one party. Nor is it easy to review the

243

first 40 years of healthcare initiatives and conclude that Labour did a better job than the Tories. One reason, according to Professor Raymond Moss, who set up the Medical Architecture Research Unit[13] in 1969, is that: "Hospital building programmes are like battleships – they take forever to stop."

Like battleships, NHS hospitals have also always taken years to plan, design and build. In the early 1970s, when the goal was to replace old hospitals with 70 huge 1,000-bed district general hospitals (DGH), the then Department of Health and Social Security (DHSS) embarked on a massive centrally piloted programme to standardise plans so that each hospital could be planned and Treasury-approved in less than five years – the life-span of a government, assuming all went well.[14]

Things did not go well. The 1973 Yom Kippur war and a national coal miners' strike put paid to the 70-DGH goal and forced DHSS architects to find new ways to deploy their systems and standards under Treasury scrutiny, much as youths on council estates were policed under the suss laws.

Margaret Thatcher, however, took denial where no man had gone before: "There is no such thing as society!" Her solution to the problems of council housing maintenance costs was the introduction of the 'right to buy' (at discount), the proceeds going to the Treasury not the boroughs. Was the simultaneous high unemployment, in which many received big enough redundancy payoffs to make down payments on their council flats, entirely circumstantial?

Normal circumstances in many inner cities included poverty, unemployment and strong-arm policing. Riots in Brixton in 1980 and Liverpool 8 in 1981 led to enquiries and brought the issue of institutional racism in the police force into the open. Thatcher's Tarzan – Michael Heseltine – did a three-week safari in Liverpool. Later he told the *Guardian:* "Alone, every night ... I would stand with a glass of wine, looking out at the magnificent view over the river, and ask myself what had gone wrong for this great English city."

Town and Country Planning had been in the firing line for over a decade, and Paul Barker had published an inspirational critique, 'Non-Plan' (co-written with planning guru Peter Hall, Reyner Banham and Cedric Price) in *New Society* in 1969.[15] Heseltine returned from Liverpool to set up special 'development corporations' for Merseyside and London Docklands. Liverpool got a branch of the Tate and London got Canary Wharf, and Britain got a new idea: regeneration, i.e. development with a frothy topping.

Thatcher retreated from wholesale privatisation of the NHS but split Social Security away from Health and disbanded the Architects Division who were told that if they wanted to design hospitals so much they were free to try their luck in

Creative Destruction

the private sector. What else could they expect from someone who had famously said: "Cut your own throats if you want to, but don't ask me for a bandage!"

Eleven years on, the Blair-Brown project is trying to resuscitate 'Tomorrow', not as dreamers and builders but as management consultants. They believe that the quality of British life can only be improved by bringing clip-boards and calculators to bear on the way that they spend over £600 billion a year. If they dream, they dream of evidence that every effect can be traced, like the cholera in Soho, to a single source and then sterilised.

Their housing policy, however, follows the rule of predictive maintenance: 'If it ain't broke, don't fix it.' Between the 'right to buy' in 1980 and Blair's victory in 1997, total housing stock rose by 2.6 million but the total rented by local authorities and charities fell by 753,000. In other words, owner-occupied and buy-to-let rose from roughly 70% to 80%. This was good news in a rising market. The average price paid by first-time buyers in the UK had doubled (£20,800-£43,650); but, since 1997, it has risen by 350% to £153,100. The fact is, however, that housing output has remained flat, despite low interest rates. House builders blame the planning system and deny they drip-feed the market to boost demand.[16]

TABLE 4: Housing production 1993-2006, with new construction shown in the right-hand column[17]

	TOTAL STOCK	NEW BUILD
1992	151,000	155,100
1993	152,000	142,500
1994	166,000	147,700
1995	163,000	158,000
1996	154,000	154,600
1997	156,000	146,200
1998	149,000	149,600
1999	148,000	138,600
2000	132,000	141,400
2001	130,000	133,100
2002	144,000	129,900
2003	132,000	137,700
2004	155,000	144,000
2005	168,000	155,900
2006	185,000	163,400

Who, in 1997, could say housing was broke and needed fixing? Who, in 1997, could say the NHS did not need fixing? Despite the massive expansion of diagnostics and treatments, and the consequential huge increase in its workload, Thatcher kept annual NHS budgets slightly below its historical level, and her successor, John Major, cut them further still to 2.6% year-on-year. The NHS had grown to over one million staff, and roughly 45% of its hospitals were built before 1948. Since NHS rules dictated which hospitals GPs had to send their patients to, hospital management still worked with a captive market. So, in 1997, over one million GP patients had to wait at least three months to be admitted to hospital and 25% had to wait six months or more.

The Blair-Brown health dream is somehow to turn the NHS from a British Leyland into a Toyota. Two key parts of the scheme are: (1) turning the NHS into an internally competitive market, and (2) giving patients the right to choose which hospital they go to. The idea is a paradigm shift and it is far too early to see what will happen. To do this, they raised health spending to 7% (year-on-year increases) and introduced a raft of controversial performance targets. One result is that waiting lists have dropped by 50% and the median wait is now 4.3 weeks.

In 2000, Blair launched his '100 New Hospitals by 2010' plan.[18] Now the NHS is organised into 260 Hospital Trusts with 150,000 beds. It adds up to 24 million square metres of hospital stock. This sits on 7,500 hectares. Over 80 Trusts now generate some renewable electricity. Since 6,300 of the 7,500 hectares are not built on, the NHS has the space (if it adopts my suggestion) to erect 2,316, 44-metre high, 660-kilowatt-hour wind turbines. That would provide all the electricity that hospitals use today, at a cost of £1.2 billion. Think of this as one Dome and one Wembley, or four Hadidesque swimming pools, or about one eighth of what Britain spends at McDonalds.[19]

They have already spent over £30 billion on new hospitals, but more relevant is that, as a whole business, NHS hospitals have an annual turnover of over £50 billion. A typical new hospital has a turnover of £190-200 million. So has Arsenal FC. Their managers face the same challenges: (1) pay the mortgage, (2) pay the staff, (3) fill the seats and beds, (4) add value to the core business, and (5) build the brand.

A new hospital will spend around 15% of its turnover on its mortgage (debt service), fuel and cleaning. The rest goes on staff, equipment, drugs, food, laundry, etc. Obviously there is much more chance of increasing efficiency by concentrating on the 85% of turnover. For example, nurses on wards walk anything from 12-20 miles a shift! But the 100 New Hospitals plan has been completely compromised because Department of Health procurement still only deals with construction contract costs.

The dangers of this are more obvious in the 30-50% of hospitals procured through Private Finance Initiatives (PFI). This has drawn flak from academics, trade unions and parliamentarians, largely because of profiteering. In 'normal' design projects, every dreamer proposing innovation to help the sufferers has to outwit the builders. In PFI, the builders are boss, the dreamers become sufferers and innovation dies.

Three facts cannot be ignored: (1) the British way of planning and approving hospitals still focuses exclusively on compliance with standard templates from days gone by; (2) unlike office buildings and retail centres, hospitals are not designed as adaptable structures – growth, shrinkage and change are as difficult to cope with in 2008 as they were in 1948; and (3) nobody has ever bothered to think about the future uses of any healthcare buildings once their historically defined missions have been completed, i.e. after things change. There are no exit strategies.

The inconvenient truth is that the ratio of GPs to population has only improved at glacial rates – from 1:2000 to 1:1650 in 60 years. Most people still have to negotiate with aggressive receptionists in badly converted semi-detached houses before they can get NHS primary care. Even for the simplest procedures like blood tests, they still have to go to a hospital. And in hospital, they are still nursed in open wards, some of them mixed-sex! Caught out when this scandal hit the headlines, Patricia Hewitt (former head of research at Anderson Consulting), who rose through Blair's ranks to Secretary of State for Health, responded with this: "The Healthcare Commission's annual surveys show that most patients do indeed feel they have their privacy respected. They also confirm that being treated with respect and dignity as a whole is *more important than just being in single-sex accommodation*" (emphasis added).

What a smokescreen! The idea that patient surveys should define the quality of nursing care is as daft as using them to select surgical procedures. The NHS has to function as a business but must operate with science. Only politicians think they can fob the public off with opinion pimped up as evidence.

At the time of writing, everything we assumed about housing is going haywire. The dreamtime of rising house prices is now a £1.3 trillion debt nightmare! Would Ebenezer Howard say something about this? In fact, yes: his spiritual decedents, the Town and Country Planning Association (TCPA), have reported that the current government target of three million new homes by 2020 may well be 750,000 too low. Gideon Amos, chief executive of the TCPA, said: "The worrying implication of this report and its picture of a burgeoning older population is the spectre of rising overcrowding, homelessness and social exclusion."

Government will have to spend more on job seekers and fuel subsidies. It will have less to target on deprivation and inequality. This year, the best way out of deprivation – employment – just got harder to find. Harder times will force people at both ends of the income spectrum to make hard decisions that affect their health. (1) What will the people who are dumped from bankrupt builders and banks do about their private health insurance? That is a £5.5 billion a year industry that NHS die-hards prefer to ignore. (2) Will hard times make people healthier? Will it change lifestyles? The public spends £7.5 billion a year at McDonalds. How many will give up Big Macs to keep their PPP?

It helps me, makes me, work rest and play
I eat a deep-fried Mars Bar every day.

'Mars Bars', The Undertones, 1979 (re-released 2009)

Hurray for David Morrison! Thanks to his tireless explorations, the rest of us now know the deep-fried Mars Bar really does exist. Dr Morrison, a consultant in public health medicine with NHS Greater Glasgow, directed a survey of 500 chip shops in 2004 and found that deep-fried Mars Bars are available in 22% of them.

In May 2006, more research from Glasgow's Centre for Population Health suggested that housing, poverty and a family history of deprivation can also play a role in people's health. Men living in some parts of Glasgow can expect to die up to 10 years younger than the average for Scotland. Researchers hope the study will reveal why people from deprived areas age faster and die younger than those from affluent areas. They think it goes far beyond the 'usual suspects' of diet, smoking, drinking and lack of exercise.

Philip Hanlon, Professor of Public Health, said: "What we're doing here is discovering something about the biology of poverty." Analysis of data on English population, housing stock and life expectancy shows that life expectancy goes up as occupants per dwelling goes down.

In the context of TINAG's Medical City salon it is a good result as it appears to connect the physicality of the city and the physiology of mind and body.

TABLE 5: Declining people per dwelling and rising life expectancy – the evidence behind the argument[20]

	ENGLISH POPULATION (MILLIONS)	ENGLISH DWELLINGS (MILLIONS)	PEOPLE PER DWELLING	LIFESPAN
1700	4	–	–	–
1801	8	1.5	5.33	
1851	16.75	3.2	5.23	
1901	30.51	6.3	4.84	50
1911	33.64	7.25	4.64	53
1921	35.23	7.45	4.73	58
1931	37.36	8.8	4.25	61
1941	39.12	–	–	–
1951	41.16	11.67	3.53	69
1961	43.46	13.83	3.14	71
1971	46.01	6.07	2.86	72
1981	46.61	17.91	2.60	74
1991	47.87	19.67	2.43	76
2001	49.18	21.2	2.32	76

But it does not mean that people living alone can safely eat all the deep-fried Mars Bars they want. And Professor Hanlon's work only adds to the evidence that if you do eat loads of deep-fried Mars Bars you will endanger your kids too, just as junkies endanger theirs.

Emile Durkheim's research in the 1890s found that suicide in German towns was much higher than in the countryside.[21] In Britain today, the opposite is true, according to DEFRA, the Ministry of Optimism. But we still need more research. For example, suicide statistics are collected by local area but not by housing type. Similarly, MRSA is recorded by NHS Trusts but not correlated with hospital age, configuration or ventilation systems. It means we still do not really know if tower blocks drive more people to suicide than semi-detached houses, and we don't know if new hospitals are safer than old ones.

Sixty years ago, when the idea that the NHS would look after you 'from cradle to grave' was introduced, the unstated clause in the deal was 'as best we can, given the limits of our medical science'. In 1948, GPs traversed the social divides making house calls, and the common sense they freely dispensed was often more important than most medicines. Today the deal is different. GPs have contracted out of night and weekend services, and common sense is inescapable on every NHS pin board, magazine, TV channel and website.

The NHS deal is still 'cradle to grave', but politicians are now warning that, sooner or later, they will have to impose some sort of sanctions against smokers and the obese. Their argument is that such people force the NHS to spend more than a fair share on needless preventable diseases. It is more than an echo of Thatcher's 'don't ask me for a bandage!' Now that Britain sees itself as a faith and ethnically inclusive society, the new politically correct agenda is looking for new minorities to pin the blame on. They have done it before, banishing the insane to asylums. Will the obese be our next lepers? Everyone agrees that inequality in health care must be eradicated. I would like to define equality as socialism without brass bands, but it looks increasingly likely that health equality will depend on public conformity. From cradle to grave *if you behave*!

So what have frogs to do with this? In his deathbed essay, Britain's great 'historian of the immediate future', Reyner Banham, reflected that design was a 'black box' process, "but when [architecture] schools were under radical pressure in the early seventies, many students will have heard something which I personally heard at that time, the blunt directive: 'Don't bother with all that environmental stuff, just get on with the architecture!'"[22]

When I learned about the paradoxical frogs (*Pseudis paradoxa*) that live in Trinidad and Tobago (home of calypso, the love songs of paradox), it struck me that their unique property – that as they grow from tadpoles into frogs they shrink in size – is what happens to the ambitions of planners and architects: "Don't bother with all that environmental stuff, just get on with the architecture!"

BIOGRAPHY

Phil Gusack is an architect and widely published critic of the architecture of public health and the health of public architecture. (www.gusack.com)

* ACKNOWLEDGEMENTS: The author would like to thank Professor Raymond Moss MBE; Noel Whiteside, Professor of Comparative Public Policy, Warwick; Dr Geoffrey Rivett www.nhshistory.net; Dr Eva Katona MD MRC Psych; Simon Mallin, Creative Industries Regeneration consultant; Judy Abel, British Medical Association; Courtney Hoilett, Labour Statistics Team; Alan Cox, Dept of Communities and Local Government.

1. www.maps-charts.com/Prints_books_photos.htm
2. For more on Haussmann and on planning, see wikipedia.
3. Data from Noel Whiteside, Professor of Comparative Public Policy, Warwick University, UK.
4. Census data, England and Wales; housing stock data, Department of Communities and Local Government, UK.
5. Wikipedia.
6. James Silk Buckingham, *National Evils and Practical Remedies, with The Plan of a Model town* (London: Peter Jackson, Late Fisher, Son, & Co., 1849) www.library.cornell.edu/Reps/DOCS/buckham.htm
7. www.library.cornell.edu/Reps/DOCS/howard.htm
8. For more on prefabs, see www.ideal-homes.org.uk/index1a.html
9. Reyner Banham, *The New Brutalism: Ethic or aesthetic?* (London: Architectural Press, 1966).
10. Statistics and information from the British Medical Association.
11. Michael Young and Peter Willmott, *Family and Kinship in East London* (London: Institute of Community Studies, 1957, then Pelican, 1962).
12. See www.open2.net/modernity/3_13.htm
13. The Medical Architecture Research Unit (MARU) was originally established at the Northern Polytechnic, Holloway Road, London, by Professor Raymond Moss MBE.
14. nuffieldtrust.org.uk/.../download.asp?f=/.../50_years_of_ideas.pdf
15. 'Non-Plan: an experiment in freedom' by Paul Barker, Reyner Banham, Peter Hall and Cedric Price, *New Society*, 20 March 1969.
16. Housing stock data from Department of Communities and Local Government; house prices data from the Nationwide Building Society.
17. Data from Department of Communities and Local Government, UK.
18. *NHS Plan: a plan for investment, a plan for reform* was published by the Department of Health, 1 July 2000.
19. All statistics about hospital buildings and grounds are from the Department of Health annual Health Estate and Facilities surveys.
20. Data compiled by Phil Gusack, 2008.
21. Emile Durkheim, *Suicide*, first published in 1897.
22. Reyner Banham, 'A Black Box: The Secret Profession of Architecture', in M. Banham *et al.* (eds), *A Critic Writes* (Berkeley: University of California Press, 1997).

Precarities and Dissensualities

Arts, Policy and Space on the Eve of an Election

SUKHDEV SANDHU

Brightly-coloured, funkily-designed, estate-agent literature bigging-up chunklets of economically needy London boroughs for the edgy cool and dynamic live-work spaces they offer. Supersized photographs of YBA artists fringed by gobbets of freedom-invoking Beat poetry draped across the exteriors of lavish retail developments on the sites of old neighbourhood markets. Public spaces across the capital, battered but resilient mesh-works of hairdressers, corner stores and independent traders, buffed up and rezoned into toney cultural quarters.

In recent years, it's been hard to miss the often-predatory ways in which policymakers and big business have sought to use the lexicons and prestige of art in order to rebrand and engineer contemporary London. What's more, local authorities, always on the lookout for opportunities to attract tourist revenue, increasingly support cultural events that purport to address the needs of minority or historically embattled groups (with sexuality, Gay Pride parades; with ethnicity, Chinese New Year festivals and Diwali; with anti-racism, the RISE festival).

How odd. Up until recently, artists were seen as metropolitan flotsam and jetsam. They represented a ragged and amorphous demographic, a puzzlingly disaggregated sector whose members sported neither blue nor white collars, a negligible bunch of idlers and dreamers who had little to contribute to serious debates about social or economic life within the capital. They were, at best, footnotes to the real story of urban development.

Things have changed. As the city's manufacturing and maritime past fades into history, invoked mainly by bespoke developers hoping to peddle a muzzy, nostalgia-tinged form of industrial aesthetics to hike up the value of old garment workshops and riverside warehouses, there is a growing desire to use art and artists as examples of knowledge-economy entrepreneurialism.

Policymakers view them as highly motivated and ambitious networkers who make relatively few demands on public funds; tangible assets generating value for neglected or abandoned parts of the capital; flexible itinerants whose vibe-seeking migration to a new postcode has the potential to presage speculation of a loftier, financial kind.

This is a global phenomenon of course. It's been described and celebrated by the likes of Richard Florida in *The Rise of the Creative Class – And How It's Transforming Work, Leisure, Community, And Everyday Life* (2002) and Elizabeth Currid in *The Warhol Economy: How Fashion, Art, and Music Drive New York* (2007). Florida has even established ranking systems allowing cities to be rated according to a 'Gay index' or a 'Bohemian index', metrics he believes will allow policymakers to foster the correct environments for attracting and retaining that class of web designers, curators, DJs and fashion students that apparently holds the key to urban prosperity.

It's a perspective that was rearticulated by The Work Foundation's 2007 report 'Staying Ahead: The Economic Performance of the UK's Creative Industries' whose preface was written by the then-Secretary of State for Culture, Media and Sport, Tessa Jowell. And it's a perspective, full of elisions and blind spots, that was deconstructed by Andy Pratt from the London School of Economics in his opening contribution to Cultural City: How Arts Policies Influence Space, a salon organised by This is Not A Gateway.

Far from seeing the growth of the cultural sector, or indeed its dominant working practices, as a desirable formula for the rest of the capital's economy, Pratt suggested that the election of the Labour Party in 1997 ushered in an era when the political classes within Britain began to valorise artists precisely because their work patterns were in sync with the forms of precariousness and insecurity that neo-liberal economists had inflicted on other industries since the early 1980s.

Seen in this light, the romantic vision of the artist as free, independent and not subject to the work vs leisure division faced by grafters and toilers in the 'straight' world makes him or her a model worker. For, typically, artists work at home or in studios which aren't covered by health and safety regulations; they have irregular but also long hours that erode the difference between day and night; they don't belong to unions; are accustomed to a system of 'free labour' where, because of the number of people trying to break into the art world and the challenges involved in monetising such an abstract, speculative sphere, a lot of services are unpaid. In short, the 'space of art' is a concept that, far from being shorthand for urban enclaves dotted with cafés, vintage-clothes stores and new galleries, refers to the topography of modern labour, one governed by contingency, illegality, casualisation and compulsory flexibility.

According to Pratt, any government or state body that wishes to engage with contemporary arts policy in serious, constructive fashion needs to think about its production as much as its consumption. It's no good talking up the role of art as an engine for personal expansion, cultural citizenship or social cohesion if the means by which it is incubated and created rely so heavily on systems of exploitation (and self-exploitation).

Currently, access to the arts is treated as a matter of finding discourses, curatorial strategies and pricing mechanisms that attract rather than intimidate socially disadvantaged groups. But, as the cost of living and working in the city has shot up in recent years, entry-level jobs in the arts sector, most of which pay a pittance at best, are serious options only for those who can afford to donate their labour freely. Even internships, long seen as a quick-fix way of introducing under-represented people into work environments, are increasingly only of use to those who have gone to university and already have cultural capital and social networks on which they can draw. Arts policies designed to address questions of diversity and social inclusion need to tackle class at least as much as race and gender.

The presence at the salon of Helen Burrows, a policy researcher for the Conservative Party, made this topic especially timely. As she herself acknowledged, the arts world tends to skew Left. As she didn't say, there are good reasons why it has done so with particular passion since the 1980s. Margaret Thatcher (who chose 'How Much Is That Doggie In the Window?' as one of her Desert Island Discs) famously claimed, "There is no such thing as society, only individuals."

Norman Tebbit, the Chairman of her Party (who said he believed there was no difference between a Titian painting and a Page-3 pin-up), urged unemployed people (though not would-be immigrants) to get on their bikes rather than bemoan the dismantling of industry in their home cities. For the last three decades, Tories, like their Republican counterparts across the Atlantic, have championed Samuel Smiles-style individualism. Instinctively hostile to experimentalism and non-instrumentalism (as evidenced by their efforts to introduce greater quantification into higher education and art schools – a move continued by New Labour), they also dismantled the Greater London Council whose commitment to subaltern and minority voices they vilified as Loony Left-ism.

Burrows spent much of her twenties working as a freelance photographer and later for the Ministry of Sound. She stressed she was not a member of the Conservative

Party, and claimed that, when it came to the arts, there was very little ideological difference between Labour and the Tories. Asked to talk about texts that had influenced her thinking on the relationship between arts policies and space, she mentioned Lewis Hyde's *The Gift* (1979), an idiosyncratic synthesis of anthropology, sociology and literary criticism that explores the nature of creativity in capitalist society.

Her summary of the book – that it deals with the challenges creative people face in order to survive; that it argues art is "beyond the market" – didn't quite capture the extent to which Hyde regards the market economy as the enemy of art. Nor did it emphasise sufficiently Hyde's belief in the spiritual, almost erotic power of gift exchange (as opposed to that of market transactions); the former, he believed, established a link with a community, while the latter was extricated within the values and social relations of commodity capitalism.

Burrows was a thoughtful speaker, and it was good to hear her assert that governments should be prepared to invest in forward-thinking institutions while, at the same time, appreciating that eight out of ten of their projects would likely fail. Still, it's not being unduly cynical to speculate about the implications of a future Conservative culture department drawing on *The Gift* for its philosophic underpinning. Undue emphasis on the supra-market qualities of art runs the risk of treating it as a neo-Romantic, transcendental sphere; or, as Andy Pratt had suggested, neglecting the extent to which, for good or for bad, the arts are a deeply embedded part of the political economy, and need just as much sympathetic understanding and long-term investment as other industries.

Perhaps the most disappointing part of Burrows' presentation, especially in light of comments she made about her belief in the importance of grassroots and ground-up experience, was her claim that the single most important factor in making the arts so successful in modern-day Britain was the introduction of the National Lottery by John Major's Conservative government. Leaving aside the difficulty of gauging that success, such top-down initiatives can hardly be said to explain the transformations (for good or for bad) in the East End of London, a place where Burrows lives and home to Rich Mix, the culture centre whose complex institutional history served as a case study for the contributions of many of the salon panellists.

More significant by far were the concerted actions taken by a generation of young Bangladeshis, alongside a clutch of left-wing groups, to tackle the British National Party thugs who used to make life miserable for local inhabitants until the 1990s. It was their bravery, day after day, in kicking out racists that made the likes of Brick Lane, Bethnal Green and Hoxton feel safe for outsiders and would-be artists to move to. It was their resolve, now clearly forgotten by the amnesia-plagued hipsters who benefited from it, that created the preconditions for the 'gritty', 'edgy' playgrounds across which they circulate.

The shifting demographics of London, in part caused by new waves of immigration, and property-boom inflation, and their knock-on effects on local populations, was an issue that cropped up in the contributions to the salon of John Pandit of Asian Dub Foundation. He entered music through anti-racist politics and community activism in the early 1980s, putting much of his energy, even after the formation and success of his band, into educational and workshop initiatives designed to help disadvantaged youths many of whom came from Bangladeshi backgrounds.

He suggested that by the time funding bodies finally made up their minds and decided to fund a centre in the East End that could speak to the educational and cultural needs of 'the local community', the nature of and dynamics within that community had morphed. Poverty still exists, levels of inequality are still very high, but other social groups – artists, lawyers from the ever-encroaching City, Polish migrants, middle-class refugees from Islington – are also part of the new picture. What's more, as Pandit pointed out, the Bangladeshi youths whom he used to train have turned in greater numbers to drugs, gangs and the politics of a particularly rigid strain of Islam.

In this changing context, can an organisation, especially one the size of Rich Mix, accommodate and adapt to the ever-mutating communities to whom they were designed to cater? How useful even is the idea of 'community' – freighted as it is with assumptions about a broadly shared critique of local issues, as well as a vision of and commitment to an ameliorated future? Might 'neighbourhood', a term that is at least as spatial as 'community', and possibly less pregnant with unhelpful ethical connotations, be a better category for policymakers to work with and around? How can arts organisations that often develop crookedly and unevenly over the course of many years, dealing in the process with an ever-changing roll-call of bureaucrats and cultural gatekeepers, cleave to their original goals *and* respond to the transformed landscapes they encounter when they finally get up and running? Clearly, any theory of urban space has to be a theory of, or at least be informed by an understanding of, time.

If the relationship between art and community requires more supple and clear-eyed conceptualisation than is currently the norm (too many organisations perceive 'social inclusion' as an add-on, a matter of tacking a couple of ethnic members onto their trustee boards, screening a few ethnic films, commissioning graffiti or mural projects; too many also talk, in the language of Christian missionaries, of bringing their work 'to the community'), it's equally important to be alert to the reductive ways in which the word 'culture' gets bandied about. Far too often it's spoken of as an artefact, a product, something to be offered to the masses. Too rarely is there an acknowledgement of culture as encompassing a way of life, what Raymond Williams called "structures of feeling".

The result is that arts policymakers, in speaking up for the need for new spaces within cities, imply that the people whose cultural poverty or limited cultural access they are trying to redress didn't already have spaces that they'd established for themselves. These spaces might be in parks, at churches, at fast-food restaurants. They might be perambulatory spaces carved out over long periods both inside and outside particular neighbourhoods. By contrast, specially customised quarters or buildings, meticulously conceived though they may be, represent a monumentality that is just as off-putting as a Victorian statue (I'm reminded of the architectural consultant to the Rich Mix who boasted that the building represented "a piece of the West End coming to the East End"). There is an ethics of scale and of texture, and of speed – both real and perceived – to which politicians and consultants need to be better attuned. This was touched upon by Sonia Mehta, a creative industries consultant with a background of working in social justice and anti-racist groups, who likened arts centres in deprived areas to gated communities, embodiments of a gentrification they were unable fully to perceive let alone work against.

A more finessed understanding of the way in which social groups fashion themselves would involve getting to grips with the role technology plays in their lives. The digital sphere, and the free software and applications available there (or available to be hacked and stolen from there), offers interfaces, platforms and networking tools rich with a potential unimaginable a decade ago. Users can talk to each other, access otherwise unaffordable information, participate in a huge range of 'communities' that speak equally to their 'real' and speculative identities. They can learn to create music, self-publish, see themselves represented on YouTube. They can seek to intensify local subjectivities, but they can also sever themselves from their surroundings. And all without leaving their bedrooms.

The internet is not a panacea, and not everyone has 24/7 access to it, but just as its unstoppable rise has had a huge impact for professionals in the music, journalism and broadcasting industries, it will also pose difficult questions for policymakers attempting to conceptualise and develop best-practice models about the relationship between space and culture. Indeed, one of the most intriguing discussions at the salon involved Tony Nwachukwu and Gavin Alexander, musicians responsible for CDR, an on-line platform for producers, artists and club-music fans to discuss and offer feedback to record producers who had submitted tracks that were still works in progress.

This commitment to collaboration chimed with their belief in the need to foster platforms that promoted creative processes rather than mere consumption. It also reflected their desire to go beyond Left/Right binaries (New Labour, in their eyes, having implemented funding cuts that an incoming Conservative Party will continue), and to develop business models that, by moving beyond the public of 'the public sector', have the potential to give rise to especially innovative projects.

The economist Paul Romer famously declared: "A crisis is a terrible thing to waste." A sense of crisis is indeed prevalent throughout our society. It's viral. It's meteorological. Economic: some financial analysts fret that the collateral damage from the current recession might last for decades. And it's political: the country is on the brink of electing a Conservative Party that has next-to-no track record on caring for art or contemplating space in anything other than property/'an Englishman's home is his castle' terms.

The current Mayor of London came to power on the basis of targeting voters living in the suburbs, men and women with little knowledge of or perhaps even interest in the kinds of social problems, demographic admixtures and motile energies that are second nature to inner-city Londoners. That sense of multiplicity, though it can oftentimes be fractious and challenging, is what has always made the capital a magnet.

This city is a series of overlapping and competing stories. It's ragged and hybrid and sometimes internecine. It's a dissensus. Any attempt to sell a narrative that smoothes and planes its splintered surfaces in the name of continuity and a pasteurised community will be a betrayal.

The crisis of contemporary London is also an opportunity as much as it is a challenge: to look closely at and imagine anew the cultural landscapes we cherish and, in the face of coming attritions, to work to hold on to them.

BIOGRAPHY

Sukhdev Sandhu is Director of Asian/Pacific/American Studies at New York University and author of *Night Haunts* (Verso, 2007) and *London Calling: How Black and Asian Writers Imagined A City* (HarperCollins, 2003).

The Cleansing of Slumland

and the Return of the Bed Bug:
Pest Infestations and the Shaping of London

BEN CAMPKIN

How have the presence and threat of pest infestations shaped the processes
and discourses of urban change in London? In the following essay I explore the
history of urban vermin, aside from the great plagues, as an everyday focus for
housing reformers and as an unwanted and problematic form of urban nature,
linked to housing quality and density. The discussion centres on the slum clearance
and flat building programmes instigated by the St Pancras House Improvement Society (SPHIS) in Somers Town in the 1920s, and the strikingly experimental propaganda work that shaped this phase of radical urban transformation. This example
provides a historical perspective from which to consider urban pests in the early
21ST-century metropolis.

After laying out a conceptual framework I examine the specific histories of infestation and disinfestation, and the discourses around vermin, through three further
sections. The first of these introduces the work of the SPHIS and the slum clearance
campaigns initiated in the mid-1920s. Particular attention is given to the role of
infestations of the common bed bug, *Cimex lectularius*, as a focus for modernising
housing and hygiene reformers and urban commentators, and as an impetus for the
construction of modern flats. Following this, I turn to the main empirical focus: the
documentation of a publicity event, staged by the SPHIS in 1931, which marked a
symbolic moment in the demolition of slums and the perceived eradication of their
pest populations. Having examined this historical example, taken from the period
when bed bug populations in the UK dramatically declined,[1] in conclusion I reflect

on contemporary relationships between pests and neo-liberal policies and processes of urban development; and in particular the implications of the current 'dramatic' return of the bed bug in Western Europe and North America.[2] This discussion centres on the London Borough of Camden, and returns, therefore, to the area that comprised the geographical focus of the SPHIS's original slum clearance work.

As a form of 'bad' or unwanted nature, pest infestations are not necessarily an urban problem. However, reconstructing the history of housing conditions in reference to vermin raises a wide range of questions of urban development. For example, issues of social struggle, class difference and inter-class representation will be encountered through a discussion of the conception, construction and occupation of 19TH-century houses, and their degradation into slums. Also key to this history of social and physical housing reconstruction are the use of architectural and urban design as forms of sanitisation, the development of hygiene aesthetics, and the use of architectural settings as propaganda in reform. As a research concern, urban pests are situated at the intersection between private domestic and public environments, highlighting tensions between state, local authority and private responsibility for housing and infrastructure. The history of urban vermin, and the study of fluctuating pest populations, highlight the city as a natural environment (rather than a territory defined against nature), and nature itself as a social and cultural product. These species threaten in particular to destabilise the security of domestic environments. In such contexts they constitute an *unheimlich* intrusion of nature, lurking in the services and structures of houses which are not normally meant to be seen, and affecting the perception of the home as a safe place.[3] As with the manipulation of other forms of nature, the control of pests constitutes one of the transformations necessary to make civilised urban life possible.

In sociological and cultural studies, a number of recent accounts have explored the connections between vermin and human life in cities.[4] For example, sociologist Gargi Bhattacharyya defines vermin as "the most human of animals, those that arrange their lives around the business and rhythm of the human world".[5] Bhattacharyya explores the relationships between the success of particular species and the arrangement of urban space, arguing that certain kinds of pests, such as pigeons, "flourish in the crevices of urban intensification",[6] and that "the urban breeds its own particular vermin".[7] In a similar vein, cultural theorist Steven Connor describes flies as "our negative species",[8] observing that houseflies are integral to home environments, intimately bound to human spaces, though "rarely seen as domesticated or *heimlich*".[9] Robert Sullivan's study of rats in New York City resonates with

Connor and Bhattacharyya's accounts when he refers to these rodents as "our mirror species".[10] Ultimately, the examples I will now explore suggest that the changing
demographics of pest species reflect human behaviours and attitudes towards the
city as a matter of shared responsibility.

Housing and pest control in the 1920s and 1930s

By the mid-1920s, what we would now call 'pest control' was a highly specialised
and organised industry offering an array of skills, expertise, new technologies and
products.[11] For example, in 1926, "expert in sanitary building construction", Ernest
G. Blake, published a manual for the protection of buildings against vermin, as part
of a series of "practical manuals for practical men" involved in the construction
industry and building crafts. In its introduction he observes:

> The word vermin is a very comprehensive term, and includes quite a number of
> different kinds of animals and insects. Some of these are the authors of a great deal of
> damage to house property, and as they consume large quantities of foodstuffs they are
> universally detested, while others are objected to, more on the score of their repulsive
> appearance, and the unsavoury conditions which they are usually associated ...
> The presence of vermin in a building, indicates, either that there is a regular sup-
> ply of food of some kind or other to which they have access, or else, that the condition
> of the place is so insanitary, that various species of insects are encouraged to breed
> and thrive in the dirt and filth that ought to be kept down.[12]

Acknowledging the wide scope of the category 'vermin', Blake emphasises the para-
sitic relationship of these pests to humans and human waste. He also highlights an
association between vermin, "dirt and filth", and "insanitary" or neglected environments. The manual focuses on vermin that can be found in enclosed areas and in-
habited structures: brown and black rats, the common house mouse, the cockroach,
ants and houseflies. For Blake, the material costs of vermin to property owners are a
central concern. These include damage to the structures of buildings and the wider
economic losses that might accrue from, for example, destruction of stock in a ware-
house or the spread of disease.

George Orwell's anthropomorphic depiction of bed bugs as soldiers on the march
in *Down and Out in London and Paris*, published in 1933, suggests the prominence
of these insects as a problem and topic of urban debate at this time. Mobilising

261

the military and sacrificial metaphors commonly deployed by modernising hygiene reformers, he writes:

> The walls were as thin as matchwood, and to hide the cracks they had been covered
> with layer after layer of pink paper, which had come loose and housed
> innumerable bugs. Near the ceiling long lines of bugs marched all day like columns of
> soldiers, and at night came down ravenously hungry, so that one had
> to get up every few hours and kill them in hecatombs. Sometimes when the bugs got
> too bad one used to burn sulphur and drive them into the next room;
> whereupon the lodger next door would retort by having his room sulphured, and
> drive the bugs back. It was a dirty place, but homelike ....[13]

Orwell emphasises, therefore, the intimately close relationship between neglected, dilapidated and overcrowded buildings and bed bug infestations. The episode suggests the insects to be integral to the decaying fabric of a poorly built and run-down boarding house occupied by service workers in low-paid jobs. The accretion of wallpapers indexes the landlord's long-term negligence. The passage also emphasises the difficulty of permanently eliminating the bugs – made near impossible through a cyclical process of infestation-disinfestation-reinfestation, in a building comprised of individual lodgings occupied by tenants with no sense of shared ownership or structures in place to orchestrate an effective, collective defence. However, what is particularly interesting is Orwell's comment that "it was a dirty place, but homelike". Disputing a simple equation of domestic cleanliness and comfort, this phrase can be read as a form of 'nostalgia for the mud'. The bed bugs' invasion of this dirty-but-homely space is presented as an uncanny intrusion of nature. As the following discussion will demonstrate, Orwell's suggestion that pest infestations and control are bound inextricably to underlying structures of property ownership, building conditions and responsibility for maintenance continues to be of central importance.

Still active as the St Pancras Housing Association, the SPHIS was originally established in 1924, two years prior to the publication of Blake's manual. Architectural historian Elizabeth Darling places the Society as one of a number of voluntary housing-sector organisations formed in the inter-war period set up to address housing issues for the working-class poor, particularly slum dwellers neglected by state housing policies concentrating primarily on housing provision for the 'labour aristocracy'.[14]

The founding SPHIS committee comprised a group of committed and energetic social workers from various existing welfare organisations, chaired by the charismatic

and locally popular Father Basil Jellicoe (1899–1935), who had been sent to Somers Town in 1921 to head up a Magdalen College Mission settlement.[15] The SPHIS committee members were united by a non-denominational Christian welfare ethic, understanding the slums, poverty, overcrowding and infestations as the "devil's work".[16] Strongly influenced by the Garden Cities and Town Planning Association, they resolved to establish a house improvement and rehousing programme, which centred initially on Somers Town.[17]

The area was known colloquially as "little hell", and was described by one journalist as a place of "vermin-ridden dens…the worst hovels in London…where mothers are afraid to put their children to bed for fear of rats and other vermin of all descriptions".[18] In this "difficult district" (*Daily Telegraph*, 1930), conditions had become particularly dire due to ineffective state housing policies, local authority inactivity and neglectful landlords. As one property commentator put it in 1930:

In Dickens' day, Somers Town had become shabby-genteel; today it is merely shabby.[19]

The SPHIS sought to tackle the housing problems and improve the area's reputation and in so doing demonstrate, as SPHIS historian Malcolm Holmes has written, "that slum clearance and rehousing was a practical proposition and could show a return on investments, despite rents for the improved properties being no greater than for the old".[20] Operating as a Public Utility Society under the *Industrial and Provident Societies Act* (1893), the committee members soon attracted the investment of a range of influential and affluent shareholders, including the Prince of Wales.[21]

A 1925 survey of housing in Somers Town detailed the conditions that the Society's members wished to highlight and overcome. These included overcrowding, lack of sanitation facilities, extreme architectural dilapidation, rot and severe infestations of vermin such as rats, fleas, cockroaches and bed bugs.[22] Of all the pests, hematophagous bed bugs caused the most anxiety because of the extent and effects of infestations.[23] Called 'wall bugs' in some countries,[24] bed bugs were (and are) a particular threat to the home where, intimately occupying a building's material core, fixtures and fittings, they "hide in cracks and crevices in beds, wooden furniture, floors, and walls".[25] The degraded slums of Somers Town and their furnishings were ridden with these insects. In the area's decaying brick and timber slums, the tenants had to develop tactics to cope with the bugs, such as sealing their clothes in paper bags and hanging them from the ceiling as soon as they arrived home – a strategy the Society recorded on film.[26]

Founding members of the SPHIS committee, architect Ian Hamilton and chartered surveyors Irene Barclay and Evelyn Perry,[27] provided an intentionally alarming
evocation of the bed bugs in an article which resonated with Orwell's description.
The piece was first published by the SPHIS and later appeared in a widely circulated
manual, *Housing: a Citizen's Guide to the Problem* (1931):

> *Ghosts and hobgoblins[28] are not legendary creatures of the past nor*
> *figments of a disordered imagination. They exist in Somers Town. Here nearly every*
> *house is a haunted house. After dark there is no place more eerie, no torture*
> *more prolonged and blood-curdling than that enacted here year after year, no atrocity*
> *more revolting than the nightly human sacrifice. For there are vampires.*
> *Not creatures of classical mythology, but solid hair-raising scientific facts. I have*
> *seen them. I have smelt them.*

Such colourful and provocative first-person accounts were an important tool for
the Society's committee members as they went about raising awareness of the problems of bed bugs and slum life in general, attempting to attract funding for their work.
This was a time of general anxiety about the state and health of the nation, with increasing, but patchy, attempts to improve the lives of the poor through early welfare
legislation.[29] The SPHIS reformers, who were either living in the area (Jellicoe) or on
the ground every day (Barclay and Perry), gained an intimate insight into the bed
bug problem. To potential donors – for whom the slums were more distant – they
described the bugs as a source of both horror and fascination, the focus of a "war
to the death, its object the extermination of this interesting species".[30] The Somers
Town residents were also presented as a source of quasi-sociological fascination,
caricatured and classified by Barclay as "cheerful cockneys" and "the wonderfully
clean to the wonderfully dirty".[31]

Through a personal evocation of the slums she visited during the 1925 survey,
Barclay later described the bed bug problem again, with equal relish:

> *For the brickwork was sodden and bulging, the chimneys were full of holes, the*
> *plaster crumbling, the staircases unsound. Then there was* Cimex lectularius, *or the*
> *common bed bug. This insect, we discovered, is a prolific breeder: the female lays 150*
> *eggs at a time, and they hatch out in ten days. They feed on blood, and attack the soft*
> *bodies of children unmercifully. They thrive on stuffy warmth, and hide in woodwork*
> *and plaster, emerging at night to gorge on their prey. Many live in iron bedsteads,*

conveniently for the source of their nourishment. They smell disgusting. Directly these old buildings were touched, clusters and bunches of these vile insects were uncovered. I remember seeing a cross taken down from a wall, and its exact outline remained for a few seconds in living bugs.[32]

Barclay's description suggests that the insects thrive in particular materials and degraded architectural conditions, as well as affecting the sensory experience of the slums.[33] Both Orwell and Barclay's evocations of bed bugs, hidden in the dilapidated architectural fabric, communicate that, for reformers, their presence indicated the landlords' neglect, and caused anxiety through signifying a troubling loss of human control over the environment and nature-city relations: a premature impulse to ruination.[34] The bed bugs were both acknowledged as a real problem, and took on a symbolic function as a metaphor for the impossibility of cleanliness in the slums, and the impotence of the state in improving conditions. The challenge of eliminating these "vampiric" pests – rendered by both authors in flesh-crawling detail – was stated to be "the most difficult problem",[35] leading to the assumption that the buildings were irreversibly infested. As a result the reconditioning of the existing properties was considered too problematic, and the insects became a principal motive in the decision to rebuild rather than renovate which, as an "Improvement Society", the SPHIS had set out to do.[36]

Ceremonial pest control: bonfire of the slums

Darling has demonstrated that the SPHIS, alongside other voluntary housing-sector organisations in this period, functioned to address the "slum problem" in multiple and often "flamboyant" ways.[37] As well as direct actions to improve the physical environment through reconditioning properties, demolishing slums and building new housing, the SPHIS conducted environmental surveys and research. However, in large part, Darling argues, it operated as a "propaganda machine" aiming to raise awareness of housing issues, provoke debate, and lobby for improved state housing and provision:

> *From the outset the Society made a point of documenting through film and still photography the process of constructing new accommodation. Each stage would be marked with special events and carefully recorded.*[38]

The events staged by the Society and the techniques of film, photographic and written documentation and dissemination they employed were both experimental and
extremely powerful.[39]

The representations and discourses associated with the slum clearances that led
to the construction of St Christopher's Flats, one wing of the SPHIS's Sydney Estate,
attest to the Society's imaginative approach to publicity and its understanding of the
value of symbolic purification. From a lot purchased in 1802, the particular houses
undergoing demolition to make way for the Sydney Estate had been developed by
John Johnson, a highly successful scavenger, builder and paviour who played a central role in the development of Somers Town, as detailed by building and labour
historian Linda Clarke.[40] The approach of Johnson and his collaborators to building was profit-led, rapid and newly regularised. It had ultimately resulted in mo-
notonous and low quality architectural environments.[41] Typically there would be
four families living in seven or eight rooms.[42] Ironically, given the poor housing
conditions, since the neighbourhood's earliest development a large proportion of
its residents were workers who were themselves directly involved with the building
industry. The houses, completed in the 1820s, were "highly standardized", with a
lack of differentiation between the four storeys, suggesting their use for single-class
tenements.[43] The overall "haphazard"[44] development was uniform and dense imply-
ing "greater concentration and quicker turnover of building capital" and "a more
regularized use of building labour and skills than in the earlier phase of the town".[45]
According to Clarke, when combined with the neglect of self-interested landlords,
this style of development reinforced the structures of poverty and exacerbated public
health problems. The houses deteriorated quickly and many of them failed to last
the length of their 99-year leases, ultimately being demolished as infested slums.

In 1929, in the course of the demolitions to make way for St Christopher's Flats,
monstrously oversized and elaborately detailed cardboard and straw models of a
cockroach, rat, flea and bed bug were made, impaled upon wooden stands and positioned at the summit of a pile of slum rubble from the surrounding half-demolished
buildings.[46] It is clear from the surviving press photographs that considerable time
and craftsmanship went into the making of these anatomically accurate but supersized creatures, which were presumably modelled by SPHIS volunteers themselves.[47]
The models – or 'effigies' as the Society's members referred to them – were then cer-
emoniously torched by a high-profile public figure, retired military leader General
Sir Ian Hamilton.[48] The impact of this symbolic community bonfire was maximised
by the setting: a site between the Society's newly completed flats and the half-ruined

slum housing undergoing demolition. The event, the setting and the effigies poignantly articulated "the transition from the old to the new" through a physical, performative and visually impressive act.[49] The ceremonial bonfire had been advertised in national newspapers;[50] and the models, and the act of their incineration in front of a sizeable audience, were carefully documented through film, photography and written accounts by the Society's members,[51] as well as through numerous articles, many illustrated, in the local and national press.

Though the making and burning of the vermin models was apparently a unique event, it found a parallel in the public dynamiting of tenement blocks which, though less playful, had previously provided a theatrical symbolic focus for slum clearances.[52] The staging of such events, their documentation and publicisation, all emphasise the skill of the Society's committee members as propagandists.[53] Reminiscent of a sacrifice or public execution,[54] the incineration was just the first act of purification in an extended sequence of ceremonies to mark the construction of St Christopher's Flats and to celebrate the Society's sixth birthday. It was followed one month later by the blessing of the first brick by Father Nigel Scott; and later in 1931 by the inauguration by Princess Helena Victoria and the blessing of the completed building by the Bishop of Truro.[55] As a spectacular publicity event, the effigy burning rated in its theatricality alongside later SPHIS productions such as their 'Chamber of Horrors' display at the *New Homes for Old* exhibition (December 1931), which included similar oversized models of common slum pests.[56] As props, intended to draw attention to slum conditions, the models also compared to another SPHIS tool discussed by Darling: a widely displayed scale model of an overcrowded slum room, used to communicate the claustrophobic domestic environments experienced by Somers Town residents to potential donors.

The Society's films, such as *Paradox City* (1934),[57] were equally powerful and experimental. As film archivist Ros Cranston has observed, in its exposé of slum life in Somers Town and its documentation of the Society's demolition and rebuilding work, this film "demands the audience's engagement … in what is an unusually direct style of filmmaking for the period".[58] Other, equally direct, SPHIS films focused specifically on the bed bug problem, showing close-ups of infested furniture covered in crawling bugs, and of the bugs themselves.[59] Like the films, the making and burning of the vermin effigies had a didactic function, bringing aspects of slum life into sharp focus for a wider (healthier and wealthier) public.

Also like the films, the models and the spectacle of their incineration were productions that had an entertainment value and provided the focus for a celebratory

IN THE NAME OF THE BABE OF BETHLEHEM

WILL
YOU
HELP US TO
RESTORE THE HOMES
WHICH HAVE BEEN
STOLEN BY THE
DEVIL?

CLOCKWISE FROM TOP

Cockroach, rat, flea and bug, site of St Christopher's Flats, Werrington Street, Somers Town, 1930 (Camden Local Studies Archive)

"The Devil's Architecture. A typical crumbling and vermin-ridden staircase", *House Happenings*, Christmas 1931

"Bugs from a Wardrobe in Somers Town", *House Happenings*, Christmas, 1931

"Sydney Estate, St Pancras, view from the air", *House Happenings*, Christmas 1931

PREVIOUS DOUBLE PAGE SPREAD

Cockroach, rat, flea and bug set alight, site of St Christopher's Flats, Werrington Street, Somers Town, 1930 (Camden Local Studies Archive) community event marking a new beginning for Somers Town's residents. Barclay's description of the infestations she witnessed during the 1925 survey seems subdued by comparison with the hyperbole and light-hearted enthusiasm of the first-hand account in the Society's magazine, House Happenings, of the burning of the "itchingly realistic" models, "magnified to the proportions of well-fed tabbies".[60] The author of the article describes the occasion in all its theatrical and sensory detail, adding to the drama evoked in the photographic records:

Fiery tongues licked the planks and reared towards the pale azure of the sky, to the tune of 'Keep the Home Fires Burning'; and the house breakers positioned in the background of the photographs drove their picks into the ruins sending bricks cascading to the ground in a cloud of dust.[61]

This animated image of the demolition men foreshadows a scene in *Paradox City* where, grim reaper-like, the SPHIS's chairman is shot from below, looming threateningly with his pickaxe, while he sets the demolition process in motion. Apocalyptic, and sensationally expressed, the imagery used in the written account demonstrates the importance of the moment in the public erasure of the existing urban environment, perceived to be impossibly infested, and the envisioning of a new (and vermin-free) neighbourhood. The SPHIS aimed to completely rework the urban environment, from the purification of the air, to the improvement of the material conditions of the architecture. However, in contrast to local authorities during this period, they were committed to rehousing people on the sites of their former slums, with their friends and families – even those they perceived as 'problem' tenants.[62]

Chiming with Orwell's military metaphors the reference in *House Happenings* to the tune of Ivor Novello's popular sentimental World War I song, 'Keep the Home Fires Burning' (1914),[63] positions the battle to reclaim the slums from the occupying forces of pests alongside the protection of the homeland by families awaiting the return of their loved ones from the battlefields. While entertaining and playfully executed, the making and burning of the models was a highly charged symbolic act, intended to project the idea that victory over the vermin had been permanently achieved. The occasion marked a triumph in the re-imagining of the neighbourhood. As reported in a contemporary newspaper account, this was to be the end of the "vermin-ridden dens".[64] However, in retrospect, the event and the discourses around it emphasise the direct, extensive and serious influence such species had on the urban environment and on the experience of living in poverty in the city; and the significant resources and constant effort required to protect people's homes from the invasions of unwanted and anxiety-inducing forms of nature.[65]

For Hamilton, the SPHIS architect responsible for the design of the new flats, the work of the 19TH-century speculative builders represented the lowest point in the history of architecture. The slums were the "devil's architecture", "crumbling and vermin-ridden". He writes that:

> To-day what is called an artistic sense has to be cultivated because there are so many
> ugly surroundings and instinct is polluted and fails ...
> With the nineteenth century and the industrial age came the speculative
> builder, cheap mechanical ornament and the utter debasement of taste, and
> we know the legacy which we, the Heirs of all the Ages, have been left in Somers Town.[66]

Within his account, Hamilton suggests vermin to be a corrupt or dirty form of nature associated with poor construction. Juxtaposed with this evocation of a contaminated and contaminating nature, his designs for the new flats incorporated a vision of a Garden Cities Movement-inspired, redemptive, cleansing nature, expressed through open spaces, courtyard gardens, trees, planting and ponds.[67] In contemporary publications, the architect depicted the new estate from the air to maximise the visual impact of its reordering of the urban environment. The new blocks surround a spacious cruciform courtyard, centering on a group of trees. The modern flats with their pitched roofs and impressively tall chimney stacks stand out above the surrounding narrow terraced streets. They are illuminated in sunlight from the left of the picture plane, their walls white, contrasting the shaded roofs of the slums. The familiar modernist architectural motif of a tiny single car parked in front of the central block, at the forefront of the drawing, reinforces the sense of modernisation.

In the drawing, a pair of trees mark out each gateway. Window boxes, though not visible in the scheme as planned, would also become an important feature.[68] These interventions were intended to redress what the architect perceived as slum tenants' starvation from 'pure' nature: "one or two at least there have told me that they have never seen grass growing", he wrote emotively in the *Sunday Times* (1931). Equally important in reorganising the city-nature dynamics of the neighbourhood were the design tactics employed by Hamilton to prevent future infestations by unwanted and intrusive pests, and the process of gas fumigation applied to furniture and bedding as tenants were moved into the new flats.[69] Drawing on up-to-date expertise of the kind in Blake's manual, Hamilton targeted these insects through the employment of specific design, material and decorative tactics including the avoidance of wallpaper and picture rails, where the bugs would be able to hide, and the use of specific kinds of plaster intended to reduce the risk of infestation.[70]

In summary, this episode demonstrates that in 1920s Somers Town the presence of specific kinds of vermin, and the extent of infestations, reflected the long-term underlying structures of urban development and property ownership; the nature and density of occupation; and the materials, quality, character and methods of the production of the houses. These slums were designated by the reformers as terminally infested in order to effect change. As a mix of socially concerned professionals and philanthropists who occupied a position of class superiority, the SPHIS sought to reorganise the poor of Somers Town. As philanthropic hygiene reformers their attitudes and actions were progressive and critical of the underlying structures that produced the conditions they witnessed and of the inadequacy of state intervention.

Through the celebratory ritual burning of the vermin effigies, the Society effectively drew attention to the pest problem. In the process they sought to attract attention and funding to address long-term neglect through innovative forms of representation, powerful imagery and juxtaposition, rather than through negative stereotyping.

Vermin in the late-modern city and the return of the bed bug

Although, as we have seen, bed bugs a high-profile problem in the 1920s, during the second half of the 20TH century they were all but eradicated from the industrialised world; eliminated, it seemed, through improved housing conditions, the use of powerful DDT-type insecticides, and increasingly sophisticated and specialised fumigation and pest control techniques.[71] However, scientists have recently expressed alarm in response to a widespread surge of infestations, particularly in the context of North America and Western Europe.[72] Further increases are now predicted in bed bug populations in developed countries, with infestations described as a "major public health concern".[73] What does the current "dramatic"[74] increase in bed bug infestations, in London and other cities internationally, suggest about contemporary urban structures? How have responses to bed bugs and other vermin, and the discourses related to pest control, changed since the 1930s?

Within London's contemporary structures of development, the distribution and treatment of pests continue to reflect property boundaries and forms of ownership; levels of investment and disinvestment and the quality of maintenance; styles of building; density of occupation; lifestyles and standards of living; as well as scientific knowledge, pest-control techniques and technologies. In the contemporary London Borough of Camden,[75] like a number of other London boroughs, pest control is now sub-contracted by the council to specialist private companies.

Camden's pest-control technicians were recently called to a 1980s council estate, prompted by the mass migration of rodents displaced by the demolition of Victorian railway arches, with light industrial uses, as part of the major Channel Tunnel Rail Link redevelopment.[76] These infestations contributed to the other pollutions – particularly dust and noise – suffered by the estate's residents during the lengthy development process.[77] This incident reinforces a continuing direct relationship between vermin and urban development.

According to Camden's chief pest-control officer, the infestation of the 1980s estate, like the slums that were demolished in the 1930s, was exacerbated by the poor quality of construction:

Modern [contemporary] buildings present the biggest problems ... There are more void areas, partition walls, gaps for insulation, trunking and cabling areas, electricity cupboards etc. and when holes are drilled they are not drilled to size but are too big for their purpose. These factors create perfect environments to host pests such as rodents.[78]

Coleman and other municipal pest-control technicians[79] contend that low architectural quality, and a lack of consideration of potential pests in the design, contribute to infestation. He argues that there should be more communication between architects, developers and pest-control companies in order that future infestations can be minimised rather than exacerbated by contemporary building techniques. In this observation Coleman raises a debate that has existed since at least the mid-19TH century over the distribution of responsibilities for vermin control alongside the management of other kinds of urban nature.[80] In these debates pests, and other kinds of 'dirt', constitute a defining point for conflicting senses of professional duty, and individual and collective responsibility for public space.

While tenants of local authority-owned housing in contemporary London are provided with a free pest-control service for certain kinds of vermin, including bed bugs, private residents and tenants now have to pay for pest control with fees determined by the species and the nature of the infestation. In Camden (as elsewhere in London) numbers of bed bug infestations have increased 'dramatically' in recent years. The insects are extremely hard to get rid of, causing psychological distress as well as allergic reactions to the insects' bites and, in some cases, secondary infection. They are still associated with insanitary and overcrowded housing conditions.[81] In the UK, scientists, media and industry commentators have suggested a number of possible reasons for the rise including, as mentioned earlier, the insects' resistance to insecticides, as well as increased international travel and immigration, and an increase in multiple-occupancy of rented dwellings, with tenants who are reluctant to report infestation because of the cost implications of fumigation.[82] The expense hits marginal low-income groups living in (often overcrowded and poorly converted) private rented accommodation. While industry commentators and journalists have claimed a rise in bed bug populations of between 300% and 1,500% in some parts of London,[83] charges for pest control introduced in recent years have been argued to deter the reporting of infestations.[84] Bed bug infestations occupy a grey area of UK law. According to the *Prevention of Damage by Pests Act* (1949) – which makes deinfestation the landlord's responsibility with regard to many pests – tenants have to prove that they did not bring the insects into the property in order to force a landlord to pay for fumigation. In contemporary London, then, the neoliberal approach to pest control raises similar issues to discourses about the Victorian city, where infestations were attributed to alien individuals rather than understood as the consequence of wider structures or conditions. Furthermore, there are tensions between the commercial interests of pest-control companies affiliated to local authority environmental health units, and their function to promote public health, which compromise the provision of permanent or long-term solutions. The fragmentation of pest control parallels that of other services, such as water and sewers, since their privatisation.

Conclusions

Urban pests provide a point of intersection between discussions of the material conditions of housing in the city and the policies and discourses of urban development. In considering the history of the SPHIS slum clearances in Somers Town, we encounter vermin, and specifically bed bug infestations, as a material problem, experienced in very tangible ways by residents. This material condition became a pretext for the innovative actions of housing reformers, while in their accounts of slum life these manifestations of 'bad' nature were mobilised as a general metaphor for the conditions of the slums, conceived as irrevocably infested, and degraded in both physical and moral terms.

More recent discourses about urban pests in Camden, and the recent return of the bed bug, are symptomatic of the contraction of the urban public realm and reflective of contemporary housing policies. Urban pests traverse: public and private realms; architectural, infrastructural and administrative borders and networks; and cultural, scientific and sociological discourses of dirt and hygiene. The lived realities of infestations, and the requirements and resources for pest control, are in increasing tension with the privatisation of infrastructure and environmental health services, and the relinquishing of state responsibility for housing and the public realm. In this respect, the example of Camden appears typical of London as a whole, rather than being an exceptional case. With a diminished conception of collective responsibility for urban infrastructure and the privatisation of public spaces and services, the management and control of vermin may become increasingly problematic in the future, just as the management of other kinds of urban nature will be.

BIOGRAPHY

Ben Campkin is Co-Director of the UCL Urban Laboratory and Lecturer in Architectural History and Theory at the UCL Bartlett School of Architecture (b.campkin@ucl.ac.uk)

*The author would like to thank Elizabeth Darling, Matthew Gandy and David Gissen for their valuable comments on draft versions of this chapter; Deepa Naik, Trenton Oldfield and Hilary Powell for their suggestions and for inviting me to participate in the TINAG Salon (2007) on urban vermin; and Dave Coleman and Effie Williams for sharing their pest control expertise so freely.

1. K. Reinhardt and M.T. Siva-Jothy, 'Biology of the Bed Bugs (Cimicidae)', *Annual Review of Entomology* 52, 2007, pp. 351-374(361).
2. Interview between the author and Dave Coleman, Environmental Health Pest Controller, London Borough of Camden, 8 April 2008.
3. A. Vidler, *The Architectural Uncanny: Essays in the Modern Unhomely* (Cambridge, MA: MIT Press, 1992).
4. For a fuller account of these debates, and theoretical work on human-animal relations in geography, see B. Campkin, *Dirt, Blight and Regeneration: Urban Change in London* (unpublished PhD thesis, UCL, 2009).
5. G. Bhattacharyya, 'Rats with Wings: London's Battle with Animals', in J. Kerr, A. Gibson and M. Seaborne (eds), *London: From Punk to Blair* (London: Reaktion, 2003), pp. 213-220(216).
6. *ibid.*, G. Bhattacharyya (2003) p. 214.
7. G. Bhattacharyya, 'Animals', in S. Pile and N. Thrift (eds), *City A-Z* (London and New York: Routledge, 2000) p. 12.
8. S. Connor, 'The antient commonwealth of flies', undated www.bbk.ac.uk/english/skc/flies/ (accessed 12/04/09).
9. S. Connor, *Fly*, (London: Reaktion, 2006) pp. 10-11.
10. R. Sullivan, *Rats: A Year With New York's Most Unwanted Inhabitants* (London: Granta, 2004) p. 2.
11. In his social history of changing concepts and practices of cleanliness in France, Georges Vigarello observes that "certain women with nimble fingers" had made a profession of delousing even in the Middle Ages. G. Vigarello, *Concepts of Cleanliness: Changing Attitudes in France Since the Middle Ages* (Cambridge: Cambridge University Press, 1988) p. 42.
12. E.G. Blake, *The Protection of Buildings against Vermin. With a Comprehensive Description of the most Effective Methods that can be adopted for the Extermination of Rats, Mice and various Insects* (London: Crosby Lockwood & Son, 1926) pp. 1-2.
13. G. Orwell, *Down and Out in Paris and London* (London: Penguin Books, 2003/1933).
14. E. Darling, 'To induce humanitarian sentiments in prurient Londoners: the propaganda activities of London's voluntary housing associations in the inter-war period', *London Journal* 27(1), 2002, pp. 42-62(43). This had already been a complaint of philanthropic model housing schemes of the 1880s which neglected the 'worst class in Somers Town', critics argued. See: John Hollingshead quoted in R. Porter, *London: A Social History* (London: Hamish Hamilton, 1994) p. 273.
15. Jellicoe served as Missioner from 1922 to 1927, see www.madg.ox.ac.uk/college/societies/trust (accessed 31/03/09). Local historian Malcolm Holmes provides an extensive history of the SPHIS (M.J. Holmes, *Housing is not enough: the story of St. Pancras Housing Association* (London: St. Pancras Housing Association, 1999) p. 10. The SPHIS was connected to the local Mary Ward Settlement through, for example, individuals such as Mrs Edith Neville, SPHIS committee member and warden of the Mary Ward Settlement in the early 1920s. See K.B. Beauman, *Women and the Settlement Movement* (London and New York: Radcliffe Press, 1996) p. 148.
16. Although the SPHIS was officially non-denominational, in practice it was essentially an Anglo-Catholic organisation.
17. The Garden Cities and Town Planning Association was directly represented on the SPHIS committee and the rules of the Society were based on those of the Association (*ibid.*, M.J. Holmes, 1999, pp. 11, 13). The SPHIS also contributed to publications on housing with other individuals and organisations associated with the Garden Cities movement, e.g. I. Hamilton, I.T. Barclay and E.E. Perry, 'The Truth About Bugs', in K.M. England (ed.), *Housing: A Citizen's Guide to the Problem* (London: Chatto and Windus, 1931), pp. 73-77. However, in many ways building flats in densely populated urban areas was the antithesis of GCTPA principles, with their focus on planned, self-contained communities, encircled by greenbelt, and with designated areas of housing, industry and agriculture.
18. Anon, 'Interesting Remarks on Present Day Problem', *Litchfield Times*, 24 January 1930.
19. Anon, 'The Rise and Fall of Somers Town', *Estates Gazette*, 22 November 1930.
20. *ibid.*, M.J. Holmes (1999) p. 11.
21. I. Barclay, *The St. Pancras Housing Association in Camden: What it is and Why: A History 1924 to 1972* (London: St Pancras Housing Association, 1972) p. 9.
22. *ibid.*, I. Barclay (1972) p. 5; *ibid.*, M.J. Holmes (1999) p. 16.

23. *Cimex lectularius* parasitise humans, while other cimicid (bed bug) species parasitise birds and bats. Despite belonging to the hematophagus cimicid taxon, in the 1920s bed bugs were frequently associated with dirt, and this association is still strong. See *ibid.*, K. Reinhardt and M.T. Siva-Jothy (2007).

24. For example, in Swedish the plural for bed bugs is *vägglöss*, which translates literally as 'wall bugs'.

25. S.W. Hwang, T.J. Svoboda, I.J.D. Jong, K.J. Kabasele and E. Gogosis, 'Bed Bug Infestations in an Urban Environment', *Emerging Infectious Diseases*, 11(4), 2005, pp. 533-538(533).

26. S. Crockford (dir.), *Somerstown* (UK: 'People to People', Thames Television for Channel 4, 1984).

27. Irene Barclay had become the first female chartered surveyor in 1922.

28. The authors trace the etymology of *Cimex lectularius* to "a Celtic word signifying ghost or goblin" because of the terror caused by its nocturnal attacks. *ibid.*, I. Hamilton, I.T. Barclay and E.E. Perry (1931) pp. 73-74.

29. E. Darling, *Re-forming Britain: Narratives of Modernity Before Reconstruction* (London and New York: Routledge, 2007) p. 52.

30. *ibid.*, I. Hamilton, I.T. Barclay and E.E. Perry (1931) p. 77.

31. I. Barclay, *People Need Roots: the Story of the St. Pancras Housing Association* (London: Bedford Square Press, National Council of Social Science and the St Pancras Housing Association, 1976) pp. 26, 18.

32. *ibid.*, I. Barclay (1976) p. 23.

33. On the noxious smell associated with bed bugs, see *ibid.*, K. Reinhardt and M.T. Siva-Jothy (2007) p. 363.

34. In a recent discussion of contemporary industrial ruins, geographer Tim Edensor has remarked that "animals and plants are always waiting in the wings, ready to transform familiar material environments at the slightest opportunity". T. Edensor, *Industrial Ruins: Spaces, Aesthetics and Materiality* (Oxford: Berg, 2005) p. 319.

35. *ibid.*, I. Hamilton, I.T. Barclay and E.E. Perry (1931) p. 75.

36. *ibid.*, E. Darling (2007) p. 21. Further incentives to build new blocks of flats were the prohibitive cost of converting and renovating the slum houses, and the organisation's commitment to re-house the slum tenants in new homes on the sites of their existing ones, rather than displace anyone (M.J. Holmes, 1999, p.18).

37. *ibid.*, E. Darling (2002) p. 45; E. Darling (2007) p. 22.

38. *ibid.*, E. Darling (2002) p. 45.

39. The SPHIS was not unique in this respect. For example, Kensington Housing Trust also made documentary films about slum life. However, the SPHIS were perhaps the most experimental.

40. L. Clarke, *Building Capitalism: Historical Change and the Labour Process in the Production of the Built Environment* (London and New York: Routledge, 1991) plate 20, p. 264.

41. *ibid.*, L. Clarke (1991) pp. 214, 264.

42. *ibid.*, I. Barclay (1972) p. 5.

43. R. Porter, *London: A Social History* (London: Hamish Hamilton, 1994) p. 217.

44. R. Dennis, 'Review of Linda Clarke, *Building Capitalism: Historical Change and the Labour Process in the Production of the Built Environment*, Routledge, London and New York', *Journal of Historical Geography*, 18(4), 1992, pp. 484-486(486).

45. *ibid.*, L. Clarke (1991) p. 214.

46. Suitably flammable, cardboard and straw are identified as the materials used in the construction of the models in a newspaper report of the event (Anon, 'Clearing the Slums: Brighter Homes in St. Pancras', *Westminster Chronicle*, 1931).

47. The striking photographs of the incineration of the vermin models have been published without commentary in two historical accounts and one photographic history of Somers Town: *ibid.*, L. Clarke (1991); M. J. Holmes, *Somers Town: A Record of Change* (London: London Borough of Camden, 1989); and, *ibid.*, M.J. Holmes (1999).

48. The St Pancras Housing Association's architect, Ian Hamilton, was the nephew of General Sir Ian Hamilton who ignited the vermin effigies. *ibid.*, I. Barclay (1976) p. 22.

49. Anon, 'Slum Clearance in Somers Town', *The Times*, 30 January 1931.

50. Anon, 'The "burning" of slumland', *Sunday Times*, 25 January 1931.

51. N. Scott, 'A Peaceable Habitation', *House Happenings*, 1931, pp. 20-22.

52. For example, as Chairman of the LCC, Lord Monk Bretton dynamited a group of slum buildings in January 1930 (*The Daily Chronicle*, 1930).

53. *ibid.*, M.J. Holmes (1999) p. 16.

54. The caption to one of the photographs of the event published in the SPHIS magazine reads: "The Criminals ready for execution before the funeral pyre was lighted" (B. Jellicoe and N. Scott (eds), *House Happenings*, 8, Easter 1931).

55. *ibid.*, M.J. Holmes (1999) p. 98.
56. *ibid.*, E. Darling (2002) p. 52.
57. G.E. Belmont and L.A. Day (dirs.), *Paradox City* (London: St Pancras House Improvement Society, 1934) 22.34 minutes.
58. R. Cranston, 'Paradox City', undated, British Film Institute Screenonline www.screenonline.org.uk/film/id/1168236/ (accessed 1/5/09).
59. A lost film, *The Terror that Waketh in the Night*, is likely to focus specifically on bed bugs. A montage of SPHIS films in Sue Crockford's 1984 documentary, *Somerstown* (UK: Thames Television for Channel 4), shows footage of infestations and live insects.
60. *ibid.*, N. Scott (1931) p. 21.
61. *ibid.*
62. Barclay quoted in Crockford, *ibid.* (1984).
63. I. Novello, 'Keep the Home Fires Burning', 1914, can be played at: www.firstworldwar.com/audio/keep-thehomefiresburning.htm (accessed 21/04/08).
64. *ibid.*, Anon, 'Interesting Remarks' (1930).
65. Darling quotes a slum tenant, a Mr Norwood, speaking directly about his living conditions in another contemporary film, *Housing Problems* (E. Anstey and A. Elton (dirs), 1935, black and white, 13 minutes, UK), focusing on Stepney, another London district. The quote communicates very clearly his sense of anger at living in a dwelling "overrun with bugs", mice and rats. *ibid.*, E. Darling (2007) pp. 128-9.
66. Hamilton quoted in Scott, *ibid.* (1930) pp. 21-23.
67. Anon, 'Burning Down the Slums. A Miniature Garden City Arising in the Heart of Somers Town', *St Pancras Chronicle*, 30 January 1931.
68. Barclay quoted in Crockford, *ibid.* (1984).
69. *ibid.*, E. Barclay (1976) p. 28. Fumigation was common practice as part of the process of moving slum tenants to new housing and became formalised as part of municipal slum clearances in a report published on the *Management of Municipal Housing Estates* (1938). Fumigation mainly targeted bed bugs, with furniture being gassed using hydrogen cyanide in removal vans, and bedding being steam cleaned. The scientific bases of these practices were later laid out in the Medical Research Council's *Report of the Committee on Bed Bug Infestation* (1935-1940). Both reports are referred to in Anon, 'Moving from the slums', Seventh Report of the Housing Management Sub-Committee of the Central Housing Advisory Committee (London: HMSO, Ministry of Housing and Local Governance, 1956).
70. *ibid.*, M.J. Holmes (1999) p. 18.
71. *ibid.*, Anon (1956) 'Moving from the slums'.
72. Anon, 'Dirty London', *Time Out* (23-30 January 2002) pp. 16-23; Anon, 'Bedbugs bounce back from oblivion', *BBC News* (14 April 2004) news.bbc.co.uk/go/pr/fr/-/1/hi/health/3622833.stm (accessed 12/04/09); A. Romero, M.F. Potter, D.A. Potter and K.F. Haynes, 'Insecticide Resistance in the Bed Bug: A Factor in the Pest's Sudden Resurgence?', *Journal of Medical Entomology* 44(2), 2007, pp. 175-178; *ibid.*, S.W. Hwang *et al* (2005); *ibid.*, K. Reinhardt and M.T. Siva-Jothy (2007).
73. *ibid.*, A. Romero *et al.* (2007).
74. *ibid.*, Interview with Dave Coleman (2008).
75. The London Borough of Camden was formed in 1965 when the Metropolitan Borough of St Pancras – including King's Cross and the neighbourhood of Somers Town – was amalgamated with the Metropolitan Boroughs of Hampstead and Holborn. It therefore subsumed control of the area that was the location of the SPHIS's slum clearances and rebuilding.
76. Camden's technicians operate from within the Council's Environmental Services division, *ibid.*, Interview with Dave Coleman (2008).
77. R. Allison, 'Residents fight to block 24-hour work on Channel Link', *The Guardian* (12 January 2004) www.guardian.co.uk/uk/2004/jan/12/london.transport (accessed 12/04/09); Anon, 'Row over 24-hour rail link work', *BBC News* (18 December 2003)) news.bbc.co.uk/go/pr/fr/-/1/hi/england/london/3330363.stm (accessed 12/04/09); Argent, 'King's Cross Central - Quarterly Monitoring Report', London, 2008; R. Haynes and A. Savage, 'Assessment of the Health Impacts of Particulates from the Redevelopment of King's Cross', *Environmental Monitoring and Assessment* 130(1-3), 2007, pp. 47-56.
78. *ibid.*, Interview with Dave Coleman (2008).
79. Correspondence with Effie Williams, Pest Control Technician, London Borough of Hammersmith and Fulham, 10 April 2008.

80. In 1846, for example, the period of the most rapid and intense industry-led development of the King's Cross area, architect Robert Kerr imagined: "[An] improved division of labour ... whereby the real Architect might be relieved from the inspection of sewers and cesspools and wells, and the shoring up of old houses, and their rating of dilapidations, and the ventilation of foul cellars, and the fitting up of stables, and the curing of smoky chimneys, and the exclusion of rats, and all such like 'Architecture'. " (R. Kerr, *The Newleafe Discourses on the Fine Art Architecture*, London: Weale, 1846.) As we have seen, by the mid-1920s, when Blake was writing his technical manual, the protection of buildings against vermin was an established sub-discipline within the construction industry; while, in the 1930s, as a socially concerned architect, Hamilton was directly engaged with pest-control techniques.
81. *ibid.*, S.W. Hwang *et al.* (2005).
82. In Camden, fees for the control of bed bugs currently start from £120, with £53 extra for each additional bed treated, with no guarantee of success. Pest-control services in London vary from borough to borough. In Hammersmith and Fulham pest control is the direct responsibility of the council, rather than being outsourced to a private company, but incurs fees comparable to those of Camden. If the council's guidelines on pre-deinfestation preparation are adhered to, service clients are given a "90 percent guarantee of success after two treatments" with further charges for repeated treatments. Correspondence between the author and Effie Williams, Pest Control Technician, London Borough of Hammersmith and Fulham, 10 April 2008; *ibid.*, Interview with Dave Coleman (2008); and *ibid.*, Anon, 'Dirty London' (2002).
83. D. Cain, 'Mapping Bed Bug Infestations in London' (London: Bed Bugs Limited, 2008).
84. D. Derbyshire, 'Rise of the rat as town halls end free pest control', *Daily Mail*, London, 5 April 2008.

Vermin

*The Future
Development of Cities...and Other Stories*

ALAN THOMPSON

Definitions

As city dwellers our experience of vermin can, at best, be described as sporadic or unpredictable: we are occasionally shocked when confronted by a house mouse or sewer rat; the sighting of the once shy urban fox is now a little more commonplace; and we may be lucky enough to see the red kite, which is gradually reintroducing itself into our metropolitan skies.

The documentation and history of vermin infestation is fluid and surprising. At the outset of this investigation it must be remarked that, despite our obviously long-lived and enduring relationship with vermin, it is shocking to discover how very little we actually know about our unwanted friends. The accumulated history of vermin is sparse; documentation and censuses are rare; predictions for future trends are piti-fully few in number. It is significant to note that the main ways in which we tend to become acquainted with vermin are not scientific, not learned, not academic; rather, they are predominantly based on tabloid scare stories, unsavoury anecdotes and myth. The OED describes 'vermin' as: "species regarded as pest or nuisance, those associ-ated with the carrying of disease, or common animals and birds of an objectionable kind, especially those that injure crops, food, or game." However, there is secondary usage: this transposes the pejorative term for animals onto an unwanted sector of so-ciety, perceived as similarly damaging. The etymology of 'vermin' (earliest mention 14th century) derives from the Latin *vermis* which means 'worm'. This immediately sets us thinking of the underworld, of dragons ... of evil. In order to talk about ver-min we must talk about fear. These fears are no less real than the repulsive sources of such anxieties? This trepidation is certainly a worthy subject for investigation.[1]

Archaeology

In her book *Purity and Danger*, Mary Douglas famously defined dirt as "matter out of place"; her point being that our repulsion to soil, hair, fingernails etc., has very little to do with the actual objects themselves, but is rather related to our discovery of those objects, unexpectedly, in contexts where they do not normally belong. Perhaps vermin ought to be thought of similarly, as "animals out of place"? Finding a mouse in the garden is appropriate, maybe even charming; finding one in the larder is another matter! This could explain the ambivalence felt towards the fox: tolerated or enjoyed by city dwellers; hated and demonised by country folk. We can also start to appreciate the somehow arbitrary division between 'clean nature' and 'dirty nature': not all wildlife seems wholesome in every situation. It very much depends on our context whether animals fall into the dirty or clean category.[2]

Alan Pipe of the Museum of London gives us an insight into the history of our ongoing relations with vermin. There are many sophisticated archaeological techniques deployed to identify the presence of vermin. In the City of London, archaeologists have a more than 13-metre depth of accumulated debris available for analysis. Through study of these sediments, whether by hand trowelling or by microfiltration, a picture soon emerges. It is clearly revealed that there has been a particular group of species that have come to share our cities with us. Excavations in London produce the most remarkable picture of urban animal populations. From one particular site a considerable number of archeological fragments from the inner ears of the herring point to a long tradition of our dietary associations with this fish. Conversely, although the ubiquitous cockroach is thought to have been with us forever, there is very little archeological evidence to support this assumption; yet it is expected that our suspicions will in fact be confirmed. Fleas, lice and mites are indisputably ancient parasites and probably will be with us for many years to come.

The usual suspects

The common house mouse has been with us since well before Roman times. The black rat, which is now very rare, was an accidental introduction by the Romans (between the 2ND and 4TH centuries AD). The brown rat came much later (1728-29) and was probably bought by ship from Scandinavia. Rats were always pests:

infesting food supplies, damaging buildings, and carrying disease. The pigeon seems to be indigenous. It certainly carries disease and adversely effects our environment; yet we are ambivalent about the pigeon's role in the city's ecology. This is demonstrated by the recent battle over the pigeon population in Trafalgar Square between Ken Livingstone (Mayor of London) and the pigeon-feed sellers (in particular Bernard Rayner's High Court challenge in 2001). The pigeon-feed sellers reached a settlement, and the pigeon population is somewhat in decline, but the city's attitude to pigeons remains a contentious issue. The red kite and the raven were most unwelcome in medieval times. In 1457 James II of Scotland decreed that the kite should be killed whenever possible; in England and Wales they were saved because of their nature as carrion feeders and hence their role in cleaning the city streets. Yet, by the time of the first Vermin Act of 1532, in the reign of Henry VIII, it was "ordeyned to dystroye Choughes, Crowes and Rookes". These birds of prey were now considered true vermin since they put game populations at risk. A further law was passed in 1566, in the reign of Elizabeth I, which outlawed a number of animals thought to be in competition with the agricultural economy; it was instituted for "the preservation of Grayne". A bounty was set: "one penney for the head of every Woodwall [woodpecker], Pye, Jaye, Raven or Kyte". This law was very effective and over the next couple of hundred years the red kite was hunted practically to extinction.[3]

Resurgence

Populations of vermin are in constant flux. The red kite, which was almost lost forever, is now reappearing in our city skies in ever increasing numbers. It is now a protected species – legislation which once attempted to eradicate it now safeguards its survival. Gulls and kittiwakes are other species that have re-occupied a niche in the city. Tall buildings offer these birds a surrogate for their natural cliff-face habitat. But these birds can be very destructive, adding considerable cost to the maintenance of property. The collared dove is an example of a vermin population that is steadily expanding. A study of breeding distributions from 1958 to 1965 (Hudson 1965/1972) clearly shows this trend. What is unclear, however, is the effect that this population will have on the city as they grow in number.

Moving onto bugs, the common house-fly is an ancient adversary, spreading disease from decaying waste and faeces. Ben Campkin reminds us of Steve Connor's characterisation of flies: they "seem to inhabit an inverse universe, in which bad is good, shit is precious, decay is useful, as though they moved through our world in negative, through the negative of our world".[4] They live with us, but occupy a parallel world. Lice and mites, although not often visible, have certainly been making their presence felt for millennia. Isolated monocultures of people are likely to have isolated monocultures of vermin. Effie Williams points out that the persistence of bed bugs is partly down to waves of infestations of ever new species arriving from abroad; these are generally brought with new communities of immigrants. Diverse populations of vermin is a price that we pay for the global nature of modern life, but this is a small price for the rich, cosmopolitan and culturally diverse life that we enjoy in cities. However, some new species can be particularly threatening to the environment and give us good reason for concern.

Emerging threats

More recent and less obvious additions to our vermin populations include some unwanted aquatic incomers: the Chinese mitten crab (*Eriocheir sinensis*) and the zebra mussel (*Dreissena polymorphia*). Each population poses a new and peculiar threat to the environment.

The mitten crab, so called because of its furry claws, first appeared in Germany in 1912 and spread throughout Europe during the 1920s and 30s. Its relatively dormant populations in the UK have suddenly expanded in the last few years, causing significant alarm. These crustaceans, which are carried across the oceans in the ballast of large ships, have been known to migrate as far as 1,500 kilometres along rivers in China under their own steam. They are responsible for serious structural damage of river banks: they burrow into the mud leaving a network of holes, which results in instability and collapse. Like all successful vermin populations, the mitten crab reproduces at an alarming rate and readily travels huge distances to set up new colonies. There are moves to control this population by fishing, but it is too early to say if this will prove successful.[5]

Similarly, the zebra mussel arrives via large ocean-going ships, attached to their hulls. The UK Government Zebra Mussel Control Group has warned of the dangers of this new infestation. This mollusc accumulates and blocks the inlet pipes at water treatment plants and is adding considerably to the running costs of these establishments. In addition, this new population is already changing the ecology of fish populations and has infiltrated freshwater fisheries.[6] Although neither the crab nor the mollusc are yet having a major affect on the city, they are a warning of the potential impact that might accompany the introduction of any further unwanted species.

Terror

From among the legions of repulsive vermin, the one that casts the longest shadow in our collective unconscious is the rat. The rat appears again and again in fairy tales, myths, stories and film; it is malevolent, it is generally threatening. For example, E.T.A. Hoffman's *Mouse King* (1892) is a mythical story of a seven-headed rodent that terrorises the fairytale world of the little girl Marie. He demands to be given sweets and dolls, threatening to gnaw to pieces her favourite toy: the nutcracker. In reality, the 'rat king' was a very rare natural phenomenon: a contorted and intertwined group of rats held together by blood, dirt and excrement. Historically, the discovery of a rat king was an extremely bad omen, a portent of plague; indeed, the rat was responsible for the spread of plague and is especially associated with the Black Death.[7] Thomas Mann's *Death in Venice* (1912) relies on rats for setting the scene of the infection of the city and metaphorically the infection of Gustav von Aschenbach's mind. Visconti's film (1971) of the novella made a point of drawing the viewer's attention to the vermin: while filming, the director had pieces of fresh meat scattered around to attract rodents into the path of the camera.

The rat again makes a significant reappearance in post-war literature. Albert Camus' *The Plague* (1947) opens with the town of Oran being overrun by a plague of rats. At first they are ignored but, as the dead rats come to litter the streets, panic sets in. Ironically, the municipal collection of the dead vermin actually spreads the disease. Only one year later, George Orwell's *Nineteen Eighty-Four* (1948) deploys the rat as the ultimate personal terror for its hero Winston Smith. Behind the ominous door of Room 101 at the Ministry of Love, it is the rat that awaits Winston. The confrontation with the rat is invoked as his path to re-education. So powerful is his fear that, when the cage of hungry vermin is placed over his head, he betrays both his love and his freedom.

Outbreak

Stories about rats are disturbing; they give rise to deep-seated fears. But what of the real threats from these monsters of our imaginations? Ben Campkin underlines Gargi Bhattacharyya's observation that vermin are: "the most human of animals, those that arrange their lives around the business and rhythm of the human world".[8] Ben adds that they are also the "most urban" of animals and closest to us in a number of ways. Effie Williams, Senior Pest Controller for Hammersmith and Fulham Borough Council, has been working in this field for over 15 years. Her team carries out 2,000 treatments per year. Effie sizes up her adversaries in a detached, matter of fact way: The rat (*Rattus rattus* and *Rattus norvegicus*): 500 grams, approximately 200-270 millimetres long. The tail is just shorter than the body. It is agile and burrows underground in a network of tunnels. There are about 10 young in a litter and they have a 5-6 week gestation period. Without control this fecundity quickly leads to an exponential increase in population. The rat infiltrates our buildings through broken airbricks or tunnels through the benching of sewers . . . and, emerging through the U-bend in toilets, heads directly for the kitchen. These intruders make their home in the fabric of the building; they carry disease and parasites harmful to human populations;[9] they damage the structure of buildings: most house fires are caused by rats gnawing electrical wires. Signs of infestation are black bean-like droppings and salty urine piles; and since they burrow into buildings, there will always be evidence of an entry hole and an exit hole. The best strategy is to avoid infestation in the first place: building and sewage fabric should be vigilantly maintained to deter their entry. Once inside the building, however, the only course of action is trapping; poisoning has the adverse effect of leaving a decaying body trapped in the fabric of the building, compounding the problem of infection, distress and discomfort.

Infestation

The house mouse (*Mus domesticus*): 10-25 grams, approximately 75-100 millimetres long with additional tail of 50-100 millimetres. Droppings are tiny black ricelike grains. They tend to live outside; but venture in during spring and autumn. They have a litter of 6-10; gestation period is about 20 days. Infestation is through tiny holes in the fabric of the building; the mouse's head and body are very small and flexible. They prefer warm secluded places; under the fridge or in the airing cupboard are the most common places to find an infestation. It is best to protect the building against entry: airbricks should have a wire mesh of a small enough gauge to repel mice; the building fabric should have no holes. Poor workmanship in modern construction is a cause of much infestation. Mice, like rats, live in communities and reproduce quickly; if you see one mouse, then you probably have at least six. Once a mouse has made it into the house, the best course of action is poison; unlike rats, the bodies, which are comparatively small, disintegrate quickly without any adverse effects. The warnings from a practitioner on the ground are to: (A) maintain our sewage system more carefully; (B) manage waste and litter more effectively; (C) avoid flooding wherever possible; (D) control the quality of new construction more tightly. Most infestation of rats is through breaks in the benching of sewage pipes; if we maintain these joints correctly, infiltration will diminish. Open waste bins, reduced frequency of collection and general litter (especially fast food) encourage vermin. If we clamp down on waste, vermin will not flourish. Flooding displaces vermin populations from their habitats; it also provides an additional means of entry into buildings and encourages vermin to proliferate. Flood prevention can prevent the worst outbreaks of vermin. The recent King's Road floods were an illustration of the connection between floods and rat infestation. Poor construction of new buildings allows pathways for entry of vermin. Greater care in construction needs to be taken to avoid infestation.

Proliferation

We might try to keep a particular population of vermin at bay; we can attempt to diminish their numbers; but ultimately, could we, or should we, ever try to totally stamp out a species altogether? Surely it is naïve to imagine that we could succeed in eradicating an entrenched population of vermin. Historically, any campaign to systematically combat vermin has inevitably succumbed to the law of diminishing marginal returns: at first, a burgeoning population will be easy to cull; yet, as numbers dwindle, the job requires more and more effort to deliver any significant results. A tiny recalcitrant population always remains, and left to its own devices it will quickly re-populate, restoring its traditional foothold within a given ecological niche. After all, most vermin owe their success to an ability to reproduce in large numbers, with disturbingly short generation cycles. Victory over vermin will only ever be an aspiration; the best we can hope for is to keep them in their place. In the image of the Somers Town slum clearance near King's Cross (1930), shown by Ben Campkin, we see the celebration of a victory over the four notorious culprits of infestation.[10] Making space for modern dwellings on top of freshly demolished rubble from slum clearance, the local people have erected carnivalesque effigies of the rat, the bed bug, the flea and cockroach. These traditional demons are being offered up in sacrifice in a primordial, quasi-pagan festival: a ritual cleansing by fire! It is well documented that Modern Movement architecture found inspiration in the principals of sanitation, health and clean living. It was a tenet of this ethos to rid our domestic habitations of age-old infestations. But these irksome beasts were not the only vermin being targeted: the objectionable, uneducated, unwashed under-class were also fair game. A privileged class in society seized the campaign of post-war slum clearances as a golden opportunity to reorganise the poor, for their own ends. And in the process, destroyed long established communities and imposed alien values.

Degeneration

During the inter-war years, the move toward the redevelopment of working-class housing was heralded by a series of political pamphlets, including the Labour Party's 'Up With the Houses, Down With the Slums' (1934). This paper was radical in its prescriptions, deriding slums as the "Cancer of the Empire" and stating: "Let it be said right away that reconditioning is neither a cure for the slums problem nor an alleviation. The only way to deal with slums is to tear them down."[11] The 1935 film *Housing Problems*[12] took a stark view of London slum clearance during the inter-war years. Behind the bravado and propagandist tone lies a story of massive social upheaval. The living conditions in the Stepney row houses of this documentary are undeniably inhuman. The filming clearly shows the buildings in a state of dilapidation: the crooked, rickety houses are clearly overcrowded by tenants and writhing with vermin. The interviews with the working–class residents tell a story of poverty, discomfort and sickness; the premature and unnecessary death of children appears commonplace and calmly accepted as a normal part of life by this stoic community. The model for replacement of slum housing proposed by the filmmakers was Leeds' Quarry Hill Estate (1935-1940), with flats modelled on the Karl Marx Hof flats (Karl Ehn, 1930), a huge social housing scheme in Vienna. New clean materials were chosen at Quarry Hill: prefabricated concrete panels were assembled over a revolutionary steel frame. Clean electric lighting was provided alongside efficient solid-fuel ranges. There was a community hall, a welfare centre, playgrounds, tennis courts and bowling greens. A suction-powered refuse collection system took waste directly to an incineration plant that produced heat for a community laundry. At the heart of the design ethos was a will to provide sanitary conditions for the poor. However, progress was slow in the inter-war years and even the visionary Quarry Hill itself was never properly finished: it lacked many of the amenities that had been promised and succumbed to demolition as early as 1978.[13]

Regeneration

Despite the best efforts of inter-war campaigners for slum clearance, the real catalyst for change came courtesy of the cleansing fires of the Luftwaffe during World
War II; many poverty-stricken and dilapidated neighbourhoods in Greater London were levelled by aerial bombing. The post-war regeneration campaigns that
followed offered a similar modernist vision to that found at Quarry Hill, only now
with an increased urgency to achieve density, deliver results rapidly, and achieve
extreme economic efficiency. Consequently, the resulting schemes found their expression in verticality, following the high-rise solution. These projects certainly
continued the crusade for sanitation. They used clean materials and technology,
but their design posed problems of a different kind. The vermin were indeed kept
at a far greater remove (to begin with) than they had been in the inter-war slums,
but through the mechanism of 'zoning of the underclass', the new urban projects
institutionalised their occupants and made a ghetto for a whole sector of society.
As living conditions collapsed under the pressure of poor maintenance, crime and
fear, vermin began to make a reappearance. Some modern developments have in-
trinsic problems with vermin. A recent report on a Hackney complex complains
that "there was a big problem with rats on the estate, particularly in the tower block
because of the chute system used to dispose of the household waste".[14] And again,
reporting on the current condition of the Ferrier Estate in Kidbrook (Greenwich)
pending redevelopment, Ayshea Buksh remarks: "The residents that I spoke to feel
unsafe and neglected. Where their neighbours have left, vermin and drug dealers
have moved in next door. Children are scared to walk in badly lit corridors as
they are the sole family living in the block."[15] Despite the noble ambitions of the
campaigners for better housing, it would seem that modern developments are not
immune from the traditional ravages of vermin.

Epidemic

At the end of the Henry James' short story *Daisy Miller* (1878), one is shocked by
the sudden death from malaria of the vivacious, if not reckless, young protagonist.
The moral overtones of James are undeniable: the girl's death can be read as her
just deserts for a wayward and objectionable lifestyle; late night liaisons with
shady Italian men at the Coliseum did not sit comfortably with the social mores
of late 19TH-century transatlantic society. It is more alarming to discover that this

tragic story is indeed based in fact. The 1883 edition of the Baedeker travel guide for Rome warned tourists of the perennial dangers of malaria: "In summer when the fever-laden *aria cattive* (bad air) prevails, all the inhabitants who can afford it make a point of leaving the city." It seems strange to think of late 19TH-century Rome as a lethal and practically uninhabited city during the hot summer months! To go out at night, into the wrong districts, would be to take your life in your hands. In the same year as the ominous warning in Baedeker, the Scottish medic Sir Patrick Manson (1844-1922) was the first to argue for the link between malaria and the mosquito. He became a founding member of the London School of Tropical Medicine (1899), an institution that still conducts research and offers treatment to unfortunate travellers returning from exotic shores. And now our climate is creeping towards the tropical, who knows? Maybe more of us will, very shortly, be making use of the school's services and receiving treatment for maladies contracted a little closer to home? There is a warning here: how might we deal with future infestations of vermin and are we ready for the diseases they bring? Not so long ago, London was a notorious centre for cholera epidemics. During the 1853 outbreak 10,675 people died in English cities. The solution to cholera was found in collective action: a better managed supply of public drinking water and the systematic provision of a city-wide sewage system. Is there a clue for us here? Ought we to be thinking of acting collectively?

Flood

An undeniable consequence of global warming will be sea levels rising at a rate that was previously unforeseen. London is a case for particular concern with respect to flooding. Historically, the global mean sea level has risen by about 0.22 metres per century.[16] Glacial melting is thought to accelerate this to 0.31 metres (some research suggests a higher figure). The Thames Barrier designers only allowed for the lower figure when they arrived at 0.4 metres maximum increase in high water in central London in the next 50 years. If the higher figure is assumed, the barrier will be at risk of failure by 2030 (less optimistic figures put this date at 2010). Flooding is not necessarily a direct consequence, but the probability is hugely increased. Given the above figures, the chances of seeing a 1,000-year event becomes likely by the year 2050, and the most pessimistic figures predict this event by around 2015. If we do nothing, we are likely to see a flood similar in scale to the floods of 1953 by 2070 (or 2040 if we believe the worst case predictions concerning rising sea level). The threat of flooding is a major worry in our battle against vermin. Effie Williams makes it clear that flooding is inevitably followed by the outbreak of vermin. During the flooding of New Orleans in September 2005, once the waters had subsided, the true damage was to be found in the levels of contamination associated with the overflowing sewage system and massive infestation of vermin, especially rats. During floods, vermin become displaced from their natural habitats and food supplies; they are pushed into closer proximity with the human population than would otherwise be the case. Given that our flood defences are based on predictions that are likely to prove woefully inadequate, unless we take action to avoid increased risk of flooding, our cities will certainly find themselves underwater. Just like New Orleans in 2005, contamination and the spread of vermin will surely result.

Eradication

The legend of the Pied Piper of Hamelin dates from 1284. The story has a chilling logic. For some time, the town of Hamelin had been plagued by an infestation of rats. These unwanted visitors had been threatening the town's survival and prosperity. So a mystical rat–catcher is engaged by the elders of the community and given the job of eradicating the vermin. For an agreed sum, the stranger obliges. The rats follow his enchanted pipe playing down to the River Weser, where they meet a watery death. With the town restored to health, the elders see no reason to pay the piper the gold that he was promised. Furious, and keen for revenge, the piper returns. And, while the town's people are assembled in church, he plays his pipe once more; only this time his victims are not rodents. On this occasion, all the children of the town follow him into the mountains; 130 innocents are lured into a secret cavern and they are never seen again! Here is a story of a malevolent stranger with mystical powers, capable of rebalancing the natural order. It is significant to ask: are we more afraid of the rat–catcher here than we are of our traditional bogeyman: the rat? Is the rat–catcher the villain of the piece? Well, perhaps not? Above all, the story speaks of loss of innocence, a betrayal of youth. The true villain here is neither rat, nor rat-catcher, but surely the greedy elders of the town. After all, the elders only ever wanted to save themselves and maintain their own comfort? Wasn't it the elders who reneged on the contract, not the piper? (One might say: a contract with the future.) Once the elders refuse to 'pay the piper' they enter into another more sinister pact, a simple trade: they betray their

children for their own continued prosperity. And for a while there is prosperity, but with the loss of a whole generation the prosperity soon subsides. And, ultimately heirless, there comes the inevitable death of the town.

Hope

In recent years, the debate with respect to sustainability all too often centres around resources and climate change; the hot issues for discussion are rising sea levels, carbon dioxide emissions, renewable energy sources etc. However, there is a much broader and more traditional way to think of sustainability. The Brundtland Commission, formally known as the World Commission on Environment and Development, headed by Gro Harlem Brundtland (1983), defined sustainable development as development that "meets the needs of the present without compromising the ability of future generations to meet their own needs". This definition places cross-generational social justice at the heart of any policy claiming to address sustainability. There are fears about the spread of vermin as a result of new policies in waste management. These policies tend to decentralise responsibility for the provision of waste collection and disposal; they put these traditionally government-controlled duties into the hands of the private sector. The consequence is a less co-ordinated and more ad hoc system of delivery. Public concern is evident in the frequency with which issues relating to the inadequacies of waste collection recur in the popular press. A recent report into waste management highlighted domestic collection as the most vulnerable part of the waste management chain: "changes in collection routine would therefore appear to be the most likely to influence fly infestation rates and the subsequent risk of disease transmission in the home environment". There is clearly a need for some proper research in this area; the report goes on to say: "there are significant gaps in knowledge to fully understand the implication of changes to collection routines". It warns that moves towards alternate weekly collections "could encourage vermin and insects into the home environment, which could potentially increase disease transmission routes".[17]

Prognosis

It is evident that patterns of vermin infestation have changed over the centuries. Historically, there have been diverse reasons for these changes; alterations in the vermin population result from many factors. There are demographic causes, influenced by influxes of foreign populations, bringing with them new vermin. There are logistical causes, stemming from changes in the way in which we manage waste. There are statutory causes, resulting from the ways that we legislate for and regulate the control of vermin. Our attitudes towards these causes and the action that we take, collectively and individually, will surely determine how we are affected by vermin in years to come. However, it is our collective 'inaction' that might well precipitate greater changes. Any ecological system finds a balance if it operates in a more or less closed way, i.e. while external factors remain constant. Given stable external factors, we can be confident that we will be able to keep the populations of vermin in check. But with the fear of imminent climate change, is the stability of these external factors to be relied upon? We expect to see severe changes in weather and sea level. Surely the traditional habitats for vermin will be altered? Could we see a resulting alteration in our relationship with our existing vermin populations? Could some of these populations be displaced by vermin more adapted to the unfamiliar, emerging climates? Could these new populations be more dangerous or more difficult to control than our existing adversaries? Our willingness to respond to the threats of climate change, together with our commitment to the responsible management of waste and the ongoing provision of an effective public health system, are central to our future stable relations with our vermin populations. But there is a growing trend to outsource these responsibilities to private business: to economise, to act irresponsibly with our future. Are we in danger of repeating the mistakes of the elders of Hamelin? Are we refusing to 'pay the piper'? Will we suffer the same fate?

BIOGRAPHY

Alan Thompson is chairman of the cultural organisation Art & Architecture and Director of the architectural design and animation company 3DWG.

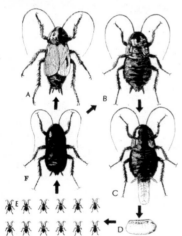

CLOCKWISE FROM TOP

The Coliseum, Vedute di Roma(Views of Rome), 1740 GIOVANNI BATTISTA PIRANESI

The Rat King (Wikipedia.org) (Scientific Museum Mauritianum Altenburg, Germany)

Life Cycle of the Common Cockroach (Norman E. Hicken, Household Insect Pests, 1974, p.48)

Creative Destruction

1. Ben Campkin discusses the etymology of 'vermin' in his unpublished paper, 'On Vermin: the most human and urban of animals', which was presented at the TINAG salon How Vermin Are Shaping Our Future Cities (26 November 2008).

2. *ibid.* Campkin distinguishes between 'dirty' and 'clean' categories of nature.

3. Richard Girling, 'The cull of the wild', *Times* online (4 March 2007), a review of Roger Lovegrove, *Silent Fields: The Long Decline of a Nation's Wildlife* (Oxford: Oxford University Press, 2007).

4. Steven Connor, www.bbk.ac.uk/english/skc/flies/ (accessed 17/11/07), as quoted by Ben Campkin, *ibid.*

5. *Nature* online, Natural History Museum, London, www.nhm.ac.uk/nature-online/life/other-invertebrates/chinese-mitten-crabs/index.html (accessed 18/01/08).

6. 'Zebra Mussels Threaten Economic Future of Waterways', Department of the Environment, www.archive.nics.gov.uk/env/040909b-env (accessed 13/01/08).

7. It was in fact fleas carried on infected black rats that transmitted the disease, which went on to kill one third of Europe's population in 1347 AD.

8. Gargi Bhattacharyya, 'Rats with Wings: London's Battle with Animals', in J.Kerr, A. Gibson and M. Seaborne (eds), *London: From Punk to Blair* (London: Reaktion, 2003) p. 216.

9. Research by Webster and McDonald (1995) on wild rats on English farms identified many common diseases carried by rats that are transmissible to human population, these include: (a) Helminthus (worms): LiverWorm (*Capillaria*), Cestodes (*Hymenolepsis diminuta* and *Hymenolepsis nana*); (b) Bacteria: *Leprospira spp.* (causes Weil's disease), *Listeria spp.* (causes listeriosis), *Yersinia enterocolitica spp.* (causes yersiniosis), *Pasturella spp.* (causes pasturellosis), *Pseudomonas spp.* (causes meilioidosis); (c) Protozoa: *Cryptosporidium Parvum* (causes cryptosporidiosis), *Toxoplasma Gondii* (causes toxoplasmosis); (d) Rickettsia: *Coxiella Burnetti* (causes infection of Q fever); (e) Viruses: *Hantavirus* (causes hantaan or hemorrhagic fever); (f) Ectoparasites: fleas, mites and lice (all potential vectors for disease themselves including typhus).

10. *ibid.*, Ben Campkin.

11. 'Up With the Houses, Down With the Slums' (London: Labour Party, 1934) p. 26.

12. Arthur Elton and E.H. Anstey (producers), *Housing Problems*, 1935 (London: BFI Archive).

13. Royal Commission on Historical Monuments (Supplementary Series), *Workers' Housing in West Yorkshire, 1750-1920* (London: HMSO, 1986).

14. 'Inner-City Food Waste Compost Scheme Set For Expansion', letsrecycle.com 30/09/04 (accessed 13/01/08).

15. Ayshea Buksh, 'Kidbrook Regeneration Clash', www.bbc.co.uk 03/01/07) (accessed 17/01/08).

16. Richard Doyle, Flood London Statistics, gathered from www.floodlondon.com/floodtb.htm (accessed 04/02/08).

17. Nicola Dennis, Andy Baxter and Nichola Darwin, 'Potential Health Risk to Humans from Birds, Mammals and Insects associated with UK Waste Management Operations: a Literature Review', Bird Management Unit, Defra (London: HMSO, 2006).